Incidents of

Travel in Yucatan

JOHN LLOYD STEPHENS

NEW EDITION BY KARL ACKERMAN

SMITHSONIAN BOOKS

WASHINGTON

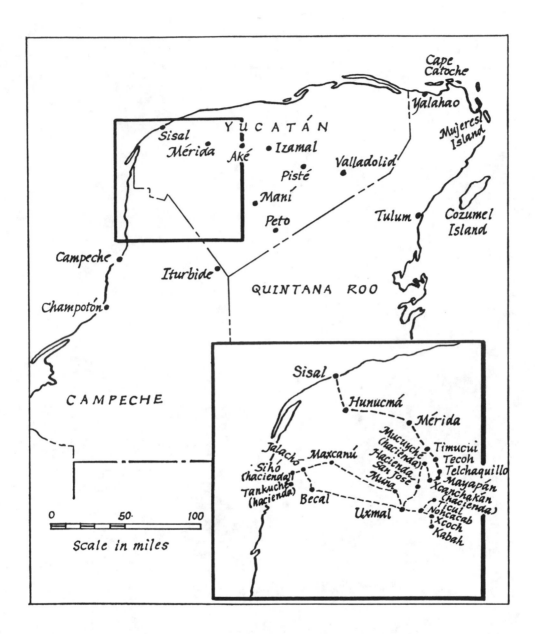

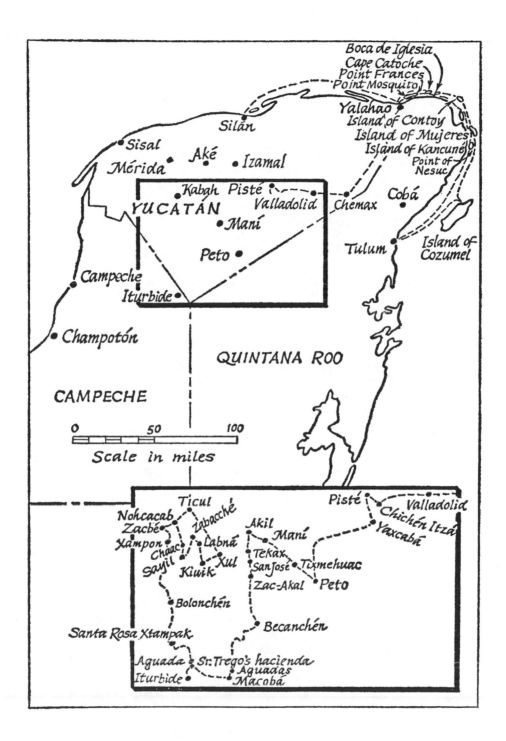

Copy Editor: Mary E. Laur
Production Editor: Duke Johns
Designer: Linda McKnight

Library of Congress Cataloging-in-Publication Data

Stephens, John Lloyd, 1805–1852.
    Incidents of travel in Yucatan / John Lloyd Stephens. — New ed. / by Karl
Ackerman.
        p.   cm.
    A condensation of the work originally published: New York : Harper,
1843.
    Includes many of the original Frederick Catherwood drawings, along with
a new selection of various 19th and 20th century prints and photographs.
    Includes index.
    ISBN 1-56098-652-2 (cloth : alk. paper). — ISBN 1-56098-651-4 (pbk. :
alk. paper)
    1. Yucatán (Mexico : State)—Description and travel. 2. Yucatán (Mex-
ico)—Antiquities. 3. Mayas—Antiquities. 4. Stephens, John Lloyd, 1805–
1852—Journeys—Mexico—Yucatán. I. Ackerman, Karl. II. Catherwood,
Frederick.
F1376.S843   1996
972'.65—dc20   95-21801

British Library Cataloguing-in-Publication Data is available

Manufactured in the United States of America
11 10 09 08 07 06 05 04   6 5 4 3 2

CONTENTS

LIST OF
ILLUSTRATIONS

ACKNOWLEDGMENTS

Once again I would like to thank the staff at the Smithsonian Institution Press for their continuing support of this project, most especially Amy Pastan and Daniel Goodwin. Thanks also to designer Linda McKnight, editors Duke Johns and Mary Laur, assistant editor Cathy Jones, and the marketing staff, including Hilary Reeves and Jeannie Ringo. I am grateful to the Smithsonian Institution's Scholarly Book Fund for the grant that made production of this book possible.

I am also grateful to Martha Labell and Barbara Isaac at Harvard University's Peabody Museum of Archaeology and Ethnology for permission to reproduce many images from their extraordinary archive, and to photographers Parney and Jacques VanKirk for once again allowing access to their extensive collection of images of the Maya ruins.

Finally, my sincere thanks to filmmakers Paul and Ellen Wagner for their interest and ongoing efforts to produce a documentary film about John Lloyd Stephens and his search for the "lost" cities of the ancient Maya civilization.

INTRODUCTION

Karl Ackerman

The Yucatán peninsula of Mexico is home to dozens of ancient cities whose quiet beauty and grand designs, even in ruin, continue to inspire awe. Millions of travelers from around the world visit these sites each year. They climb the stairways of the Castillo at Chichén Itzá and the Pyramid of the Magician at Uxmal; they stand transfixed before the Palace of the Masks at Kabáh, grasping at once the artistic achievement and the political power of a civilization that has passed from the scene. All who have walked the length of Uxmal's House of the Governor, or circled the courtyard of the nearby Nunnery Quadrangle, are forever struck by the intricate mosaics and the architectural genius of the Maya. They are struck, too, by the silence.

To explore these sites is to walk in the footsteps of people who lived at the time of Charlemagne, unknown to—and unaware of—the men and women of Europe, highly cultured and intellectual, and as contentious and warlike as the rest of humanity. It is also to walk in the footsteps of the Spanish conquistadors and priests, who came upon these ruined cities some five hundred years ago, and in the steps of intrepid later explorers such as John Lloyd Stephens. Today Stephens is best remembered for two books, *Incidents of Travel in Central America, Chiapas, and Yucatan* (1841) and *Incidents of Travel in Yucatan* (1843), both lively accounts of his explorations of the Maya region. These volumes ignited the popular and scholarly interest in this ancient culture of the Americas. Scientists today credit Stephens with launching the field of Maya archaeology. His books stand as the first guides to the ruined cities of the Maya.

Incidents of Travel in Central America, Chiapas, and Yucatan is the gripping adventure story of the rediscovery of a number of ruined cities in the forests of Honduras, Guatemala, and Mexico. Stephens had little grasp of the cultures or history of the region (Central America was then engulfed in a bloody civil war), and the tone of the narrative reflects his naïveté. *Incidents of Travel in Yucatan* reveals a different narrator: seasoned, and with the focused approach of a self-taught field archaeologist. During a survey that lasted from November 1841 to May 1842, Stephens set as his goal to visit and describe as many ruined cities on the Yucatán peninsula as he could find—forty-four, by his own count. The results astounded American and European readers, who had just begun to consider the idea that a sophisticated, artistic people had once flourished in the jungles and dry forests of this region.

Time and the tide of humanity have changed the look of the ruins of Yucatán but not their character. Today even the casual tourist is moved by the sight of ancient limestone buildings set like pieces of sculpture against a blue sky. So it was for Stephens. Of his first view of Uxmal, he wrote: "We took another road, and, emerging suddenly from the woods, to my astonishment came at once upon a large open field strewed with mounds of ruins, and vast buildings on terraces, and pyramidal structures, grand and in good preservation, richly ornamented, without a brush to obstruct the view, in picturesque effect almost equal to the ruins of Thebes. . . . " He began as all visitors to Uxmal begin, wandering among the ruined buildings, climbing the Pyramid of the Magician, and pondering the view before him: "I stood in the doorway when the sun went down, throwing from the buildings a prodigious breadth of shadow, darkening the terraces on which they stood, and presenting a scene strange enough for a work of enchantment."

3. *Page xiv*: Modern view of stacked Chaac masks decorating the west side of the Pyramid of the Magician, Uxmal

I first arrived at Uxmal in late July 1994, the beginning of a rainy season that had produced little rain. For much of the day the skies above the ruins remained pale blue, almost white. But late in the day, clouds the color of pewter gathered in the south. Lightning flickered on the horizon. I climbed the steep stairway of the Pyramid of the Magician, past the long row of snout-nosed masks depicting the Maya god Chaac. At the top, as the storm hit, I ducked into a doorway shaped to resemble the mouth of a dragon. There were pellets of hail first, then huge raindrops that mottled the buff-colored stone. Soon sheets of water were blowing sideways through the ruins, bending the isolated trees, rippling the edge of the low forest that surrounds Uxmal. The Nunnery Quadrangle at my feet and the House of the Governor in the distance disappeared behind curtains of water and I felt truly alone, mesmerized by the raw power of Chaac, destroyer and life-giver, the god of lightning and rain.

I stood where generations of Maya kings once stood, walked

through a ruined ball court where athletes once played a sacred game, wandered among house mounds, climbed walls and temples, and gazed at fantastic images of feathered serpents, stylized jaguars, and the ubiquitous Chaac. I was informed by the groundbreaking research of today's Maya scholars, whose insights have begun to explain the rise and fall of these ancient cities. But at Uxmal I came to appreciate that science alone has not—and perhaps cannot—bridge the divide that separates modern travelers such as myself from the ancient Maya. We come to Uxmal with more wonder and awe than real understanding of the people who once lived here. We still see with the eyes of the earliest explorers. "The place . . . was beyond all doubt once a large, populous, and highly civilized city," Stephens wrote. "Who built it, why it was located on that spot, away from water or any of those natural advantages which have determined the sites of cities whose histories are known, what led to its abandonment and destruction, no man can tell."

The first explorers of the Maya region concluded without much evidence that these cities were not built by the peoples of the New World. They looked instead to seafaring Greeks or Egyptians, one of the Lost Tribes of Israel, or survivors fleeing the submerged continent of Atlantis. In the late 1830s, John Lloyd Stephens, hungry for new adventure, was drawn into the debate.

Born in 1805 to a prosperous family, Stephens had grown up in New York City and embarked on a life in law and politics. But in 1834 he abandoned the settled life, seeking instead the thrill of traveling in the "barbarous countries" of the Middle East, Europe, and Russia. Two books chronicling his adventures among the ruins of Greece, Egypt, and the Holy Land established Stephens' literary reputation and earned him a fortune. He had struck a chord with American readers, satisfying a hunger for something that seemed absent from the New World: although the American landscape held great natural wonders, it seemed empty of human history. Wandering among the ruins of Greece, Stephens lamented, "We have no old monuments, no classical associations; and our history hardly goes beyond the memory of . . . the oldest inhabitant."

News of monumental ruins in the jungles of Mexico and Central America challenged this idea. After poring through the available literature on the region, including Alexander von Humboldt's account of his explorations in Mexico and the sketchy reports of Spanish soldiers who had visited such sites as Copán and Palenque, Stephens decided to mount his own expedition and to attempt to settle the question of who had built them. He hired British artist Frederick

4. John Lloyd Stephens in
1845

Catherwood, who had spent the previous ten years drawing the ruins
of Italy, Greece, Egypt, and Jerusalem, to accompany him. In October
1839, the two men set out to find the "lost" cities of the Maya. After
months of work at the ruins of Copán in Honduras, Quiriguá in Guatemala, and Palenque and Uxmal in Mexico, Stephens returned to
New York and wrote his first best-selling book on the Maya, *Incidents of Travel in Central America, Chiapas, and Yucatan.* "The
work is certainly a magnificent one," wrote Edgar Allan Poe, "perhaps the most interesting book of travel ever published." Today the
book is considered a classic.

At Copán, the first stop, Stephens was overwhelmed by the size
of the ruins and the richness of the sculptured monuments. He wrote:
"We sat down on the very edge of [a] wall and strove in vain to pene-

trate the mystery by which we were surrounded. Who were the people who built this city?" By the end of the journey, Stephens had the beginning of an answer to this question: "[W]e have a conclusion far more interesting and wonderful than that of connecting the builders of these cities with the Egyptians or any other people. It is the spectacle of a people skilled in architecture, sculpture, and drawing, and beyond doubt, other more perishable arts, . . . not derived from the Old World, but originating and growing up here, . . . like the plants and fruits of the soil, indigenous."

Stephens flatly rejected the notion that these ruins were thousands of years old. "[T]hey are not the works of people who have passed away and whose history is lost," he wrote, but were constructed by "the races who inhabited the country at the time of the Spanish conquest, or some not very distant progenitors." His examination of the hieroglyphic inscriptions led him to make a bold assertion that there was once a single language in the Maya lowlands, extending from Copán in the east to Palenque in the west to Uxmal in the north. "The intermediate country is now occupied by races of Indians speaking many different languages, and entirely unintelligible to each other; but there is room for the belief that the whole of this country was once occupied by the same race, speaking the same language, or, at least, having the same written characters." Further, he believed that these hieroglyphic inscriptions recorded the history of Maya nobles and kings. Of one monument at Copán, he noted that "in its medallion tablets the people who reared it had published a record of themselves, through which we might one day . . . unveil the mystery that hangs over the city."

The task of unveiling that mystery was left for the scholars of the future; Stephens largely confined his explorations to the field of ruins. His initial survey of Uxmal had been aborted after two days when Frederick Catherwood came down with malaria. The abrupt departure left Stephens unable to follow up on the news that the entire peninsula of Yucatán was dotted with ruined cities. "I have no doubt that a year may be passed with great interest in Yucatan," he wrote. Within months of the publication of these words, Stephens and Catherwood, accompanied by a young doctor and amateur ornithologist named Samuel Cabot, returned to Yucatán to survey the region for themselves. Again, Stephens knew little about the history or archaeology of the region—he carried only Jean-Frédéric Waldeck's contemporary (and unreliable) account of an exploration of Uxmal and a few early Spanish accounts of the region, among them Diego López de

Cogolludo's *Historia de Yucatán* (1688) and Antonio de Herrera's *Historia general de los hechos de los Castellanos en las Indias* (1615).

Stephens viewed his survey as a race against time: at each site, it seemed, ancient buildings were collapsing into piles of rubble before his eyes. The structures of Labná were under "the sentence of irretrievable ruin," he declared. "In a few years, even these will be gone; and, as it has been denied that such things ever were, doubts may again arise whether they indeed existed. So strong was this impression that we determined to fortify in every possible way our proofs."

Except for brief forays into the religious and municipal archives in Yucatán, Stephens confined himself to scouting and surveying sites, uncovering buildings and artwork for Catherwood to draw, measuring palaces and temples, and clambering to the tops of mounds and descending into subterranean rooms and caves in search of pottery and bones. At a few stops he removed artifacts to ship home. The carved wooden lintels from Kabáh and Uxmal were lost almost immediately in a fire that consumed Catherwood's Panorama of Jerusalem in New York City in July 1842; the sculpted stone panels and figures that Stephens removed from Kabáh now reside in the American Museum of Natural History in New York City.

Reviews of Stephens' second book about the Maya ruins, *Incidents of Travel in Yucatan,* published in March 1843, matched those of the first. The *Democratic Review* pronounced it "superb." A notice in the *North American Review* called it "magnificent," adding: "[T]he sale is reckoned by thousands; and . . . our discourse is not likely to fall into the hands of many . . . who have not read the book for themselves." William Hickling Prescott, whose classic *History of the Conquest of Mexico* appeared the same year, wrote this to Stephens: "I believe that there is but one opinion of the work here and all agree. It is better than its brother."

Stephens wrote *Incidents of Travel in Yucatan* quickly, completing the 622-page book in less than six months. This speed of composition resulted in inconsistencies: Stephens criticized his Yucatec Maya guides for lacking "traditionary" knowledge of their ancestors, yet time and again he recorded insights and information obtained from these same Indians (for example, the fact that the chambers carved into the limestone rock beneath palaces, called chultuns, were used to store water). And Stephens made mistakes: he incorrectly assumed that the city of Mayapán was older than Uxmal, that Uxmal was inhabited during the era of the conquest, and that the wooden lintels at Kabáh were carved with copper tools. But these are minor

errors. Today, few scholars would quarrel with the statement of Maya-
nists Linda Schele and Mary Ellen Miller that Stephens' reports rank
among "the best books written about the Maya."

This new edition of *Incidents of Travels in Yucatan,* like my edition
of Stephens' *Incidents of Travel in Central America, Chiapas, and Yucatan* (Smithsonian Institution Press, 1993), reduces the text by two-
thirds but aims to preserve the spirit and essence of the original
work. Thus I have eliminated Stephens' description of the journeys to
and from the region and have focused and organized the text around
the archaeological sites that Stephens and Catherwood visited. As
with the previous volume, I have tightened Stephens' prose, eliminated the detailed measurements of buildings and mounds, and ex-
cised long historical digressions and anecdotes addressed to the readers of Stephens' day. I have not used ellipses to indicate compression
and have used brackets only where I have introduced words for clar-
ity. In one case I moved a block of text in order to present Stephens'
survey of Uxmal in a single chapter.

In Spanish and English, Stephens was a creative speller (*comeder*
for *comedor,* "moschctocs" for "mosquitoes"). These mispronuncia-
tions and misspellings (and, often, British spellings) reveal Stephens'
character and time, and have thus been retained. Chapter titles, cap-
tions, and running heads reflect current spellings: Stephens' city of Ja-
lachó is Halachó; his Salli or Zayi is Sayil; Schoolhoke is Xculoc; Labphak is Xtampak; Tuloom is Tulum.

Many of the sites that Stephens visited—Uxmal, Kabáh, Labná,
Sayil, Chichén Itzá, and Tulum, for example—have been excavated
and restored, and they attract crowds of visitors today; other sites—
Kiuic, Sabacché, and Macobá, among others—remain off the tourist
track and have, as Stephens once predicted, fallen to ruin. To show
how all of these Maya sites have changed over time, I have included a
variety of illustrations: Catherwood drawings from the original work,
nineteenth-century photographs, modern photographs, and reconstruction drawings. This new edition of *Incidents of Travel in Yucatan* is meant for those readers and travelers who wish to walk in the
footsteps of the man who brought news to the world of the cultural
richness of the Maya region.

Incidents of Travel in Yucatan

CHAPTER ONE

Mérida

We had arrived at Merida at an opportune moment. The fête of San Cristoval, an observance of nine days, was then drawing to its close, and that evening a grand function was to be performed in the church dedicated to that saint. We had no time to lose, and, after a hasty supper, under the guidance of an Indian lad, we set out for the church. In every house a lantern hung from the balconied windows, or a long candle stood under a glass shade. At the head of the street was a large plaza, on one side of which stood the church, with its great front brilliantly illuminated. On the platform and steps, and all the open square before it, was a great moving mass of men, women, and children, mostly Indians, dressed in white.

We worked our way up to the door, and found the church within a blaze of light. Two rows of high candlesticks, with wax candles ten feet high, extended the whole length from the door to the altar. On each side hung innumerable lamps, dotting the whole space from the floor to the ceiling. Standing on an elevated platform was an altar thirty feet high, rich with silver ornaments and vases of flowers, and hung with innumerable lamps brilliantly burn-

5. *Page 10:* West side of
the corbelled portal arch,
the ruins of Labná (Edward
H. Thompson, 1886)

ing. Priests in glittering vestments were officiating before it, music
was swelling through the corridor and arches, and the floor of the immense church was covered with women on their knees, dressed in
white, with white shawls over their heads. Through the entire body
of the church not a man was to be seen. Near us was a bevy of young
girls, beautifully dressed, with dark eyes, and their hair adorned with
flowers, sustaining my previous impressions of the beauty of the ladies of Merida.

Early the next morning the carreta arrived with our luggage. To
avoid the trouble of loading and unloading, we directed it to remain
at the door, and set out immediately to look for a house. We had not

13   *House in Mérida*

6. Modern view of an unexcavated mound at the ruins of Xlapak

much time, and, consequently, but little choice; but in half an hour we found one that answered our purpose.

Our house was in the street of the Flamingo. Like most of the houses in Merida, it was built of stone, and had one story. The front was about thirty feet, and had a sala covering the whole. The ceiling was perhaps eighteen feet high, and the walls had wooden knobs for fastening hammocks. Behind the sala was a broad corridor, opening on a courtyard, at one side of which was a sleeping room, and at the back of that a comeder or eating-room. The floors were all of hard cement. The courtyard was about thirty feet square, with high stone walls, and a well in the centre. In order that my inquiring fellow-citizens may form some idea of the comparative value of real estate in Merida and New York, I mention that the rent was four dollars per month, which for three persons we did not consider extravagant. We had our own travelling beds, the table, washhand-basin, and chairs set up, and before breakfast our house was furnished.

The next day was Sunday, the last day of the fiesta, which opened in the morning with grand mass in the church of San Cristoval. The great church, the paintings and altars, the burning of incense, the music, the imposing ceremonies of the altar, and the kneeling figures, inspired, as they always do, if not a religious, at least a solemn feeling. Among the kneeling figures of the women my eyes rested upon one with a black mantle over her head, a prayer-book in her hand, and an Indian woman by her side, whose face exhibited a purity and intellectual softness which it was easy for the imagination to invest with all those attributes that make woman perfect. Whether she was maid, wife, or widow, I never learned.

At four o'clock in the afternoon we set out for the procession and paseo. The intense heat of the day was over, there was shade in the streets, and a fresh evening breeze. The streets through which the procession was to pass were adorned with branches, and at the corners were large collections of them, forming groves of green. The balconies of the windows were hung with silk curtains and banners, and in the doorways and along the walks sat rows of ladies simply but beautifully dressed, without hats, their hair adorned with flowers, and their necks with jewels. Near the church of San Cristoval we waited till the procession came up.

It was headed by three priests, all richly dressed, one supporting a large silver cross ten feet high, and each of the others bearing a tall silver candlestick. They were followed by an Indian band, a motley group, the leaders of which were three Indians, one supporting the head and another the foot of a large violoncello. Next came a party of Indians, bearing on their shoulders a barrow supporting a large silver cross. At the foot of the cross sat the figure of Mary Magdalen, large as life, dressed in red. Over her head was a blue silk mantilla, with a broad gold border, and across her lap the figure of the dead Christ.

When the crowd had passed by we strolled to the Alameda. This is the great place of promenade and paseo in Merida. It consists of a broad paved avenue, with a line of stone seats on each side, and beyond, on both sides, are carriage roads, shaded by rows of trees. In full sight, and giving a picturesque beauty to the scene, rises the Castillo, a ruined fortress, with battlements of dark gray stone, and the spires of the old Franciscan church rising inside, romantic in its appearance, and identified with the history of the Spanish conquest. Regularly every Sunday there is a paseo around the castle and along the Alameda, and this day, on account of the fête, it was one of the best and gayest of the year.

The most striking feature, the life and beauty of the paseo, were the calesas. The body is somewhat like that of an oldfashioned gig, only much larger, and resting on the shaft a little in front of the wheels. It is painted red, with light and fancifully coloured curtains for the sun, drawn by one horse, with a boy riding him—simple and peculiar to Yucatan. Each calesa had two, and sometimes three ladies, in the latter case the prettiest sitting in the middle and a little in front, all without hats or veils, but their hair beautifully arranged and trimmed with flowers. We sat down on one of the stone benches in the Alameda, with the young, and gay, and beautiful of Merida. Not less attractive were the great crowds of Mestizas and Indian women, some of the former being extremely pretty, and all having the same mild and gentle expression. They wore a picturesque costume of white, with a red border around the neck and skirt, and [had] that extraordinary cleanness characteristic of the poorest in Merida. For an

15   *The Alameda*

7. Plaza at Mérida (Désiré Charnay, circa 1880)

hour, one continued stream of calesas passed us. As the sun sank behind the ruins of the Castillo, we thought that there were few places in the world where it went down upon a prettier or happier scene.

One fiesta was hardly ended when another began. On Monday was the great fête of Todos Santos. Grand mass was said in all the churches, and in every family prayers were offered up for the souls of the dead; and, besides the usual ceremonies of the Catholic Church throughout the world, there is one peculiar to Yucatan, derived from the customs of the Indians, and called Mukbipoyo. On this day every

Indian, according to his means, purchases and burns a certain number of consecrated candles, in honour of his deceased relatives, and in memory of each member of his family who has died within the year. Besides this, they bake in the earth a pie consisting of a paste of Indian corn, stuffed with pork and fowls, and seasoned with chili, and during the day every good Yucateco eats nothing but this. In the interior, where the Indians are less civilized, they religiously place a portion of this composition out of doors, under a tree, or in some retired place, for their deceased friends to eat, and they say that the portion thus set apart is always eaten, which induces the belief that the dead may be enticed back by appealing to the same appetites which govern when living. But this is sometimes accounted for by malicious and skeptical persons, who say that in every neighborhood there are other Indians, poorer than those who can afford to regale their deceased relatives, and these consider it no sin to step between the living and the dead.

We have reason to remember this fête from one untoward circumstance. A friendly neighbour, who, besides visiting us frequently with his wife and daughter, was in the habit of sending us fruit and dulces more than we could eat, this day, on the top of a large, undisposed-of present, sent us a huge piece of mukbipoyo. It was as hard as an oak plank, and as thick as six of them. Having already overtasked ourselves to reduce the pile on the table, when this came, in a fit of desperation we took it out into the courtyard and buried it. There it would have remained till this day but for a malicious dog which accompanied them on their next visit. He passed into the courtyard, rooted it up, and, while we were pointing to the empty platters as our acknowledgment of their kindness, this villainous dog sneaked through the sala and out at the front door with the pie in his mouth, apparently grown bigger since it was buried.

The population of Merida is probably about twenty-three thousand. The city stands on a great plain, on a surface of limestone rock, and the temperature and climate are very uniform. The general aspect of the city is Moorish, as it was built at a time when the Moorish style prevailed in Spanish architecture. The houses are large, generally of stone, and one story in height, with balconies to the windows and large courtyards. In the centre of the city stands the plaza major, a square of about six hundred feet. The whole of the east side is occupied by the cathedral and the bishop's palace. On the west stand the house of the municipality and that of the Doña Joaquina Peon. On the north is the palace of the government, and on the south a building which on our first visit arrested our attention the moment we entered the plaza. It is distinguished by a rich sculptured façade of curious design and workmanship. In it is a stone with this inscription:

Esta obra mando hacerla el
Adelantado D. Francisco de Montejo
Año de MDXLIX.

The Adelantado Don Francisco Montejo
caused this to be made
in the year 1549.

The subject represents two knights in armour, with visors, breastplates, and helmets, standing upon the shoulders of crushed naked figures, probably intended to represent the conquering Spaniard trampling upon the Indian. Mr. Catherwood attempted to make a drawing of it, and, to avoid the heat of the sun, went into the plaza at daylight for that purpose; but he was so annoyed by the crowd that he was obliged to give it up. There is reason to believe that it is a combination of Spanish and Indian art. The design is certainly Spanish. But five years after the foundation of Merida, Spaniards were but few, and probably there were none who practised the mechanic arts. The execution was no doubt the work of Indians; and perhaps the carving was done with their own instruments.

Besides the inscription on the stone, the only information that exists in regard to this building is a statement in Cogolludo, that the façade cost fourteen thousand dollars. It is now the property of Don Simon Peon, and is occupied by his family. It has been lately repaired, and some of the beams are no doubt the same which held up the roof over the adelantado.

Eight streets lead from the plaza, two in the direction of each cardinal point. In every street, at the distance of a few squares, is a gate, now dismantled, and beyond are the barrios, or suburbs.

The streets are distinguished in a manner peculiar to Yucatan. In the angle of the corner house, and on the top, stands a painted wooden figure of an elephant, a bull, a flamingo, or some other visible object, and the street is called by the name of this object. On one corner there is the figure of an old woman with large spectacles on her nose, and the street is called la Calle de la Vieja, or the Street of the Old Woman. That in which we lived had on the corner house a flamingo, and was called the Street of the Flamingo; and the reason of the streets being named in this way gives some idea of the character of the people. The great mass of the inhabitants, universally the Indians, cannot read. Printed signs would be of no use, but every Indian knows the sign of an elephant, a bull, or a flamingo.

The most interesting and remarkable edifice in Merida is the old Franciscan convent. It stands on an eminence in the eastern part of the city, and is enclosed by a high wall, with turrets, forming what is now called the Castillo. These walls and turrets are still erect, but within is ruin irretrievable.

In 1820 the new constitution obtained by the patriots in Spain reached the colonies, and Don Juan Rivas Vertiz, then Gefe Politico, published it in the plaza. The church sustained the old order of things, and the Franciscan friars, confident in their hold upon the feelings of the populace, endeavoured to put down this demonstration of liberal feeling. A mob gathered in the plaza; friars appeared among them, urging them on; field-pieces were brought out, the mob dispersed, and Don Juan Rivas marched to the Franciscan convent, opened the doors, drove out the monks, above 300 in number, at the point of the bayonet, and gave up the building to destruction. The superior and some of the brothers became seculars or regular priests; others turned to worldly pursuits; and of this once powerful order, but eleven are now left who wear the garb of the Franciscan monks.

It was in company with one of these that I paid my last visit to this convent. We entered by the great portal of the castle wall into an overgrown courtyard. In front was the convent, with its large corridors and two great churches, the walls of all three standing, but without doors or windows. The roof of one of the churches had fallen, and the broad glare of day was streaming into the interior. We entered the other—the oldest, and identified with the times of the conquerors. Near the door was a blacksmith's forge. A Mestizo was blowing at the bellows, hauling out a red-hot bar of iron, and hammering it into spikes. All along the floor were half-naked Indians and brawny Mestizoes, hewing timber, driving nails, and carrying on the business of making gun-carriages for artillery. The altars were thrown down and the walls defaced; half way up were painted on them, in coarse and staring red characters (in Spanish) "First squadron," "Second squadron"; and at the head of the church, under a golden gloria, were the words "Comp'y Light Infantry." The church had been occupied as barracks, and these were the places where they stacked their arms.

As we passed through, the workmen stared at my companion, or rather at the long blue gown, the cord around his waist, and the cross dangling from it—the garb of his scattered order. It was the first time he had visited the place since the expulsion of the monks. To me it was mournful to behold the destruction and desecration of this noble building; what, then, must it have been to him? In the floor of the church near the altar and in the sacristia were open vaults, but the bones of the monks had been thrown out and scattered on the floor. Some of these were the bones of his earliest friends. We passed into the refectory, and he pointed out the position of the long table at which the brotherhood took their meals, and the stone fountain at which they performed their ablutions. His old companions in their long blue gowns rose up before him, now scattered forever, and their home a desolation and ruin.

But this convent contains one memorial far more interesting than any connected with its own ruin; one that carries the beholder back through centuries of time, and tells the story of a greater and a sadder fall. In one of the lower cloisters going out from the north, and under the principal dormitory, are two parallel corridors. The outer one faces the principal patio, and this corridor has that peculiar arch so often referred to in my previous volumes, two sides rising to meet each other, and covered, when within about a foot of forming an apex, by a flat layer of stones. There can be no mistake about the character of this arch; it cannot for a moment be supposed that the Spaniards constructed anything so different from their known rules of architecture; and beyond doubt it formed part of one of those mysterious buildings which have given rise to so much speculation; the construction of which has been ascribed to the most ancient people in the Old World, and to races lost, perished, and unknown.

I am happy thus early in these pages to have an opportunity of recurring to the opinion expressed in my former volumes, in regard to the builders of the ancient American cities. The conclusion to which I came was, that "there are not sufficient grounds for belief in the great antiquity that has been scribed to these ruins"; "that we are not warranted in going back to any ancient nation of the Old World for the builders of these cities; that they are not the works of people who have passed away, and whose history is lost; but that there are strong reasons to believe them the creation of the same races who inhabited the country at the time of the Spanish conquest, or of some not very distant progenitors."

This opinion was not given lightly, nor without due consideration. It was adverse to my feelings, which would fain have thrown around the ruins the interest of mystery and hoary age. Even now, though gratified at knowing that my opinion has been fully sustained, I would be willing to abandon it did circumstances warrant me in so doing. But I am obliged to say that subsequent investigations have fortified and confirmed my previous conclusions, and, in fact, have made conviction what before was mere matter of opinion.

When I wrote the account of my former journey, the greatest difficulty attending the consideration of this subject was the absence of all historical record concerning the places visited. Copan had some history, but it was obscure, uncertain, and unsatisfactory. Quirigua, Palenque, and Uxmal had none whatever; but a ray of historic light beams upon the solitary arch in the ruined convent of Merida.

In the account of the conquest of Yucatan by Cogolludo it is stated, that on the arrival of the Spaniards at the Indian town of Tihoo, on the site of which, it will be remembered, Merida now stands, they found many cerros hechos a mano, i.e., hills made by hand, or artificial mounds, and that on one of these mounds the Spaniards encamped. This mound, it is stated, stood on the ground now occupied by the plaza major. East of it was another large mound, and the Spaniards laid the foundation of the city between these two, because the stones in them were a great convenience in building, and economized the labour of the Indians. These mounds were so large that with the stones the Spaniards built all the edifices in the city, so that the ground which forms the plaza major remained level.

Other mounds are mentioned as obstructing the laying out of streets according to the plan proposed, and there is one circumstance which bears directly upon this point, and, in my opinion, is conclusive.

In the history of the construction of the Franciscan convent, which was founded in the year 1547, five years after the arrival of the Spaniards in Tihoo, it is expressly stated that it was built upon a small artificial mound, one of the many that were then in the place, on which mound, it is added, were *some ancient buildings*. Now we must either suppose that the Spaniards razed these buildings to the ground, and then constructed this strange arch themselves, which supposition is utterly untenable, or that this corridor formed part of the ancient buildings which, according to the historical account, stood on this artificial mound, and that for some purpose or other the monks incorporated it with their convent.

There is but one way to overthrow this conclusion, and that is by contending that these mounds were all ruined, and this building too, at the time it was made to form part of the convent. But then we are reduced to the necessity of supposing that a great town, the fame of which reached the Spaniards at Campeachy, and which made a desperate and bloody resistance to their occupation of it, was a mere gathering of hordes around the ruined buildings of another race. It is a matter of primary importance to note that these artificial mounds are mentioned, not in the course of describing the Indian town, for no description whatever is attempted, but merely incidentally, as affording conveniences to the Spaniards in furnishing materials for building the city, or as causing obstructions in the laying out of streets regularly and according to the plan proposed. Cogolludo mentions particularly one [mound] that completely obstructed the running of a particular street, which, he says, was called *El grande de los Kues, adoratorio que era de los idolos.* Now the word "Kues," in the Maya language, as spoken by the Indians of Yucatan at the present day, means their ancient places of worship, and the word "adoratorio," as defined in the Spanish dictionary, is the name given by the Spaniards to the temples of idols in America. So that when the historian describes this mound as *El grande de los Kues el adoratorio de los idolos,* he means to say that it was the greatest among the places of worship of the Indians, or the temples of their idols.

It is called the "great one" of their places of worship, in contradistinction to the smaller ones around, among which was that now occupied by the Franciscan convent. In my opinion, the solitary arch found in this convent is very strong, if not conclusive, evidence that all the ruined buildings scattered over Yucatan were erected by the very Indians who occupied the country at the time of the Spanish conquest, or, to fall back upon my old ground, that they were the work "of the same race of people," or "their not very distant progenitors."

Who these races were, whence they came, or who were their progenitors, I did not undertake to say, nor do I now.

CHAPTER TWO

Mayapán and Uxmal

The day was overcast, which saved us from the scorching sun. The road was straight, level, stony, and uninteresting. On both sides were low, thick woods, so that there was no view except that of the road before us. Already, in the beginning of our journey, we felt that, if we were safe from the confusion and danger which had attended us in Central America, we had lost, too, the mountains, valleys, volcanoes, rivers, and all the wild and magnificent scenery that gave a charm to the country in spite of the difficulties and dangers.

I would remark that no map of Yucatan at all to be depended on has ever been published. Doña Joaquina Peon had one in manuscript, which she was kind to place at our disposal, but with notice that it was not correct. In order to keep a record of our own track from the time we left Merida until we returned to it, we took the bearings of the roads, noted the number of hours on each day's journey, and the pace of our horses, and at some places Mr. Catherwood took an observation for latitude.

At the distance of a league we passed a fine cattle hacienda, and at twenty minutes past one reached Timucui, a small village five leagues from

Merida. This village consisted of a few Indian huts, built around a large open square, and on one side was a sort of shed for a casa real. It had no church or cura. The population consisted entirely of Indians, who in general throughout the country speak nothing but the Maya. There was not a white man in the place, nor any one who could speak in any tongue that we could comprehend. Fortunately, a muleteer from the interior on his way to Merida was swinging in a hammock in the casa real. He was surprised at our undertaking alone a journey into the interior, seeing that we were brought to a stand at the first village from the capital. Finding us somewhat rational in other respects, he assisted us in procuring ramon leaves and water for the horses. His life had been passed in driving mules from a region of country called the Sierra, to the capital; but he had heard strange stories about foreign countries, and, among others, that in El Norte a man could earn a dollar a day by his labour. He was comforted when he learned that a real in his country was worth more to him than a dollar would be in ours; and as he interpreted to his nearly naked companions, crouching in the shade, nothing touched them so nearly as the idea of cold and frost, and spending a great portion of the day's earnings for fuel to keep from freezing.

At three o'clock we left the hamlet, and at a little after four we saw the towers of the church of Tekoh. The village consisted of a long, straight street, with houses or huts almost hidden by foliage. We rode up to the plaza without meeting a single person. At one side of the plaza, on a high stone platform, stood a gigantic church, with two lofty towers, and in front and on each side was a broad flight of stone steps. Crossing the plaza we saw an Indian woman, to whom we uttered the word *convento*, and, following the direction of her hand, rode up to the house of the cura. The gate was closed, but we opened it without knocking. The convent stood on the same platform with the church, and had a high flight of stone steps. A number of Indian servants ran out to the corridor, to stare at such strange-looking persons, and we understood that the padre was not at home; but we were too well pleased with the appearance of things to think of going elsewhere. We tied our horses in the yard and strolled through the corridor of the convent and along the platform of the church, overlooking the village.

The top of the church commanded a view of a great plain, covered by an almost boundless forest, extending on one side to the sea, and on the other to the sierra which crosses the peninsula of Yucatan, and runs back to the great traversing range in Guatimala, broken

8. *Page 22:* Roadway and limestone fence on the outskirts of Mérida (Thompson, circa 1890)

only by a high mound, which at three leagues' distance towered above the plain, a mourning monument of the ruins of Mayapan, the capital of the fallen kingdom of Maya.

On our return we found the cura waiting to receive us. We had again made a beginning with the padres, and this beginning, in heartiness of welcome and goodness of cheer, corresponded with all that we had before received at their hands. We had the choice of cot or hammock for the night, and at breakfast a group of Indian musicians were seated under the corridor, who continued making a noise, which they called la musica, till we mounted to depart. The cura accompanied us, mounted on one of the best horses we had seen in the country; and as it was a rare thing for him to absent himself a day from his parochial duties, he set out as for a holy-day excursion, worrying our poor nags, as well as ourselves, to keep up with him.

The padre took a lively interest in the zeal lately awakened for exploring the antiquities of the country, and told us that this particular region abounded with traces of the ancient inhabitants. At a short distance from the camino real we came to a line of fallen stones, forming what appeared to be the remains of a wall which crossed the road, and ran off into the forest on both sides, traversing, he said, the country for a great distance in both directions. A short distance beyond, we turned off to a large hollow basin perfectly dry, which he called an aguada, and said it was an artificial formation, excavated and walled around, and had been used by the ancients as a reservoir for water. At the time, we did not agree with him, but considered the basin a natural formation, though, from what we saw afterward, we are induced to believe that his account may have been correct.

At ten o'clock we reached the small village of Telchaquillo, containing a population of six hundred souls, all Indians. In the square of this little village was a great senote, or subterraneous well, which supplied all the inhabitants with water. At a distance the square seemed level and unbroken; but women walking across it with cantaros or water-jars suddenly disappeared, and others seemed to rise out of the earth. Nearer, we found a great opening in the rocky surface, like the mouth of a cave. The descent was by irregular steps cut and worn in the rocks. Over head was an immense rocky roof, and at a distance from the mouth was a large basin of water. Directly over the water the roof was perhaps sixty feet high; and there was an opening above which threw down light. The water had no current, and its source was a mystery. During the rainy season it rises a little, but never falls below a certain point, and at all times it is the only source of supply to the inhabitants. Women, with their water-jars, were constantly ascending and descending; swallows were darting through the cave in every direction. At this village we found waiting for us the major domo of the hacienda of San Joaquin, on which stand the ruins of Mayapan. Leaving the senote, we mounted and followed him.

At the distance of half a mile he stopped near a great cave that had lately been discovered, and which, he said, had no end. The major domo cut a path a short distance into the woods, following which we came to a large hollow, overgrown with trees, and, descending, entered a great cavern with a lofty roof, and gigantic passages branching off in different directions, and running no one knew whither. The cave had been discovered by the major domo and some vaqueros while in pursuit of robbers who had stolen a bull; and no robber's cave in romantic story could equal it in wildness. The major domo said he had entered it with ten men, and had passed four hours in exploration without finding any end. The cave, its roof, base, and passages, were an immense fossil formation. Marine shells were conglomerated together in solid masses, many of them perfect, showing a geological structure which indicated that the whole country, or, at least, that portion of it, had been once, and probably at no very remote period, overflowed by the sea.

We could have passed a day with much satisfaction in rambling through this cave, but, remaining only a few minutes, and taking away some curious and interesting specimens, we remounted, and very soon reached mounds of earth, fragments of sculptured stones, broken walls, and fallen buildings, indicating that we were once more treading upon the sepulchre of an aboriginal city. At eleven o'clock we came to a clearing, in which was situated the hacienda of San Joaquin. The building was a mere rancho, but there was a fine clearing around it. In the platform of the well were sculptured stones taken from the ancient buildings of Mayapan.

The ruins of Mayapan cover a great plain, which was at that time so overgrown that hardly any object was visible until we were close upon it, and the undergrowth was so thick that it was difficult to work our way through it. Our's was the first visit to examine these ruins. For ages they had been unnoticed, almost unknown, and left to struggle with rank tropical vegetation. The major domo, who lived on the principal hacienda, and had not seen them in twenty-three years, was more familiar with them than any other person we could find. He told us that within a circumference of three miles, ruins were found, and that a strong wall once encompassed the city, the remains of which might still be traced through the woods.

At a short distance from the hacienda, but invisible on account of the trees, rises the high mound which we had seen from the top of the church at Tekoh. It is sixty feet high; and like the mounds at Palenque and Uxmal, it is an artificial structure, built up solid from the plain. Though seen from a great distance above the tops of the trees, the whole field was so overgrown that it was scarcely visible until we reached its foot. The mound itself appeared a mere wooded hill, but peculiar in its regularity of shape. Four grand staircases ascended to an esplanade within six feet of the top, and on each side was a smaller staircase leading to the top. The steps are almost entirely gone, and we climbed up by means of fallen stones and trees growing out of its sides. As we ascended, we scared away a cow, for the wild cattle roaming on these wooded wastes pasture on its sides.

The summit was a plain stone platform. It had no structure upon it, nor were there vestiges of any. Probably it was the great mound of sacrifice, on which the priests, in the sight of the assembled people, cut out the hearts of human victims. The view commanded from the top was a great desolate plain, with here and there another ruined mound rising above the trees, and far in the distance could be discerned the towers of the church at Tekoh.

Around the base of this mound, and throughout the woods, wherever we moved, were strewed sculptured stones. Most of them were square, carved on the face, and having a long stone tenon or stem at the back. Doubtless they had been fixed in the wall, so as to form part of some ornament, or combination of ornaments, in the façade, in all respects the same as at Uxmal.

Besides these, there were more curious remains. These were representations of human figures, or of animals, with hideous features and expressions, in producing which the skill of the artist seems to have been expended. The sculpture of these figures was rude, the stones were timeworn, and many were half buried in the earth. One seems intended to represent a warrior with a shield, the arms broken off. Probably, half buried as they lie, they were once objects of adoration and worship, and now exist as mute and melancholy memorials of ancient paganism.

At a short distance from the base of the mound was an opening in the earth, forming another of those extraordinary caves. The cura, the major domo, and the Indians called it a senote, and said that it had supplied the inhabitants of the old city with water. The entrance was by a broken, yawning mouth, steep, and requiring some care in the descent. The mouth opened into an extensive subterranean chamber, with a high roof, and passages branching off in every direction.

In different places were remains of fires and the bones of animals, showing that it had at times been the place of refuge or residence of men. In the entrance of one of the passages we found a sculptured idol, which excited us with the hope of discovering some altar or sepulchre, or perhaps mummied figures. With this hope, we sent the Indians to procure torches; and while Mr. Catherwood was making some sketches, Doctor Cabot and myself passed an hour in exploring the recesses of the cave. In many places the roof had fallen, and the passages were choked up. We followed several of them with much toil and disappointment, and at length fell into one, low and narrow, along which it was necessary to crawl on the hands and feet, and where, from the flame and smoke of the torches, it was desperately hot. We at length came to a body of water, which, on thrusting the hand into it, we found to be incrusted with a thin coat of sulphate of lime, that had formed on the top of the water, but decomposed on being brought into the air.

Leaving the cave or senote, we continued rambling among the ruins. The mounds were all of the same general character, and the buildings had entirely disappeared on all except one; but this was different from any we had at that time seen, though we afterward found others like it.

What the shape of the mound had been was difficult to make out, but the building was circular. The exterior is of plain stone. The door faces the west, and over it is a lintel of stone. The outer wall is five feet thick; the door opens into a circular passage three feet wide, and in the centre is a cylindrical solid mass of stone. The whole diameter of the building is twenty-five feet. The walls had four or five coats of stucco, and there were remains of painting, in which red, yellow, blue, and white were distinctly visible.

On the southwest side of the building, and on a terrace projecting from the side of the mound, was a double row of columns eight feet apart, of which only eight remained. Probably, from the fragments around, there had been more, and, by clearing away the trees, more might have been found still standing. In our hurried visit to Uxmal, we had seen objects which we supposed might have been intended for columns; and though we afterward saw many, we considered these the first columns we had seen. They were two feet and a half in diameter, and consisted of five round stones, ten inches thick, laid one upon another. They had no capitals, and what particular connexion they had with the building did not appear.

So far, although the fragments of sculpture were of the same general character as at Uxmal, we had not found any edifice sufficiently entire to enable us to identify that peculiar arch which we had found in all the ruined buildings of this country; but it was not wanting. At some distance from this place, and on the other side of the hacienda, were long ranges of mounds. These had once been buildings, the tops of which had fallen, and almost buried the structures. At the end was a doorway, encumbered and half filled with rubbish, crawling through which, we stood upright in apartments exactly similar to those at Uxmal, with the arch formed of stones overlapping, and a flat stone covering the top.

The day was now nearly spent; with the heat and labour we were exceedingly fatigued, and the Indians insisted that we had seen all the principal remains. The place was so overgrown with trees that it would have taken a long time to clear them away, and for the present at least it was out of the question. Besides, the only result we could promise ourselves was the bringing to light of fragments and single pieces of buried sculpture. Of one thing, however, we had no doubt: the ruins of this city were of the same general character with those at Uxmal, erected by the same builders, probably of older date, and suffering more from the corrosion of the elements, or they had been visited more harshly by the destroying hand of man.

Fortunately, at this place again we have a ray of historic light. According to the best accounts, the region of country now called Yucatan was known to the natives, at the time of the Spanish invasion, by the name of Maya, and before that time it had never been known by any other. The name of Yucatan was given to it by the Spaniards. It is entirely arbitrary and accidental, and its origin is not known with certainty. It is supposed by some to be derived from the plant known in the islands by the name of *Yuca*, and *tal* or *thale*, the heap of earth in which this plant grows; but more generally it is derived from certain words supposed to have been spoken by the natives in answer to a question asked by the Spaniards on their first arrival. The supposed question is, "What is the name of this country?" or, "How is this country called?" and the conjectured answer, "I do not understand those words," or, "I do not understand your words," either of which expressions, in the language of the natives, has some resemblance in pronunciation to the word Yucatan. But whatever was its origin, the natives have never recognised the name, and to this day, among themselves, they speak of their country only under its ancient name of Maya. No native ever calls himself a Yucateco, but always a Macegual, or native of the land of Maya.

One language, called the Maya, extended throughout the whole peninsula; and though the Spaniards found the country parcelled into different governments, under various names and having different caciques, hostile to each other, at an earlier period of its history the whole land of Maya was united under one head or supreme lord. This great chief or king had for the seat of his monarchy a very populous city called Mayapan, and had under him many other lords and caciques, who were bound to pay him tribute of cotton clothes, fowls, cacao, and gum or resin for incense; to serve him in wars, and day and night in the temples of the idols, at festivals and ceremonies. These lords, too, had under them cities and many vassals. Becoming proud and ambitious, and unwilling to brook a superior, they rebelled against the power of the supreme lord, united all their forces, and besieged and destroyed the city of Mayapan. This destruction took place in the year of our Lord 1420, about one hundred years before the arrival of the Spaniards in Yucatan; and, according to the computation of the ages of the Indians, two hundred and seventy years from the foundation of the city. The account is confused and indistinct; but the existence of a principal city called Mayapan, and its destruction by war at about the time indicated, are mentioned by every historian. This city was occupied by the same race of people who inhabited the country at the time of the conquest, and its site is identified as that just presented, retaining, through all changes and in its ruins, its ancient name of Mayapan.

The interest of our day at Mayapan came near being marred by an unlucky accident. Just as we were leaving the ruins a messenger came to inform us that one of our pistols had shot an Indian. These pistols had never shown any particular antipathy to Indians, and had never shot one before. Hurrying back to the hacienda, we found the poor fellow with two of his fingers nearly shot off. The ball had passed through his shirt, making two holes in it, fortunately without hitting his body. The Indians said that the pistol had gone off itself while they were only looking at it. We felt sure that this was not exactly the case, knowing that pistols are not free agents, and laid the blame upon them. But it was a great satisfaction that the accident was no worse, and also that Doctor Cabot was at hand to dress the wound. The Indian seemed to think less of it than we did.

It was late when we left the hacienda. Our road was a mere bridle-path through a wilderness. At some distance we crossed a broken range of stones, rising on each side to a wall, which the major domo said was the line of wall that encompassed the ancient city.

It was nearly dark when we reached the stately hacienda of

Xcanchakan, one of the three finest in Yucatan, and containing nearly seven hundred souls. Our friend the cura of Tekoh was still with us, and, in order to entertain us, requested the major domo to get up a dance of the Indians. Very soon we heard the sound of the violins and the Indian drum. This latter consists of a hollow log with a piece of parchment stretched over the end, on which an Indian, holding it under his left arm, beats with his right hand. It is the same instrument known to the inhabitants at the time of the conquest by the name of *tunkúl* and is the favourite now. Going out into the back corridor, we saw the musicians sitting at one end, before the door of the chapel; on one side of the corridor were the women, and on the other the men.

For some time there was no dancing, until, at length, at the instance of the cura, the major domo gave his directions, and a young man stood up in the middle of the corridor. Another, with a pocket-handkerchief in his hand having a knot tied in one end, walked along the line of women, threw the handkerchief at one, and then returned to his seat. This was considered a challenge or invitation. With a

31   *A Hacienda*

9. Catherwood drawing of the hacienda of Xcanchakan

proper prudery, as if to show that she was not to be had for the asking, she waited some minutes, then rose, and slowly taking the shawl from her head, placed herself opposite the young man, at a distance of about ten feet, and commenced dancing. The dance was called the toros, or the bull. The movements were slow; occasionally the performers crossed over and changed places. When the time ended the lady walked deliberately off, which either brought the young man to a standstill, or he went on dancing, as he liked. The master of ceremonies, who was called the *bastonero,* again walked along the line, and touched another lady in the same way with the handkerchief. She again, after waiting a moment, removed her shawl and took her place on the floor. In this way the dance continued, the dancing man being always the same, and taking the partner provided for him. Afterward the dance was changed to a Spanish one, in which, instead of castanets, the dancers from time to time snapped their fingers. This was more lively, and seemed to please them better than their own, but throughout there was nothing national or characteristic.

Stopping but a few minutes at the hacienda of Uxmal, we mounted again, and in ten minutes came out upon the open field in which, grand and lofty as when we saw it before, stood the House of the Dwarf. The first glance showed us that a year had made great changes. The sides of the lofty structure, then bare and naked, were now covered with high grass, bushes, and weeds, and on the top were bushes and young trees twenty feet high. The House of the Nuns was almost smothered, and the whole field was covered with a rank growth of grass and weeds, over which we could barely look as we rode through. The foundations, terraces, and tops of the buildings were overgrown, weeds and vines were rioting and creeping on the façades. A strong and vigorous nature was struggling for mastery over art, wrapping the city in its suffocating embraces, and burying it from sight. It seemed as if the grave was closing over a friend, and we had arrived barely in time to take our farewell.

Amid this mass of desolation, grand and stately as when we left it, stood the Casa del Gobernador, but with all its terraces covered, and separated from us by a mass of impenetrable verdure. On the left of the field was an overgrown milpa, along the edge of which a path led in front of this building. Following this path, we turned the corner of the terrace, and on the farthest side dismounted, and tied our horses. The grass and weeds were above our heads, and we could see nothing. The mayoral broke a way through them, and we reached the foot of the terrace. Working our way over the stones with much toil, we reached the top of the highest terrace. Here, too, the grass and weeds were of the same rank growth. We moved directly to the wall at the east end, and entered the first open door. Here the mayoral wished us to take up our abode; but we knew the localities better than he did, and, creeping along the front as close to the wall as possible, cutting some of the bushes, and tearing apart and trampling down others, we reached the centre apartment. Here we stopped. Swarms of bats, roused by our approach, fluttered and flew through the long chamber, and passed out at the doors.

Throughout Yucatan "el campo," or the country, is considered unhealthy in the rainy season. We had arrived in Yucatan counting upon the benefit of the whole dry season, which generally begins in November and lasts till May; but this year the rains had continued longer than usual, and they were not yet over. The proprietors of haciendas were still cautious about visiting them, and confined themselves to the villages and towns. Among all the haciendas, Uxmal had a reputation pre-eminent for its unhealthiness. Every person who had ever been at work among the ruins had been obliged by sickness to leave them. Mr. Catherwood had had sad experience, and this unhealthiness was not confined to strangers. The Indians suffered every season from fevers; many of them were at that time ill, and the major

10. View of the ruins of Uxmal from the North Structure of the Nunnery Quadrangle (Charnay, 1860)

domo had been obliged to go away. All this we had been advised of in Merida, and had been urged to postpone our visit. But as this would have interfered with our plan, and as we had with us a "medico," we determined to risk it. On the spot, however, we felt that we had been imprudent; but it was too late to draw back. We agreed that we were better on this high terrace than at the hacienda, which stood low, and had around it great tanks of water, mantled with green, and wearing a very fever-and-aguish aspect. We therefore set to work immediately to make the best of our condition.

The mayoral left us to take the horses back to the hacienda, and give directions about the luggage, and we had only a little Indian boy to help us. We intimated to him by signs that we wanted a fire. He began with a scrap of cotton, which he picked up from the ground, and, lighting it with a match, blew it gently in his folded hands till it was all ignited. He then laid it on the floor and gathered up some little sticks, not larger than matches, which he laid against the ignited cotton, with one point on the ground and the other touching the fire. Then kneeling down, he encircled the nascent fire with his two hands, and blew gently on it, with his mouth so close as almost to touch it. A slight smoke rose above the palms of his hands. He had a few little sticks with a languishing fire at one end, which might be extinguished by dropping a few tears over it. Still there was a steadiness, an assurance in his manner that seemed to say he knew what he was about. The wood seemed to feel the influence of his cherishing care. A gentle blaze rose in the whole centre of the pile. Still he coaxed it along, and by degrees brought on sticks as large as his arm, which, by a gentle waving of his hat, in a few minutes were all ignited.

Perhaps half an hour elapsed, when we saw a single Indian ascend the platform of the second terrace, with his machete slowly working his way toward us. Very soon the top of a long box was seen rising above the same terrace, apparently tottering and falling back, but rising again and coming on steadily, with an Indian under it, visible from time to time through the bushes. Holding on with both hands to the strap across his forehead, with every nerve strung, and the veins of his forehead swelled almost to bursting, his face and his whole body dripping with sweat, he laid his load at our feet. A long line followed; staggering, panting, and trembling, they took the loads from their backs, and deposited them at the door. They had carried these loads three leagues, or nine miles, and we paid them eighteen and three quarter cents. We gave them a medio extra for bringing the things up the terrace, and the poor fellows were thankful and happy.

At nightfall the Indians left us, and we were again alone in the palace of unknown kings.

We had reached the first point of our journey; we were once more at the ruins of Uxmal. It was nearly two years since we originally set out in search of American ruins, and more than a year since we were driven from this place. The freshness and enthusiasm with which we had first come upon the ruins of an American city had perhaps gone, but our feelings were not blunted, and all the regret which we had felt in being obliged to leave was more than counterbalanced by the satisfaction of returning.

Early in the evening a few straggling moschetoes had given us notice of the existence of these free and independent citizens of Yucatan; but while we were swinging in our hammocks and the fire burned brightly, they had not troubled us much. Our heads, however, were hardly upon our pillows, before the whole population seemed to know exactly where they could have us, and, dividing into three swarms, came upon us as if determined to lift us up and eject us bodily from the premises. The flame and volumes of smoke which had rolled through the building, in ridding us of the damp, unwholesome atmosphere, seemed only to have started these torments from their cracks and crevices, and filled them with thirst for vengeance or for blood. I spare the reader farther details of our first night at Uxmal, but we all agreed that another such would drive us forever from the ruins.

Morning brought with it other perplexities. We had no servant, and wanted breakfast, and altogether our prospects were not good. The mayoral of the hacienda had received special orders from his master to do everything in his power to serve us, but the power of his master had limits. He could not make the Indians, who knew only the Maya, speak Spanish. Besides this, the power of the master was otherwise restricted. In fact, except as regards certain obligations which they owed, the Indians were their own masters, and, what was worse for us, their own mistresses, for one of our greatest wants was a woman to cook, make tortillas, and perform those numerous domestic offices without which no household can go on well. The mayoral had given us no hope of being able to procure one. But in the midst of our anxieties, and while we were preparing breakfast for ourselves, we perceived him coming across the terrace, followed by a train of Indians, and closing the procession was a woman, at that time really a welcome visiter.

She was taller than most of the Indian women, and her complexion was somewhat darker. Her dress fitted more closely to her body, and she had more of it. Her character was unimpeached, her bearing would have kept presumption at a distance, and, as an additional safeguard, she had with her a little grandson, whose complexion indicated that the descending line of her house had no antipathies to the white race. Her age might be a little over fifty, and her name was Chaipa Chi.

The preliminaries being settled, we immediately installed her as *chef de cuisine*. The first essay of Chaipa Chi was in boiling eggs, which, according to the custom of the country, she boiled para beber, or to drink; that is, by breaking a small hole in the shell, into which a stick is inserted to mix together the white and yolk; the egg is to be disposed of through this hole in the primitive way which nature indicates to the new-born babe. This did not suit us, and we wished the process of cooking to be continued a little longer, but Chaipa Chi was impenetrable to hints or signs. We were obliged to stand over her, and, but for the name of the thing, we might as well have cooked them ourselves. This over, we gave up, and left our dinner to the mercies of our chef.

Before we were in a condition to begin an examination and exploration of the ruins, we had a serious business before us in making the necessary clearings. We determined first to clear the terrace of the Casa del Gobernador, and cut roads from ruin to ruin, until we had a complete line of communication. Our Indians made a good beginning, and by the afternoon we had the upper terrace cleared. Toward evening they all left us, including Chaipa Chi, and at night, while the moon was glimmering mournfully over the ruins, we had a stroll along the whole front of the Casa del Gobernador.

The next day we made a valuable addition to our household. Among the Indians who came out to work was a lad who spoke Spanish. He was the puniest, lankest, and leanest of any we had seen on the hacienda, and his single garment was the dirtiest. His name was Bernaldo. He was but fifteen, and he was already experiencing the vicissitudes of fortune. For confounding some technical distinctions in the laws of property, he was banished from a hacienda near Merida to the deserts of Uxmal. We were in such straits for want of an interpreter that we overlooked entirely Bernaldo's moral weakness, withdrew him from the workmen, and led him to the sala of the palace, where, in the course of conveying some instructions to Chaipa Chi, he showed such an interest in the subject that Doctor Cabot immediately undertook to give him a lesson in cookery. In his first essay he was so apt that we forthwith inducted him as ruler over the three stones that composed our kitchen fireplace, with all the privileges and emoluments of sipping and tasting, and left Chaipa Chi to bestow all her energies upon the business that her soul loved, the making of tortillas.

CHAPTER THREE

Halachó and Maxcanú

*A*ving made such advances in the clearing that Mr. Catherwood had abundance of occupation, I set out, under the guidance of the mayoral, on an excursion to meet Don Simon Peon at the fair of Jalacho, and visit some ruins on another hacienda of his in that neighbourhood. We started at half past six, our course being west by north. At ten minutes past seven we crossed a range of hills, and came down upon an extensive savanna of low, flat land. The road was the worst I had found in the country, being simply a wet and very muddy path. My horse sunk up to his saddle-girths, and it was with great exertion that he dragged himself through. Every moment I had fear of his rolling over in the mud. Occasionally the branches were barely high enough to allow mules to pass, and then I was obliged to dismount, and trudge through the mud on foot. At eight o'clock we came to an open savanna, and saw a high mound with ruins on the top, bearing south, about a mile distant. It was called Senuisacal. I was strongly tempted to turn aside and examine it, but, on account of the thickness of the cane-brake and the mud, it would have been impossible to reach it, and the mayoral said that it was entirely in ruins.

At ten we entered the camino real for Jalacho, a broad and open road, passable for calesas. Up to this time we had not seen a single habitation or met a human being, and now the road was literally thronged with people moving on to the fair. There were Indians, Mestizoes, and white people on horseback, muleback, and on foot, men, women, and children, many carrying on their backs things to sell; whole families, sometimes half a village moving in company. I fell in behind a woman perched on a loaded horse, with a child in her arms, and a little fellow behind. We passed parties sitting in the shade to rest or eat, and families lying down by the roadside to sleep, without any fear of molestation from the rest.

At half past eleven we reached the village of Becal, conspicuous, like all the others, for a large plaza and church with two towers. In an hour I reached Jalacho, where I met Don Simon and two of his brothers; Don Lorenzo, who had a hacienda in that neighbourhood, and Don Alonzo, then living in Campeachy, who was educated in New-York, and spoke English remarkably well.

The village of Jalacho lies on the main road from Merida to Campeachy, and, next to that of Yzamal, its fair is the greatest in Yucatan, while in some respects it is more curious. It is not attended by large merchants with foreign goods, nor by the better classes from Merida, but it is resorted to by all the Indians from the haciendas and villages. It is inferior in one respect: gambling is not carried on upon so large a scale as at Yzamal. The fair of Jalacho was an observance of eight days, but the first two or three were marked only by the arrival of scattering parties, and the business of securing places to live in and to display wares. The great gathering did not begin till the day of my arrival, and then it was computed that there were assembled in the village ten thousand persons.

The plaza was the grand point of concentration. Along the houses fronting it was a range of tables set out with looking-glasses in frames of red paper, rings and necklaces, cotton, and toys and trinkets for the Indians. On the opposite side of the street, along the square of the church, were rustic arbours, occupied by venders having similar commodities spread before them. The plaza was partitioned, and at regular intervals was a rude stick fixed upright in the ground, and having another crosswise at the top, covered with leaves and twigs, thus forming a sort of umbrella, to protect its sitting occupant from the sun. These were the merchants of dulces and other eatables.

Night came on, and the plaza was alive with people and brilliant

11. *Page 38*: East face of the House of the Governor, Uxmal (Augustus Le Plongeon, circa 1880)

with lights. On one side, opposite the church, were rows of tables, with cards and dice, which were very soon crowded with players, whites and Mestizoes; but the great scene of attraction was the gathering of Indians in the centre of the plaza. It was the hour of supper, and the small merchants had abundant custom for their eatables. Turkeys which had stood tied by one leg all day, inviting people to come and eat them, were now ready. For a medio two men had a liberal allowance.

I remarked, what I had heard of, but had not seen before, that grains of cacao circulated among the Indians as money. Every vender of eatables, most of whom were women, had on the table a pile of these grains, which they were constantly counting and exchanging with the Indians. There is no copper money in Yucatan, nor any coin whatever under a medio, or six and a quarter cents, and this deficiency is supplied by these grains of cacao. The medio is divided into twenty parts, generally of five grains each. As the earnings of the Indians are small, and the articles they purchase are the mere necessaries of life, which are very cheap, these grains of cacao are the coin in most common use among them. The currency has always a real value, and is regulated by the quantity of cacao in the market. These grains had an interest independent of all questions of political economy, for they illustrate a page in the history of this unknown and mysterious people. When the Spaniards first made their way into the interior of Yucatan, they found no circulating medium, either of gold, or silver, or any other species of metal, but only grains of cacao. It seemed a strange circumstance, that while the manners and customs of the Indians have undergone an immense change, while their cities have been destroyed, their religion dishonoured, their princes swept away, and their whole government modified by foreign laws, no experiment has yet been made upon their currency.

The next day I had as a guide a major domo of another hacienda, who, being, as I imagined, vexed at being obliged to leave the fiesta, and determined to get me off his hands as soon as possible, set out at a swinging trot. The sun was scorching, the road broad, straight, and stony, and without a particle of shade. In forty minutes, both considerably heated, we reached the hacienda of Sijoh. This hacienda belonged to a brother of Don Simon, then resident in Vera Cruz. Here my guide passed me over into the hands of an Indian, and rode back as fast as he could to the fair. The Indian mounted another horse, and, continuing a short distance on the same road, we turned off, and in five minutes saw in the woods a high mound of ruins of that distinctive character once so strange, but now so familiar to me, proclaiming the existence of another unknown, nameless, desolate, and ruined city.

We continued on to another mound, where we dismounted and tied our horses to the bushes. This mound was a solid mass of masonry, about thirty feet high, and nearly square. On the top was a stone building, with its wall as high as the cornice standing. Above this the façade had fallen, but the mass of stone and mortar which formed the roof remained, and within the apartment was precisely like the interior of the buildings at Uxmal. There were no remains of sculpture, but the base of the mound was encumbered with fallen stones.

Leaving this, we returned through the woods to the mound we had first seen. Whatever it might have been, its features were entirely lost. The mass of stone was so solid that no vegetation could take root upon it. Its sides were bare and bleached, and the pieces, on being disturbed, slid down with a metallic sound like the ringing of iron. Climbing up I received a blow from a sliding stone, which nearly carried me back to the bottom, and from which I did not recover until some time afterward.

It was now about one o'clock. The heat was intense, and sweating and covered with briers and burrs, which stuck to every part of my clothes, I came out into the open road, where my Indian was waiting for me with the horses. We mounted immediately, and continued on a gallop to the hacienda of Tankuché, two leagues distant.

This hacienda was a favourite with Don Simon, as he had created it out of the wilderness, and the entire road from the village he had made himself. It was a good logwood country, and here he had erected machinery for extracting the dye. The huts of the Indians were closed and locked up; no barebodied children were playing around them, and the large gate was locked. We tied our horses, and, ascending by a flight of stone steps, entered the lane and walked up to the house. Every door was locked, and not a person in sight. Moving on to the high stone structure forming the platform of the well, I saw a little boy, dressed in a straw hat, dozing on an old horse, which was creeping round with the well-beam, drawing in broken buckets a slow stream of water, for which no one came. At sight of me he rose from the neck of his horse, and tried to stop him, but the old animal seemed so used to going round that he could not stop, and the little fellow looked as if he expected to be going till some one came to take him off. I sat down under a large seybo tree overshadowing the well, and ate a roll of bread and an orange, after which I strolled back to the gate, and, to my surprise, found only one horse. My guide had mounted his and returned to his hacienda. I walked into the factory, returned to the well, and attempted speech with the boy, but the old horse started forward and carried him away from me. I lay down on the platform of the well. The creaking of the beam served as a sort of lullaby, and I was not very eager to be interrupted, when an Indian lad arrived, who had been hunted up by my missing guide, and directed to show me the ruins. Fortunately, he was accompanied by an Indian who spoke Spanish. Through him I had an understanding with my new guide, and set out again.

After leaving the hacienda, we passed between two mounds of ruins, and, from time to time having glimpses of other vestiges in the woods, we came to a mound, on the top of which was a ruined building. Here we dismounted, tied our horses, and ascended the mound. The front wall had fallen, together with the front half of the arch; the interior chamber was filled with dirt and rubbish nearly up to the cornice, and the arch of the back wall was the only part above ground. This, instead of being of smooth stones, like all the others we had seen in Yucatan, was plastered and covered with paintings, the colours of which were still bright and fresh. The principal colours were red, green, yellow, and blue, and at first the lines and figures seemed so distinct that I thought I could make out the subjects. The apartment being filled up with dirt, I stood above the objects, and it was only by sitting, or rather lying down, that I could examine them. One subject at first sight struck me as being a representation of the mask found at Palenque. I was extremely desirous to get this off entire, but found, by experiments upon other parts of the plaster with the machete, that it would be impossible to do so, and left it untouched.

In the interest of the work, I did not discover that thousands of garrapatas were crawling over me. These insects are the scourge of Yucatan, and altogether they were a more constant source of annoyance and suffering than any we encountered in the country. I had seen something of them in Central America, but at a different season, when the hot sun had killed off the immensity of their numbers, and those left had attained such a size that a single one could easily be seen and picked off. These, in colour, size, and numbers, were like grains of sand. They disperse themselves all over the body, get into the seams of the clothes, and, like the insect known among us as the tick, bury themselves in the flesh, causing an irritation that is almost intolerable. The only way to get rid of them effectually is by changing all the clothes. In Uxmal we had not been troubled with them, for they are said to breed only in those woods where cattle pasture, and

12. Modern view of an
unrestored interior
chamber showing limestone
construction and plaster
finish, Labná

the grounds about Uxmal had been used as a milpa, or plantation of corn.

It was now nearly dark. My day's work had been a severe one. I was tired and covered with garrapatas, but the next day was Sunday, the last of the fiesta. There was a brilliant moonlight, and, hurrying on, at eleven o'clock I saw, at the end of a long straight road, the illuminated front of the church of Jalacho. Very soon, I passed by the tables of the gamblers, worked my way through the plaza and through a crowd of Indians, who fell back in deference to the colour of my skin, and, unexpectedly to my friends, presented myself at the baile. For the last night of the fiesta the neighbouring villages had sent forth their all. The ball was larger and gayer of whites and those in whose veins white blood ran, while outside, leaning upon the railing, looking in, but not presuming to enter, were close files of Indians, and beyond, in the plaza, was a dense mass of them—natives of the land and lords of the soil, that strange people in whose ruined cities I had just been wandering, submitting quietly to the dominion of strangers, bound down and trained to the most abject submission, and looking up to the white man as a superior being. Could these be the descendants of that fierce people who had made such bloody resistance to the Spanish conquerors?

At no time since my arrival in the country had I been so struck with the peculiar constitution of things in Yucatan. Originally portioned out as slaves, the Indians remain as servants. Veneration for masters is the first lesson they learn, and these masters, the descendants of the terrible conquerors, in centuries of uninterrupted peace have lost all the fierceness of their ancestors. Gentle, and averse to labour themselves, they impose no heavy burdens upon the Indians, but understand and humour their ways, and the two races move on harmoniously together, with nothing to apprehend from each other, forming a simple, primitive, and almost patriarchal state of society. So strong is the sense of personal security, that, notwithstanding the crowds of strangers, and although every day Don Simon had sat with doors open and piles of money on the table, so little apprehension was there of robbery, that we slept without a door or window locked.

At four o'clock the next day I set off with Don Lorenzo Peon for Maxcanú. Our mode of conveyance, much used in Yucatan, but new to me, was called a caricoché. It was a long wagon, on two large wheels, covered with cotton cloth as a protection against the sun, and on the bottom was stretched a broad mattress, on which two persons could recline at full length. It was drawn by one horse, with a driver riding as postillion, and another horse followed to change. The road was broad, even, and level. It was the camino real between Merida and Campeachy, and would pass in any country for a fair carriage road. In an hour we came in sight of the sierra which traverses at that point the whole peninsula of Yucatan from east to west. The sight of hills was cheering, and with the reflection of the setting sun upon them, they presented almost the first fine scenery I had encountered in the country. In an hour and ten minutes we reached Maxcanú.

In the evening, when notice was given of my intention to visit the cave, half the village was ready to join me, but in the morning my volunteers were not forthcoming, and I was reduced to the men procured for me by Don Lorenzo. From the time consumed in getting the men together and procuring torches, cord, &c., I did not get off till after nine o'clock. Our direction was due east till we reached the sierra, ascending which through a passage overgrown with woods, we arrived at the mouth, or rather door, of the cueva, about a league distant from the village.

I had before heard so much of caves, and had been so often disappointed, that I did not expect much from this; but the first view satisfied me in regard to the main point, viz., that it was not a natural cave, and that, as had been represented to me, it was hecha à mano, or made by hand.

La Cueva de Maxcanú has a marvellous and mystical reputation. It is called by the Indians Satun Sat, which means in Spanish El Laberinto or El Perdedero, the Labyrinth, or place in which one may be lost. Notwithstanding its wonderful reputation, and a name which alone, in any other country, would induce a thorough exploration, it is a singular fact, and exhibits more strikingly than anything I can mention the indifference of the people of all classes to the antiquities of the country, that up to the time of my arrival at the door, this Laberinto had never been examined. My friend Don Lorenzo Peon would give me every facility for exploring it except joining me himself. Several persons had penetrated to some distance with a string held outside, but had turned back, and the universal belief was, that it contained passages without number and without end.

My retinue consisted of eight men, who considered themselves in my employ, besides three or four supernumeraries. As I considered it important to have a reliable man outside, I stationed the mayoral of Uxmal at the door with a ball of twine. I tied one end round my left wrist, and told one of the men to light a torch and follow me, but he refused absolutely, and all the rest, one after the other, did the same. They were all ready enough to hold the string; and I was curious to know, and had a conference with them on the interesting point, whether they expected any pay for their services in standing out of doors. One expected pay for showing me the place, others for carrying water, another for taking care of the horses, and so on, but I terminated the matter abruptly by declaring that I should not pay one of them a medio. Ordering them all away from the door, which they were smothering, and a little infected with one of their apprehensions of starting some wild beast, which might be making his lair in the recesses of the cave, I entered with a candle in one hand and a pistol in the other.

The entrance faces the west. The mouth was filled up with rubbish, scrambling over which, I stood in a narrow passage or gallery, constructed, like all the apartments above ground, with smooth walls and triangular arched ceiling. It ran due east, and at the distance of six or eight yards opened into another, or rather was stopped by another crossing it, running north and south. I took first that on the right hand, running south. At the distance of a few yards, I found a door, filled up, and at the distance of thirty-five feet the passage ended, and a door opened into another gallery running due east. Following this, I found another gallery, and beyond it, at the end, still another, four yards long, and then walled up, with only an opening in it about a foot square. Turning back, I entered the gallery which I had passed. At the end was a doorway on the right, opening into a gallery. In utter ignorance of the ground, I found myself turning and doubling along these dark and narrow passages, which seemed really to have no end, and justly to entitle the place to its name of El Laberinto.

I was not entirely free from the apprehension of starting some wild animal, and moved slowly and very cautiously. In the mean time, in turning the corners, my twine would be entangled, and the Indians, moved by the probability of getting no pay, entered to clear it, and by degrees all came up with me in a body. I got a glimpse of their torches behind me just as I was turning into a new passage. At the moment I was startled by a noise which sent me back rather quickly, and completely routed them. It proceeded from a rushing of bats. Having a sort of horror of these beastly birds, this was an ugly place to meet them in, for the passage was so low, and there was so little room for a flight over head, that in walking upright there was great danger of their striking the face. It was necessary to move with the head bent down, and protecting the lights from the flapping of their wings. Nevertheless, every step was exciting, and called up recollections of the Pyramids and tombs of Egypt. I could not but believe that these dark and intricate passages would introduce me to some large saloon, or perhaps some royal sepulchre. Belzoni, and the tomb of Cephrenes and its alabaster sarcophagus, were floating through my brain, when all at once I found the passage choked up and effectually stopped. The ceiling had fallen in, crushed by a great mass of superincumbent earth, and farther progress was utterly impossible.

I was not prepared for this abrupt termination. The walls and ceiling were so solid and in such good condition that the possibility of such a result had not occurred to me. I was sure of going on to the end and discovering something, and I was arrested without knowing any better than when I entered to what point these passages led, or for what purposes they had been constructed. My first impulse was to dig a way through; but the impossibility of accomplishing anything in this way soon presented itself. For the Indians to carry out the earth on their backs through all these passages would be a never-ending work. Besides, I had no idea how far the destruction extended.

In exploring that part to the left of the door, I made an important discovery. In the walls of one of the passages was a hole eight inches square, which admitted light, and looking through it, I saw some plump and dusky legs, which clearly did not belong to the antiguos, and which I easily recognised as those of my worthy attendants.

Having heard the place spoken of as a subterraneous construction, and seeing, when I reached the ground, a half-buried door with a mass of overgrown earth above it, it had not occurred to me to think otherwise. But on examining outside, I found that what I had taken for an irregular natural formation, like a hill-side, was a pyramidal mound of the same general character with all the rest we had seen in the country. Making the Indians clear away some thorn-bushes, with the help of the branches of a tree growing near I climbed up it. On the top were the ruins of a building, the same as all the others. The door of El Laberinto, instead of opening into a hill-side, opened into this mound, and was, as near as I could judge from the ruins along the base, ten feet high. Heretofore it had been our impression that these mounds were solid and compact masses of stone and earth, without any chambers or structures of any kind. The discovery of the Laberinto gave rise to the exciting idea that all the great mounds scattered over the country contained secret, unknown, and hidden chambers, presenting an immense field for exploration and discovery, and, ruined as the buildings on their summits were, perhaps the only source left for acquiring knowledge of the people by whom the cities were constructed.

In the account which I had received of this Labyrinth, no mention had been made of any ruins, and probably, when on the ground, I should have heard nothing of them, but from the top of this mound I saw two others, both of which, with a good deal of labour, I reached under the guidance of the Indians, crossing a patch of beans and milpa. On the top of one was a building a hundred feet long. The front wall had fallen, and left exposed the inner part of the back wall, with half the arch, as it were, supporting itself in the air. The Indians then led me to a fourth mound, and told me that there were others in the woods, but all in the same ruinous condition. Considering the excessive heat and the desperate toil of clambering, I did not think it worth while to visit them. I saw no sculptured stones, except those dug out like troughs, called pilas, though the Indians persisted in saying that there were such all over, but they did not know exactly where to find them.

At three o'clock I resumed my journey toward Uxmal. About an hour before dark, I saw near the road, a high mound, with an edifice on its top, which at that distance, through the trees, seemed almost entire. It stood in a cornfield. I was not looking out for anything of the kind, and but for the clearing, I could not have seen it at all. Beyond the milpa all was forest, and what lay buried in it I had no means of ascertaining. The place was silent and desolate; there was no one of whom I could ask any questions. I never heard of these ruins till I saw them from the back of my horse, and I could never learn by what name they are called. At half past six we reached the village of Opocheque. We stopped for a cup of water, and then, pushing on by a bright moonlight, at nine o'clock reached the village of Moona.

Early the next morning we resumed our course. Immediately behind the village we crossed the sierra, the same broken and stony range, commanding on both sides the same grand view of a boundless wooded plain. In an hour we saw at a distance on our left the high mound of ruins visible from the House of the Dwarf, known under the Indian name of Xcoch. About five miles before arriving at Uxmal, I saw another high mound. At twelve o'clock I reached Uxmal. The extent of my journey had been thirteen leagues, or thirty-nine miles; for though I had varied my route in returning, I had not increased the distance, and I had seen seven different places of ruins, memorials of cities which had been and had passed away, and such memorials as no cities built by the Spaniards in that country would present.

CHAPTER FOUR

Uxmal: Explorations

The ruins of Uxmal presented themselves to me as a home, and I looked upon them with more interest than before. I had found the wrecks of cities scattered more numerously than I expected, but they were all so shattered that no voice of instruction issued from them; here they still stood, tottering and crumbling, but living memorials, more worthy than ever of investigation and study, and as I then thought, perhaps the only existing vestiges that could transmit to posterity the image of an American city.

As I approached, I saw on the terrace our beds, with moscheto-nets fluttering in the wind, and trunks and boxes all turned out of doors, having very much the appearance of a forcible ejectment for non-payment of rent. On arriving I found that my companions were *moving*. In the great sala, with its three doors, they had found themselves too much exposed to the heavy dews and night air, and they were about removing to a smaller apartment, being that next to the last on the south wing, which had but one door, and could more easily be kept dry by a fire.

The next day opened with a drizzling rain, the beginning of the prevailing storm of the country, called El Norte. This storm, we were told, rarely occurred at this season, and the mayoral said that after it was over, the regular dry season would certainly set in. The thermometer fell to fifty-two, and to our feelings the change was much for the better. In fact, we had begun to feel a degree of lassitude, the effect of the excessive heat, and this change restored and reinvigorated us.

This day, too, Don Simon arrived from Jalacho to pay us a visit. He was not in the habit of visiting Uxmal at this season, and though less fearful than other members of his family, he was not without apprehensions on account of the health of the place. His visit was a fortunate circumstance for us; his knowledge of localities, and his disposition to forward our views, gave us great facilities in our exploration of the ruins. At the same time our presence and co-operation induced him to satisfy his own curiosity in regard to some things which had not yet been examined.

Throughout the ruins circular holes were found at different places in the ground, opening into chambers underneath, which had never been examined. We had noticed them, at the time of our former visit, on the platform of the great terrace. Though this platform was now entirely overgrown, and many of them were hidden from sight, in opening a path to communicate with the hacienda we had laid bare two. The mayoral had lately discovered another at some distance outside the wall, so perfect at the mouth, and apparently so deep on sounding it with a stone, that Don Simon wished to explore it.

The next morning he came to the ruins with Indians, ropes, and candles, and we began immediately with one of those on the platform before the Casa del Gobernador. The opening was a circular hole, eighteen inches in diameter. The throat consisted of five layers of stones, a yard deep, to a stratum of solid rock. As it was all dark beneath, before descending, in order to guard against the effects of impure air, we let down a candle, which soon touched bottom. The only way of descending was to tie a rope around the body, and be lowered by the Indians. In this way I was let down, and almost before my head had passed through the hole my feet touched the top of a heap of rubbish. Clambering down it, I found myself in a round chamber, so filled with rubbish that I could not stand upright. With a candle in my hand, I crawled all round on my hands and knees. The chamber was in the shape of a dome, and had been coated with plaster, most of which had fallen, and now encumbered the ground. The depth could not be ascertained without clearing out the interior. In

13. *Page 50:* East face of the Pyramid of the Magician (Stephens' House of the Dwarf), from the road (Thompson, circa 1888–89)

groping about I found pieces of broken pottery, and a vase of terra cotta, having upon it a coat of enamel, which, though not worn off, had lost some of its brightness. It had three feet, each about an inch high, one of which is broken. In other respects it was entire.

The discovery of this vase was encouraging. Not one of these places had ever been explored. Neither Don Simon nor any of the Indians knew anything about them. Entering them now for the first time, we were excited by the hope that we had discovered a rich mine of curious and interesting fabrics wrought by the inhabitants of this ruined city. Besides this, we had already ascertained one point in regard to which we were doubtful before. This great terrace was not entirely artificial. The substratum was of natural rock, and showed that advantage had been taken of a natural elevation, so far as it went, and by this means some portion of the immense labour of constructing the terrace had been saved.

On the same terrace, directly at the foot of the steps, was another opening of the same kind, and, on clearing around, we found near by a circular stone about six inches in thickness, which fitted the hole, and no doubt had served as a cover. This hole was filled up with dirt to within two feet of the mouth, and setting some Indians at work to clear it out, we passed on in search of another. The Indians looked upon our entering these places as senseless and foolhardy, and, besides imaginary dangers, they talked of snakes, scorpions, and hornets, the last of which, from the experience we had had of them in different parts of the ruins, were really objects of fear. A swarm of them coming upon a man in such a place would almost murder him before he could be hauled out.

We went on to a third, which was exactly the same, except that it was a little smaller. The fourth was the one which had just been discovered, and which had excited the curiosity of the mayoral. It was a few feet outside of a wall which, as Don Simon said, might be traced through the woods, broken and ruined, until it met and enclosed within its circle the whole of the principal buildings. The mouth was covered with cement, and in the throat was a large stone filling it up. A rope was passed under the stone, and it was hauled out. The throat was smaller than any of the others, and hardly large enough to pass the body of a man. In shape and finish it was exactly the same as the others, with perhaps a slight shade of difference in the dimensions. The smallness of this mouth was, to my mind, strong proof that these subterraneous chambers had never been intended for any purposes which required men to descend into them. The throat was so small that there was no play for the arms, to enable me to raise myself up by the rope, and the stones around the mouth were insecure and tottering. I was obliged to trust to the Indians, and they involuntarily knocked my head against the stones, let down upon me a shower of dirt, and gave me such a severe rasping that I had no disposition at that time to descend another.

We were extremely disappointed in not finding any more vases or relics. We could not account for the one found in the chamber under the terrace, and were obliged to suppose that it had been thrown in or got there by accident.

These subterraneous chambers are scattered over the whole ground covered by the ruined city. There was one in the cattleyard before the hacienda, and the Indians were constantly discovering them at greater distances. Dr. Cabot found them continually in his hunting excursions, and once, in breaking through bushes in search of a bird, fell into one, and narrowly escaped a serious injury. Indeed, there were so many of them, and in places where they were so little to be expected, that they made rambling out of the cleared paths dangerous, and to the last day of our visit we were constantly finding new ones.

That they were constructed for some specific and uniform purpose, there was no doubt. But what it was, in our ignorance of the habits of the people, it was difficult to say. Don Simon thought that the cement was not hard enough to hold water, and hence that they were not intended as cisterns or reservoirs, but for granaries or storehouses of maize, which, from our earliest knowledge of the aborigines down to the present day, has been the staff of life. In this opinion, however, we did not concur, and from what we saw afterward, believe that they were intended as cisterns, and had furnished, in part at least, a supply of water to the people of the ruined city.

We returned to our apartments to dine, and in the afternoon accompanied Don Simon to see the harvest of the maize crop. The great field in front of the Casa del Gobernador was planted with corn, and on the way we learned a fact which may be interesting to agriculturists in the neighbourhood of those numerous cities throughout our country which, being of premature growth, are destined to become ruins. The debris of ruined cities fertilize and enrich land. Don Simon told us that the ground about Uxmal was excellent for milpas or corn-fields. He had never had a better crop of maize than that of the last year. Indeed, it was so good that he had planted a part of the same land a second time, unprecedented under their system of agriculture. Don Simon had another practical view of the value of these ru-ins. Pointing to the great buildings, he said that if he had Uxmal on the banks of the Mississippi, it would be an immense fortune, for there was stone enough to pave every street in New-Orleans, without sending to the North for it. We suggested that if he had it on the banks of the Mississippi, easy of access, preserved from the rank vege-tation which is now hurrying it to destruction, it would stand like Herculaneum and Pompeii, a place of pilgrimage for the curious; and that it would be a much better operation to put a fence around it and charge for admission, than to sell the stone for paving streets.

By this time we had reached the foot of the terrace, and a few steps brought us into the corn-field. The system of agriculture in Yu-catan is rather primitive. Besides hemp and sugar, which the Indians seldom attempt to raise on their own account, the principal products of the country are corn, beans, and calabazas, like our pumpkins and squashes, camotes, which are perhaps the parent of our Carolina po-tatoes, and chili or pepper, of which an inordinate quantity is con-sumed, both by the Indians and Spaniards. Indian corn, however, is the great staple, and the cultivation of this probably differs but little now from the system followed by the Indians before the conquest. In the dry season, generally in the months of January and February, a place is selected in the woods, from which the trees are cut down and burned. In May or June the corn is planted. This is done by making little holes in the ground with a pointed stick, putting in a few grains of corn and covering them over. Once in the ground, it is left to take care of itself, and if it will not grow, it is considered that the land is not worth having. The corn has a fair start with the weeds, and they keep pace amicably together. The hoe, plough, and harrow are en-tirely unknown. In general neither of the last two could be used, on account of the stony face of the country: the machete is the only in-strument employed.

The milpa around the ruins of Uxmal had been more than usu-ally neglected. The crop turned out badly, but such as it was, the Indi-ans from three of Don Simon's adjoining haciendas, according to their obligation to the master, were engaged in getting it in. They were distributed in different parts of the field; and of those we came upon first, I counted a small group of fifty-three. As we drew near, all stopped working, approached Don Simon, bowed respectfully to him, and then to us as his friends. The corn had been gathered, and these men were engaged in threshing it out. A space was cleared of about a hundred feet square, and along the border of it was a line of small hammocks hanging on stakes fixed in the ground, in which the Indians slept during the whole time of the harvest, each with a little fire underneath to warm him in the cool night air, and drive away the moschetoes.

Don Simon threw himself into one of the hammocks, and held out one of his legs, which was covered with burrs and briers. These men were free and independent electors of the State of Yucatan; but one of them took in his hand Don Simon's foot, picked off the burrs, pulled off the shoe, cleaned the stocking, and restoring the shoe, laid the foot back carefully in the hammock, and then took up the other. It was all done as a matter of course, and no one bestowed a thought upon it except ourselves.

The threshing machine was a rude scaffold about twenty feet square, made of four untrimmed upright posts for corners, with poles lashed to them horizontally three or four feet from the ground. Across these was a layer of sticks, about an inch thick, side by side. The whole might have served as a rude model of the first bedstead ever made. The parallel sticks served as a threshing floor, on which was spread a thick layer of corn. On each side a rude ladder of two or three rounds rested against the floor, and on each of these ladders stood a nearly naked Indian, with a long pole in his hand, beating the corn. The grains fell through, and at each corner under the floor was a man with a brush made of bushes, sweeping off the cobs. The shelled corn was afterward taken up in baskets and carried to the hacienda.

In both my expeditions into that region of country our medical department was incomplete. On the former occasion we had a medicine-chest, but no doctor, and this time we had a doctor, but no medicine-chest. This necessary appendage had been accidentally left on board the ship, and did not come to our hands till some time afterward. We had only a small stock purchased in Merida, and on this account, as well as because it interfered with his other pursuits, the doctor had avoided entering into general practice. He was willing to attend to cases that might be cured by a single operation, but the principle diseases were fevers, which could not be cut out with a knife. The day before, however, a young Indian came to the ruins on an errand to Don Simon, who had a leg swollen with varicose veins. He had a mild expression, meek and submissive manners, and was what Don Simon called, in speaking of his best servants, muy docil, or very docile. He stood at that time in an interesting position, being about to be married. Don Simon had had him at Merida six months, under the care of a physician, but without any good result, and the young man was taking his chance for better or worse, almost with the certainty of becoming in a few years disabled, and a mass of corruption. Dr. Cabot undertook to perform an operation, for which purpose it was necessary to go to the hacienda.

Don Simon had breakfast ready for us, but we found some deficiencies. The haciendas of that country never have any surplus furniture, being only visited by the master once or twice a year, and then only for a few days, when he brings with him whatever he requires for his personal comfort. Uxmal was like the rest, and at that moment it was worse off, for we had stripped it of almost every movable to enlarge our accommodations at the ruins. Our greatest difficulty was about seats. All contrived to be provided for, however, except Don Simon, who finally, as it was an extreme case, went into the church and brought out the great confessional chair.

Breakfast over, the doctor's patient was brought forward. He was not consulted on the subject of the operation, and had no wish of his own about it, but did as his master ordered him. At the moment of beginning, Doctor Cabot asked for a bed. He had not thought of asking for it before, supposing it would be ready at a moment's notice; but he might almost as well have asked for a steamboat or a locomotive engine. Who ever thought of wanting a bed at Uxmal? was the general feeling of the Indians. They were all born in hammocks, and expected to die in them, and who wanted a bed when he could get a hammock? A bed, however, was indispensable, and the Indians dispersed in search, returning, after a long absence, with tidings that they had heard of one on the hacienda, but it had been taken apart, and the pieces were in use for other purposes. They were sent off again, and at length we received notice that the bed was coming, and presently it appeared advancing through the gate of the cattle-yard in the shape of a bundle of poles on the shoulder of an Indian. For purposes of immediate use, they might as well have been on the tree that produced them, but, after a while, they were put together, and made a bedstead that would have astonished a city cabinetmaker.

In the mean time the patient was looking on, perhaps with somewhat the feeling of a man superintending the making of his own coffin. His right leg, which was almost as thick as his body, was covered with ulcers. The distended veins stood out like whipcords. Doctor Cabot considered it necessary to cut two veins. The Indian stood up, resting the whole weight of his body on the diseased leg, so as to bring them out to the fullest, and supporting himself by leaning with his hands on a bench. One vein was cut, the wound bound up, and then the operation was performed on the other by thrusting a stout pin into the flesh under the vein, and bringing it out on the other side, then winding a thread round the protruding head and point, and leaving the pin to cut its way through the vein and fester out. The leg was then bound tight, and the Indian laid upon the bed. During the whole time not a muscle of his face moved. Except at the moment when the pin was thrust under the vein, when his hand contracted on the bench, it could not have been told that he was undergoing an operation of any kind.

We set out on our return to the ruins, but hardly left the gate of the cattle-yard, when we met an Indian with his arm in a sling, coming in search of Doctor Cabot. A death-warrant seemed written in his face. His little wife, a girl about fourteen years old, soon to become a mother, was trotting beside him. His case showed how, in those countries, human life is the sport of accident and ignorance. A few days before, he had given his left arm a severe cut near the elbow with a machete. To stop the bleeding, his wife had tied one string as tightly as possible around the wrist, and another in the hollow of the arm, and so it had remained three days. The treatment had been pretty effectual in stopping the bleeding, and it had very nearly stopped the circulation of his blood forever. The hand was shrunken to nothing, and seemed withered. The part of the arm between the two ligatures was swollen enormously, and the seat of the wound was a mass of corruption. Doctor Cabot took off the fastenings, and endeavoured to teach her to restore the circulation by friction, or rubbing the arm with the palm of the hand, but she had no more idea of the circulation of the blood than of the revolution of the planets.

The wound gave out a foul and pestilential discharge, and, when that was cleared away, out poured a stream of blood. The man had cut an arterial vein. Doctor Cabot had no instruments with him with which to take it up, and, grasping the arm with a strong pressure on the vein, so as to stop the flow of blood, he transferred the arm to me, fixing my fingers upon the vein, and requesting me to hold it in that position while he ran to the ruins for his instruments. This was by no means pleasant. If I lost the right pressure, the man might bleed to death. Having no regular diploma warranting people to die on my hands, and knowing the imperturbable character of the Indians, I got the arm transferred to one of them, with a warning that the man's life depended upon him. Doctor Cabot was gone more than half an hour, and during all that time, while the patient's head was falling on his shoulder with fainting fits, the Indian looked directly in his face, and held up the arm with a fixedness of attitude that would have served as a model for a sculptor. Doctor Cabot dressed the wound, and the Indian was sent away, with an even chance for life or death. The next that we heard of him, however, he was at work in the fields. Certainly, but for the accidental visit of Doctor Cabot, he would have been in his grave.

Sickness was increasing on the hacienda. Two days after Don Simon left us we received notice that Doctor Cabot's leg patient was ill with fever, and also that a woman had died that day of the same disease, and was to be buried the next morning. We ordered horses to be sent up to the ruins, and early in the morning Dr. Cabot and myself rode to the hacienda, he to visit his patient, and I to attend the funeral, in the expectation that such an event, on a retired hacienda, without any priest or religious ceremonies, would disclose some usage or custom illustrative of the ancient Indian character. Leaving my horse in the cattle-yard, in company with the mayoral I walked to the campo santo. This was a clearing in the woods at a short distance from the house, square, and enclosed by a stone fence. It had been consecrated with the ceremonies of the church, and was intended as a burial-place for all who died on the estate. When we entered we saw a grave half dug, which had been abandoned on account of the stones. Some Indians were then occupied in digging another.

Only one part of the cemetery had been used as a burial-place, and this was indicated by little wooden crosses. In this part of the cemetery was a stone enclosure about four feet high, which was intended as a sort of charnel-house, and was then filled with skulls and bones, whitening in the sun. I began examining the skulls, and found that they were all known and identified. The campo santo had been opened but about five years, and every skull had once sat upon the shoulders of an acquaintance.

The graves were all on one side, and on the other no dead had been buried. I suggested to the mayoral, that by beginning on the farther side, and burying in order, every corpse would have time to decay and become dust before its place was wanted for another, which he seemed to think a good idea, and communicated it to the Indians, who stopped their work, looked at him and at me, and then went on digging. In the mean time I had overhauled the skulls, and placed on the top two which I ascertained to be those of full-blooded Indians, intending to appropriate and carry them off at the first convenient opportunity.

The Indians worked as slowly as if each was digging his own grave, and at length the husband of the deceased came out, measured the grave, and finding all right, returned to the house. The Indians picked up a rude barrow made of two long poles with crosspieces, which had been thrown down by the side of the last corpse it had carried, and went off for the dead body. They were gone so long that we thought they wished to wear out our patience, and told the mayoral to go and hurry them. Presently we heard a shuffling of feet, and the sound of female voices, heralding a tumultuous procession of women. On reaching the fence of the cemetery they all stopped, and, seeing us, would not come in, except one old Beelzebub, who climbed over, walked directly to the foot of the grave, leaned down, and, looking into it, made some exclamation which set all the women outside laughing. This so incensed the old woman that she picked up a handful of stones, and began pelting them, at which they all scattered with great confusion and laughter. In the midst of this, the corpse, attended by an irregular crowd of men, women, and children, made its appearance.

The barrow was lifted over the fence and laid down beside the grave. The body had no coffin, but was wrapped from head to foot in a blue cotton shawl with a yellow border. The head was uncovered, and the feet stuck out, and had on a pair of leather shoes and white cotton stockings, probably a present from her husband on his return from some visit to Merida, which the poor woman had never worn in life, and which he thought he was doing her honour by placing in her grave.

The Indians passed ropes under the body; the husband himself supported the head, and so it was lowered into the grave. The figure was tall, and the face was that of a woman about twenty-four years old. The expression was painful, indicating that in the final struggle the spirit had been reluctant to leave its mortal tenement. There was but one present who shed tears, and that was the old mother of the deceased, who doubtless had expected this daughter to lay her own head in the grave. She held by the hand a bright-eyed girl, who looked on with wonder, happily unconscious that her best friend on earth was to be laid under the sod. The shawl was opened, and showed a white cotton dress under it; the arms, which were folded across the breast for the convenience of carrying the body, were laid down by the sides, and the shawl was again wrapped round. The husband himself arranged the head, placed under it a cotton cloth for a pillow, and composed it for its final rest as carefully as if a pebble or a stone could hurt it. He brushed a handful of earth over the face. The Indians filled up the grave, and all went away. No romance hangs over such a burial scene, but it was not unnatural to follow in imagination the widowed Indian to his desolate hut.

CHAPTER FIVE

Uxmal and Ticul

ithin the whole circumference of Uxmal there is no well, stream, or fountain, and nothing which bears the appearance of having been used for supplying or obtaining water. All the water required for our own use we were obliged to procure from the hacienda. We felt the inconvenience of this during the whole of our residence at the ruins, and very often, in spite of all our care to keep a supply on hand, we came in, after hard work in the sun, and, parched with thirst, were obliged to wait till we could send an Indian to the hacienda, a distance, going and returning, of three miles.

Very soon after our arrival our attention and inquiries were directed particularly to this subject, and we were not long in satisfying ourselves that the principal supply had been drawn from aguadas in the neighbourhood. These aguadas are now neglected and overgrown, and perhaps are the cause of the unhealthiness of Uxmal. The principal of them we saw first from the top of the House of the Dwarf, a mile and a half distant. The whole intervening space was overgrown with woods, the ground was low and muddy, and the aguada was a fine sheet of water. It was completely imbosomed among trees, still and desolate, with tracks of deer on its banks. A few ducks were swimming on its surface, and a kingfisher was sitting on the bough of an overhanging tree, watching for his prey. The mayoral told us that this aguada was connected with another more to the south, and that they continued, one after the other, to a great distance; to use his own expression, there were a hundred of them.

The general opinion with regard to these aguadas is that they were "hechas á mano," artificial formations or excavations made by the ancient inhabitants as reservoirs for holding water. The mayoral told us that in the dry season, when the water was low, the remains of stone embankments were still visible in several places. There was nothing we longed for so much as a bath, and it was no unimportant part of our business at the aguada to examine whether it would answer as a bathing-place. We selected a little cove shaded by a large tree, had a convenient space cleared around it, a good path cut all the way through the woods to the terrace of the Casa del Gobernador, and on the first of December we consecrated it by our first bath. The mayoral, shrunken and shattered by fever and ague, stood by protesting against it, and warning us of the consequences. But we had attained the only thing necessary for our comfort at Uxmal, and had no apprehensions.

All that was on the hacienda belonging to the master was ours, as were also the services of the Indians. The property of the master consisted of cattle, horses, mules, and corn, of which only the last could be counted as provisions. Some of the Indians had a few fowls, pigs, and turkeys of their own, which they were in general willing to sell, and every morning those who came out to work brought with them water, fowls, eggs, lard, green beans, and milk. Occasionally we had a haunch of venison, and Doctor Cabot added to our larder several kinds of ducks, wild turkeys, chachalachas, quails, pigeons, doves, parrots, jays, and other smaller birds. Besides these, we received from time to time a present from Doña Joaquina or Don Simon, and altogether our living was better than we had ever known in exploring ruins.

A pig arrived from Don Simon, the cooking of which enlisted the warmest sympathies of all our heads of departments, Albino (a dark Mestizo servant from Merida), Bernaldo, and Chaipa Chi. They had their own way of doing it, national, and derived from their forefathers, being the same way in which those respectable people cooked men and women, as Bernal Dias says, "dressing the bodies in their manner, which is by a sort of oven made with heated stones, which are put under ground." They made an excavation on the terrace, kin-

14. *Page 62:* Modern view of four stacked Chaac masks beneath an image of Tlaloc, the rain god of central Mexico, the North Structure of the Nunnery Quadrangle, Uxmal

dled a large fire in it, and kept it burning until the pit was heated like an oven. Two clean stones were laid in the bottom, the pig (not alive) was laid upon them, and covered over with leaves and bushes, packed down with stones so close as barely to leave vent to the fire, and allow an escape for the smoke.

While this bake was going on I set out on a business which I had postponed from day to day. On a line with the back of the Casa del Gobernador rises one of the grandest and most imposing structures among all the ruins of Uxmal. It was at that time covered with trees and a thick growth of herbage, which gave a gloominess to its grandeur of proportions. But for its regularity, and a single belt of sculptured stones barely visible at the top, it would have passed for a wooded and grass-grown hill. Taking some Indians with me, I ascended this mound, and began clearing it for Mr. Catherwood to draw. I found that its vast sides were all incased with stone, in some places richly ornamented, but completely hidden from view by the foliage.

The height of this mound was sixty-five feet. On the top was a great platform of solid stone, three feet high and seventy-five feet square. The walls of the platform were of smooth stone, and the corners had sculptured ornaments. The area consisted entirely of loose rough stones, and there are no remains or other indications of any building. The great structure seemed raised only for the purpose of holding aloft this platform. Probably it had been the scene of grand religious ceremonies, and stained with the blood of human victims offered up in sight of the assembled people. Near as it was, it was the first time I had ascended this mound. It commanded a full view of every building. The day was overcast, the wind swept mournfully over the desolate city, and since my arrival I had not felt so deeply the solemnity and sublimity of these mysterious ruins.

Around the top of the mound was a border of sculptured stone ten or twelve feet high. Following it round, and clearing away the trees and bushes, on the west side, opposite the courtyard of the Casa de Palomos, my attention was arrested by an ornament, the lower part of which was buried in rubbish fallen from above. From its position, and the character of the ornament, I was immediately impressed with the idea that it was over a doorway, and that underneath was an entrance to an apartment in the mound. The Indians had cleared beyond it, and passed on, but I called them back, and set them to excavating the earth and rubbish that buried the lower part of the ornament. It was an awkward place to work in: the side of the mound was steep, and the stones composing the ornament were insecure and tottering. The Indians, as usual, worked as if they had their lifetime for the job. They were at all times tedious and trying, but now, to my impatient eagerness, more painfully so than ever. Urging them, I got them to work four long hours without any intermission, until they reached the cornice. The ornament proved to be a hideous face, with the teeth standing out. Throwing up the dirt upon the other side of them, the Indians had made a great pile outside, and stood in a deep hole against the face of the ornament. At this depth the stones seemed hanging loosely over their heads, and the Indians intimated that it was dangerous to continue digging, but by this time my impatience was beyond control.

I threw myself into the hole, and commenced digging with all my strength. The stones went rolling and crashing down the side of the mound, striking against roots and tearing off branches. The perspiration rolled from me in a stream. I was so completely carried away by the idea of entering some chamber that had been closed for ages, that I stopped at nothing; I resolved, as soon as I reached the doorway, to stop and send for Mr. Catherwood and Doctor Cabot, that we might all enter together, and make a formal note of everything exactly as it was found. But I was doomed to a worse disappointment than at El Laberinto de Maxcanú. Before getting below the cornice I thrust the machete through the earth, and found no opening, but a solid stone wall. I felt a heaviness and depression, and was actually sick at heart, so that, calling off the Indians, I was fain to give over and return to our quarters. Descending the mound my limbs could scarcely support me. My strength and elasticity were gone. With great difficulty I dragged myself to our apartments. My thirst was unquenchable. I threw myself into my hammock, and in a few moments a fiery fever was upon me. Disease had stalked all around us, but it was the first time it had knocked at our door.

On the third day, while in the midst of a violent attack, the cura Carillo of Ticul arrived. We had heard of him as a person who took more interest in the antiquities of the country than almost any other, and who possessed more knowledge on the subject. He had been in the habit of coming to Uxmal alone to wander among the ruins, and we had contemplated an excursion to Ticul on purpose to make his acquaintance. His first words to me were, that it was necessary for me to leave the place and go with him to Ticul. He would not consent to my going alone, or with his servant, and the next morning, instead of a pleasant visit to the ruins, he found himself trotting home with a sick man at his heels. It was my interval day, and the bare absence of pain was a positively pleasant sensation. In this humour, I listened with much interest to the cura's exposition of different points and localities, but by degrees my attention flagged, and finally my whole soul was fixed on the sierra, which stood out before us. My pains increased as we advanced, and I dismounted at the hacienda in a state impossible to be described. The mayoral was away, the doors were all locked, and I lay down on some bags in the corridor. There was but one Indian to be found. It was impossible to continue on horseback, and, fortunately, the mayoral came, and in a few minutes had men engaged in making a coché. In an hour my coché was ready, and at five o'clock I crawled in. My carriers were loth to start, but, once under way, they set off on a trot. Changing shoulders frequently, they never stopped till they carried me into Ticul, nine miles distant, and laid me down on the floor of the convent.

For three days I did not leave my bed; but on the fourth I breathed the air from the balcony of the convent. It was fresh, pure, balmy, and invigorating.

In the afternoon of the next day I set out with the cura for a stroll. We had gone but a short distance, when an Indian came running after us to inform us that another of the caballeros had arrived sick from the ruins. We hurried back, and found Doctor Cabot lying in a coché on the floor of the corridor at the door of the convent. He crawled out labouring under a violent fever, increased by the motion and fatigue of his ride, and I was startled by the extraordinary change a few days had made in his appearance. His face was flushed, his eyes were wild, his figure lank. He had not strength to support himself, but pitched against me, who could barely keep myself up, and both nearly came down together.

Our situation and prospects were now gloomy. If Mr. Catherwood was taken ill, work was at an end, and perhaps the whole expedition frustrated; but the poor cura was more to be pitied than any of us. His convent was turned into a hospital. But the more claims we made upon him, the more he exerted himself to serve us.

The third day the cura alarmed me by the remark that the expression of the doctor's face was *fatál*. In Spanish this only means very bad, but it had always in my ears an uncomfortable sound. He added that there were certain indices of this disease which were mortal, but, happily, these had not yet exhibited themselves in the doctor. The bare suggestion, however, alarmed me. I inquired of the cura about the mode of treatment in the country, and whether he could not prescribe for him.

He administered a preparation which I mention for the benefit of future travellers who may be caught without a medicine-chest. It was a simple decoction of the rind of the sour orange flavoured with cinnamon and lemon-juice, of which he administered a tumblerful warm every two hours. At the second draught the doctor was thrown into a profuse perspiration. For the first time since his attack the fever left him, and he had an unbroken sleep. On waking, copious draughts of tamarind water were given. When the fever came on again the decoction was repeated, with tamarind water in the intervals. The effect of this treatment was particularly happy, and it is desirable for strangers to know it, for the sour orange is found in every part of the country. From what we saw of it then and afterward, it is, perhaps, a better remedy for fever in that climate than any known in foreign pharmacy.

Like all the Spanish villages, Ticul was laid out with its plaza and streets running at right angles, and was distinguished among the villages of Yucatan for its casas de piedra, or stone houses. These were on the plaza and streets adjoining; and back, extending more than a mile each way, were the huts of the Indians. These huts were generally plastered, enclosed by stone fences, and imbowered among trees, or, rather, overgrown and concealed by weeds. The population was about five thousand, of which about three hundred families were vecinos, or white people, and the rest Indians. Fresh meat can be procured every day; the tienda grande, or large store of Guzman, would not disgrace Merida. The bread is better than at the capital. Altogether, for appearance, society, and conveniences of living, it is perhaps the best village in Yucatan, and famous for its bullfights and the beauty of its Mestiza women.

The church and convent occupy the whole of one side of the plaza. The convent is connected with the church by a spacious corridor. It is a gigantic structure, built entirely of stone, with massive walls, and four hundred feet in length. On each side are cloisters, once occupied by a numerous body of Franciscan friars. The first two and principal of these cloisters are occupied by the cura, and were our home. Another is occupied by one of his ministros, and in the fourth was an old Indian making cigars. The rest are untenanted, dismantled, and desolate. The doors and windows are broken, and grass and weeds are growing out of the floors. The great garden had once been in harmony with the grandeur and style of the convent, and now shares its fortunes. Its wells and fountains, parterres and beds of flowers, are all there, but neglected and running to waste, weeds, oranges, and lemons growing wildly together. Our horses were turned into it loose, as into a pasture.

Associated in my mind with this ruined convent, so as almost to form part of the building, is our host, the pride and love of the village, the cura Carillo. He was past forty, tall and thin, with an open, animated, and intelligent countenance, manly, and at the same time mild, and belonged to the once powerful order of Franciscan friars, now reduced in this region to himself and a few companions. After the destruction of the convent at Merida, and the scattering of the friars, his friends procured for him the necessary papers to enable him to secularize, but he would not abandon the brotherhood in its waning fortunes, and still wore the long blue gown, the cord, and cross of the Franciscan monks. The quiet and seclusion of his village did not afford sufficient employment for his active mind, but, fortunately for science and for me, he had turned his attention to the antiquities of the country. As it was a rare thing for him to associate with persons who took the slightest interest in his hobby, he mourned that he could not throw up all his business and accompany us in our exploration of the ruins.

It is worthy of remark, that even to a man so alive to all subjects of antiquarian interest, the history of the building of this convent is entirely unknown. In the pavement of the great corridor, in the galleries, walls, and roof, both of the church and convent, are stones from ancient buildings, and no doubt both were constructed with materials furnished by the ruined edifices of another race, but when, or how, or under what circumstances, is unknown. On the roof the cura had discovered, in a situation which would hardly have attracted any eyes but his own, a square stone, having roughly engraved on it this inscription:

26
Marzo,
1625.

Perhaps this had reference to the date of the construction, and if so, it is the only known record that exists in relation to it. Where such obscurity exists in regard to a building constructed by the Spaniards but little more than two hundred years ago, how much darker must be the cloud that hangs over the ruined cities of the aborigines, erected, if not ruined, before the conquest.

During the first days of my convalescence I had a quiet and almost mournful interest in wandering about this venerable convent. I passed, too, some interesting hours in looking over the archives. The books had a time-worn aspect, with parchment covers, tattered and worm-eaten. In some places the ink had faded, and the writing was illegible. They were the records of the early monks, written by their own hands, and contained a register of baptisms and marriages, including, perhaps, the first Indian who assented to these Christian rites. It was my hope to find in these archives some notice, however slight, of the circumstances under which the early fathers set up the standard of the cross in this Indian town, but the first book has no preamble or introduction of any kind, commencing abruptly with the entry of a marriage.

This entry bears date in 1588, but forty or fifty years after the Spaniards established themselves in Merida. This is thirty-eight years anterior to the date on the stone before referred to, but it is reasonable to suppose that the convent was not built until some time after the beginning of the archives. The monks doubtless commenced keeping a register of baptisms and marriages as soon as there were any to record, but as they were distinguished for policy and prudence as well as zeal, it is not likely that they undertook the erection of this gigantic building until they had been settled in the country long enough to understand thoroughly its population and resources, for these buildings had not only to be erected, but to be kept up, and their ministers supported by the resources of the district. Besides, the great churches and convents found in all parts of Spanish America were not built by means of funds sent from Spain, but by the labour of the Indians themselves, after they were completely subdued and compelled to work for the Spaniards, or, more generally, after they had embraced Christianity, when they voluntarily erected buildings for the new worship and its ministers. It is not probable that either of these events occurred in this interior village so early as 1588.

In running over the archives, it appeared that there was in those days an unusual number of widowers and widows disposed to marry again. In fact, the business of this kind was in a great measure confined to them. Probably, as the relation of husband and wife was not very clearly defined among the Indians, these candidates for Christian matrimony had only parted from former companions, and, through the charity or modesty of the monks, were called widowers and widows.

The first baptisms are on the twentieth of November, 1594, when considerable business seems to have been done. There are four entries on that day, and, in looking over the pages, from my acquaintance with the family I was struck with the name of Mel Chi, probably an ancestor of our Chaipa Chi. This Mel seems to have been one of the pillars of the padres, and a standing godfather for Indian babies.

There was no instruction to be derived from these archives, but the handwriting of the monks, and the marks of the Indians, seemed almost to make me a participator in the wild and romantic scenes of the conquest. At all events, they were proof that, forty or fifty years after the conquest, the Indians were abandoning their ancient usages and customs, adopting the rites and ceremonies of the Catholic Church, and having their children baptized with Spanish names.

Near the village of Ticul, almost in the suburbs, are the ruins of another ancient and unknown city. From the time of our arrival the memorials of it had been staring us in the face. The cura had some sculptured stones of new and exceedingly pretty design; and heads, vases, and other relics, found in excavating the ruins, were fixed in the fronts of houses as ornaments. My first stroll with the cura was to these ruins. At the end of a long street leading out beyond the campo santo we turned to the right by a narrow path, overgrown with bushes covered with wild flowers, and on which birds of beautiful plumage were sitting, but so infested with garrapatas that we had to keep brushing them off continually with the bough of a tree.

This path led us to the hacienda of San Francisco. A short distance in the rear of the hacienda were the ruins of another city, desolate and overgrown, having no name except that of the hacienda on which they stand. At this time a great part of the city was completely hidden by the thick foliage of the trees. Near by, however, several mounds were in full sight, dilapidated, and having fragments of walls on the top. We ascended the highest, which commanded a magnificent view of the great wooded plain, and at a distance the towers of the church of Ticul rising darkly above. The cura told me that in the dry season, when the trees were bare of foliage, he had counted from this point thirty-six mounds, every one of which had once held aloft a building or temple, and not one now remained entire. For generations the place had served as a mere quarry to furnish the inhabitants with building-stone. The present proprietor was then excavating and selling, and he lamented to me that the piedra labrada, or worked stone, was nearly exhausted, and his profit from this source cut off.

We have clear and authentic accounts of the existence of a large Indian town called Ticul, certainly in the same neighbourhood where the Spanish village of that name now stands. It must have been either on the site now occupied by the latter, or on that occupied by the ruins of San Francisco. Supposing the first supposition to be correct, not a single vestige of the Indian city remains. Now it is incontestible that the Spaniards found in the Indian towns of Yucatan, mounds, temples, and other large buildings of stone. If those on the hacienda of San Francisco are of older date, and the work of races who have passed away, why has every trace of the stone buildings in the Indian city disappeared?

It appears in every page of the history of the Spanish conquest that the Spaniards never attempted to occupy the houses and villages of the Indians as they stood. Their habits of life were inconsistent with such occupation, and, besides, their policy was to desolate and destroy them, and build up others after their own style and manner. It is not likely that at the early epoch at which they are known to have gone to Ticul, with their small numbers, they would have undertaken to demolish the whole Indian town, and build their own upon its ruins. The probability is, that they planted their own village on the border, and erected their church as an antagonist and rival to the heathen temples. The monks, with all the imposing ceremonies of the Catholic Church, battled with the Indian priests. Gradually overthrowing the power of the caciques, or putting them to death, they depopulated the old town and drew the Indians to their own village. It is my belief that the ruins on the hacienda of San Francisco are those of the aboriginal city of Ticul.

In the excavations constantly going on, objects of interest were from time to time discovered, one of which, a vase, was loaned to us. On one side is a border of hieroglyphics, with sunken lines running to the bottom, and on the other the face portrayed bears a strong resemblance to those of the sculptured and stuccoed figures at Palenque: the headdress, too, is a plume of feathers, and the hand is held out in the same stiff position. The vase is four and a half inches high, and five inches in diameter. It realizes the account given by Herrera of the markets at the Mexican city of Tlascala. "There were goldsmiths, feather-men, barbers, baths, and *as good earthenware as in Spain.*"

The sight of these vases induced me to devote a few days to excavating among the ruins. Amid the great waste it was difficult to know what to do or where to begin. In Egypt, the labours of discoverers have given some light to subsequent explorers, but here all was dark. My great desire was to discover an ancient sepulchre, which we had sought in vain among the ruins of Uxmal. These were not to be looked for in the large mounds, or, at all events, it was a work of too much labour to attempt opening one of them. At length, after a careful examination, the cura selected one, upon which we began.

It was a square stone structure, with sides four feet high, and the top was rounded over with earth and stones bedded in it. It stood in a small milpa, or corn-field, midway between two high mounds,

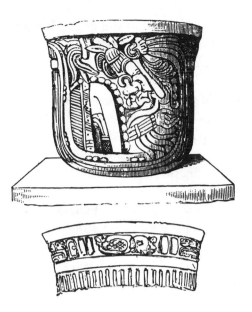

which had evidently been important structures, and from its position seemed to have some direct connexion with them. Unlike most of the ruined structures around, it was entire, with every stone in its place, and probably had not been disturbed since the earth and stones had been packed down on the top.

The Indians commenced picking out the stones and clearing away the earth with their hands. Fortunately, they had a crowbar, indispensable here on account of the stony nature of the soil. The cura gave them directions in their own language, and under his eye they worked actively. Nevertheless, the process was unavoidably slow. In digging down, they found the inner side of the outer wall, and the whole interior was loose earth and stones, with some layers of large flat stones. The sun was beating upon us. Some of the people of the village came down to look on and have an inward smile at our folly.

We continued the work six hours, and the whole appearance of things was so rude that we began to despair of success, when, on prying up a large flat stone, we saw underneath a skull. It had no covering or envelope of any kind; the earth was thrown upon it as in a common grave, and as this was removed it all fell to pieces. It was in a sitting posture, with its face toward the setting sun. The knees were bent against the stomach, the arms doubled from the elbow, and the hands clasping the neck or supporting the head. The skull was unfortunately broken, but the facial bone was entire, with the jaws and

15. Catherwood drawing of a vase found near Ticul

teeth, and the enamel on the latter still bright, but when the skull was handed up many of them fell out. The Indians picked up every bone and tooth, and handed them to me. It was strangely interesting, with the ruined structures towering above us, after a lapse of unknown ages, to bring to light these buried bones. Whose were they? The Indians were excited, and conversed in low tones. The cura interpreted what they said. The burden of it was, "They are the bones of our kinsman," and "What will our kinsman say at our dragging forth his bones?" But for the cura they would have covered them up and left the sepulchre.

In collecting the bones, one of the Indians picked up a small white object, which would have escaped any but an Indian's eye. It was made of deer's horn, about two inches long, sharp at the point, with an eye at the other end. They all called it a needle, and the reason of their immediate and unhesitating opinion was the fact that the Indians of the present day use needles of the same material, two of which the cura procured for me on our return to the convent. One of the Indians, who had acquired some confidence by gossiping with the cura, jocosely said that the skeleton was either that of a woman or a tailor.

The position of this skeleton was not in the centre of the sepulchre, but on one side, and on the other side of it was a very large rough stone or rock firmly imbedded in the earth, which it would have taken a long time to excavate with our instruments. In digging round it and on the other side, at some little distance from the skeleton we found a large vase of rude pottery, resembling very much the cantaro used by the Indians now as a water-jar. It had a rough flat stone lying over the mouth, so as to exclude the earth, on removing which we found, to our great disappointment, that it was entirely empty, except some little hard black flakes, which were thrown out and buried before the vase was taken up. It had a small hole worn in one side of the bottom, through which liquid or pulverized substances could have escaped. It may have contained water or the heart of the skeleton.

One idea presented itself to my mind with more force than it had ever possessed before, and that was the utter impossibility of ascribing these ruins to Egyptian builders. The magnificent tombs of the kings at Thebes rose up before me. It was on their tombs that the Egyptians lavished their skill, industry, and wealth, and no people descended from Egyptians would ever have constructed so rude a sepulchre. Besides this, finding these bones in so good a state of preservation, at a distance of only three feet from the surface of the earth, completely destroys all idea of the extreme antiquity of these buildings. Again there was the universal and unhesitating exclamation of the Indians, "They are the bones of our kinsman."

But whosesoever they were, little did the pious friends who placed them there ever imagine the fate to which they were destined. I had them carried to the convent, thence to Uxmal, and thence I bore them away forever from the bones of their kindred. In their rough journeys on the backs of mules and Indians they were so crumbled and broken that in a court of law their ancient proprietor would not be able to identify them, and they left me one night in a pocket-handkerchief to be carried to Doctor S. G. Morton of Philadelphia. Known by the research he has bestowed upon the physical features of the aboriginal American races, and particularly by his late work entitled "Crania Americana," this gentleman says that this skeleton, dilapidated as it is, has afforded him some valuable facts, and has been a subject of some interesting reflections.

The bones are those of a female. Her height did not exceed five feet four inches. The teeth are perfect, and not appreciably worn, while the *epiphyses,* those infallible indications of the growing state, have just become consolidated, and mark the completion of adult age. The bones of the hands and feet are remarkably small and delicately proportioned, which observation applies also to the entire skeleton. The skull was crushed into many pieces, but, by a cautious manipulation, Doctor Morton succeeded in reconstructing the posterior and lateral portions. The occiput is remarkably flat and vertical, while the lateral or parietal diameter measures no less than five inches and eight tenths. On the upper part of the left tibia there is a swelling of the bone, called a *node,* an inch and a half in length, and more than half an inch above the natural surface. This morbid condition may have resulted from a variety of causes, but possesses greater interest on account of its extreme infrequency among the primitive Indian population of the country.

On a late visit to Boston I had the satisfaction of examining a small and extremely interesting collection of mummied bodies in the possession of Mr. John H. Blake, dug up by himself from an ancient cemetery in Peru. The graves are all of a circular form. In one of them Mr. Blake found the mummies of a man, a woman, a child twelve or fourteen years old, and an infant. They were all closely wrapped in woollen garments of various colours and degrees of fineness, secured by needles of thorn thrust through the cloth.

Mr. Blake visited many other cemeteries between the Andes and the Pacific Ocean as far south as Chili, all of which possess the same general features with those found in the elevated valleys of the Peruvian Andes. No record or tradition exists in regard to these cemeteries, but woollen cloths similar to those found by Mr. Blake are woven at this day, and probably in the same manner, by the Indians of Peru. In the eastern part of Bolivia, south of where these mummies were discovered, he found, on the most barren portion of the Desert of Atacama, a few Indians who retain more of their primitive customs. Their dress at this day resembles closely that which envelops the bodies in his possession, both in the texture and the form.

Doctor Morton says that these mummies from Peru have the same peculiarities in the form of the skull, the same delicacy of the bones, and the same remarkable smallness of the hands and feet, with that found in the sepulchre at San Francisco. He says, too, from an examination of nearly four hundred skulls of individuals belonging to older nations of Mexico and Peru, and of skulls dug from the mounds of our western country, that he finds them all formed on the same model, and conforming in a remarkable manner to that brought from San Francisco; and that this cranium has the same *type* of physical conformation which has been bestowed with amazing uniformity upon all the tribes on our continent, from Canada to Patagonia, and from the Atlantic to the Pacific Ocean. He adds, that it affords additional support to the opinion which he has always entertained, that, notwithstanding some slight variation in physical conformation, and others of a much more remarkable character in intellectual attainments, all the aboriginal Americans of all known epochs belong to the same great and distinctive race.

If this opinion is correct, and I believe it—if this skeleton does present the same *type* of physical conformation with all the tribes of our continent—then these crumbling bones declare, as with a voice from the grave, that we cannot go back to any ancient nation of the Old World for the builders of these cities. They are not the works of people who have passed away, and whose history is lost, but of the same great race which, changed, miserable, and degraded, still clings around their ruins.

Among the ruins of San Francisco were circular holes in the ground like those at Uxmal. At Uxmal the character of these was mere matter of conjecture; but at this short distance, the Indians had specific notions in regard to their objects and uses, and called them chultunes, or wells. In all directions, too, were seen the oblong stones hollowed out like troughs, which at Uxmal were called pilas, or fountains, but here the Indians called them hólcas or piedras de molir, stones for grinding, which they said were used by the ancients to

16. Modern view of an ancient stone metate used for grinding corn found in the Palace at Labná

mash corn upon. The proprietor showed us a round stone like a bread roller, which they called kabtum, brazo de piedra, or arm of stone, used, as they said, for mashing the corn. The different names they assigned in different places to the same thing, and the different uses ascribed to it, show, with many other facts, the utter absence of all traditionary knowledge among the Indians; and this is perhaps the greatest difficulty we have to encounter in ascribing to their ancestors the building of these cities.

The last day we returned from the ruins earlier than usual, and stopped at the campo santo. In front stood a noble seybo tree. I had been anxious to learn something of the growth of this tree, but had never had an opportunity of doing it before. The cura told me that it was then twenty-three years old. There could be no doubt or mistake on this point. Its age was as well known as his own, or that of any other person in the village. The trunk at the distance of five feet from the ground measured 17½ feet in circumference, and its great branches afforded on all sides a magnificent shade. We had found trees like it growing on the tops of the ruined structures at Copan and Palenque, and many had for that reason ascribed to the buildings a very great antiquity. This tree completely removed all doubts which I might have entertained, and confirmed me in the opinion I had before expressed, that no correct judgment could be formed of the antiquity of these buildings from the size of the trees growing upon them.

I bade farewell to the cura, with an understanding, that as soon as Doctor Cabot was able to return, the good padre would accompany him to finish his interrupted visit to us at Uxmal. In an hour I reached the top of the sierra. On the other side my first view of the great plain took in the church of Nohcacab, standing like a colossus in the wilderness.

The village was under the pastoral charge of the cura of Ticul, and in the suburbs I met his ministro on horseback, waiting to escort me to the ruins of Nohpat. I saw at a glance that it would be indispensable for Mr. Catherwood to visit them. Nevertheless, I passed three hours on the ground, toiling in the hot sun, and at four o'clock, with strong apprehensions of another attack of fever, I mounted to continue my journey. A little before dark I emerged from the woods, and saw Mr. Catherwood standing on the platform of the Casa del Gobernador, the sole tenant of the ruins of Uxmal. It had happened most fortunately for our operations that Mr. Catherwood had held out. Without any resources or anything to occupy him except work, he had accomplished an enormous deal, and from being so much better provided with the comforts of living than at any former time while exploring ruins, he had continued in good health and spirits.

At dark the Indian arrived with my luggage, sweating at every pore, having carried it twenty-one miles, for which I paid him three shillings and sixpence. As he was going away we gave him a roll of bread, and he asked by signs if he was to carry it to the cura. Being made to comprehend that he was to eat it himself, he sat down and commenced immediately, having probably never eaten so much bread before in his life. We then gave him half a cup of Habanero, some plantains and a cigar, and, as the dew was heavy, told him to sit by the fire. When he had finished these we repeated the portion, and he seemed hardly to believe his good fortune real. But he had an idea that he was well off, and either from being a stranger, and free from the apprehensions felt by the Indians at Uxmal, or else from a fancy he had taken to us, he asked for a costal, a piece of hemp bagging, to sleep upon. We gave him one, and he lay down by the fire. For a while he endeavoured to protect his naked body against the moschetoes, and kept up a continued slapping, lighter or heavier according to the aggravation, changed his position, and tried the back corridor, but it was all in vain. Finally, with a sad attempt at a smile, he asked for another drink of Habanero and a cigar, and went away.

On the twenty-fourth of December Doctor Cabot returned from Ticul, bringing back with him Albino, who was in a rueful plight. Unfortunately, the cura Carillo was unwell, and unable to accompany him, but had promised to follow in a few days. On Christmas eve we were all once more together, and Christmas Day, in spite of ourselves, was a holyday. No Indians came out to work. Chaipa Chi, who had moved regularly as the sun, for the first time failed.

Unable to do anything at the ruins, I walked down to the hacienda to see one of our horses which had a sore back. I walked on to the campo santo, for the purpose of carrying away two skulls which I had selected and laid aside on the charnel pile at the time of the funeral. I had taken some precautions, for the news of the carrying off the bones from San Francisco had created some excitement among the Indians all over the country. The skulls I had selected had been displaced and mingled with the others, so that I could not identify them. I examined the whole heap, but could recognise only the huge skull of an African and that of the woman I had seen dug up. The latter was the skull of a full-blooded Indian, but it had been damaged by the crowbar; besides, I had seen all her bones and her very flesh taken piecemeal out of the grave. I had heard so much of her that she seemed an acquaintance, and I had some qualms of conscience about carrying her skull away. In fact, alone in the stillness and silence of the place, something of a superstitious feeling came over me about disturbing the bones of the dead and robbing a graveyard. Not wishing to run the risk of creating a disturbance on the hacienda, I left the graveyard with empty hands. The mayoral afterward told me that it was fortunate I had done so, for that if I had carried any away, it would have caused an excitement among the Indians, and perhaps led to mishchief.

CHAPTER SIX

Uxmal: The Survey

The account of our residence at Uxmal is now drawing to a close, and it is time to bring before the reader the ruins. But before doing so I shall make one remark in regard to the work of Mr. Waldeck, which was published in folio at Paris in 1835, and, except my own hurried notice, is the only account that has ever been published of the ruins at Uxmal. I had this work with me on our last visit. Our plans and drawings differ materially from his, but Mr. Waldeck was not an architectural draughtsman, and he complains that his drawings were taken from him by the Mexican government. I differ from him, too, in the statement of some facts, and almost entirely in opinions and conclusions. These things occur of course, and the next person who visits these ruins will perhaps differ in many respects from both of us. It is proper to say, moreover, that Mr. Waldeck had much greater difficulties to encounter than we, for at the time of his visit the ground had not been cleared for a milpa, and the whole field was overgrown with trees. He is justly entitled to the full credit of being the first stranger who visited these ruins, and brought them to the notice of the public.

The front is three hundred and twenty-two feet long. Don Simon Peon told us that in the year 1825 the whole was almost entire. The fragments now lie as they fell, forming a great mass of mortar, rude and sculptured stones, all imbedded together, which had never been disturbed until we dug into it for the purpose of disinterring and bringing to light some of the fallen ornaments.

This building was constructed entirely of stone. Up to the cornice, which runs round it the whole length and on all four of its sides, the façade presents a smooth surface; above is one solid mass of rich, complicated, and elaborately sculptured ornaments, forming a sort of arabesque.

The grandest ornament is over the centre doorway. Around the head of the principal figure are rows of characters, which, in our first hurried visit, we did not notice as essentially different from the other incomprehensible subjects sculptured on the façade; but we now discovered that these characters were hieroglyphics. We had ladders made, by means of which Mr. Catherwood climbed up and made accurate drawings of them. They differ somewhat from the hieroglyphics before presented, and are more rich, elaborate, and complicated, but the general character is the same. From their conspicuous posi-

17. *Page 80:* Façade of the East Building, Nunnery Quadrangle, with the Pyramid of the Magician in the distance (Charnay, 1860)

18. *Right:* East façade of the House of the Governor with the Pyramid of the Magician in the distance, Uxmal (Thompson, circa 1888–89)

tion, they no doubt contain some important meaning: probably they were intended as a record of the construction of the building, the time when and the people by whom it was built.

The part immediately over the doorway shows the remaining portion of a figure seated on a kind of throne. This throne was formerly supported by a rich ornament, still forming part of similar designs over other doorways in this building. From the head-dress proceed enormous plumes of feathers, dividing at the top, and falling symmetrically on each side, until they touch the ornament on which the feet of the statue rest. Each figure was perhaps the portrait of some cacique, warrior, prophet, or priest, distinguished in the history of this unknown people.

83 *House of the Governor*

19. Detail above the main doorway of the House of the Governor, Uxmal (Charnay, 1860)

Immediately above [is an] ornament [that] appears throughout the ruins. It measures one foot seven inches in length from the stem by which it is fixed in the wall to the end of the curve, and resembles somewhat an elephant's trunk, which name has, perhaps not inaptly, been given to it by Waldeck, though it is not probable that as such the sculptor intended it, for the elephant was unknown on the Continent of America. This projecting stone appears all over the façade and at the corners; and throughout all the buildings it is met with, sometimes in a reversed position, oftener than any other design in Ux-

mal. It is a singular fact, that though entirely out of reach, the ends of nearly all of them have been broken off. Among the many remains in every part of the walls throughout the whole ruins, there are but three that now exist entire. Perhaps they were wantonly broken by the Spaniards. The Indians believe these old buildings are haunted, and that all the monefatos or ornaments are animated, and walk at night. In the daytime, it is believed, they can do no harm, and for ages the Indians have been in the habit of breaking and disfiguring them with the machete, believing that by so doing they quiet their wandering spirits.

The [ornament] is probably intended to represent a hideous human face; the projecting stone is perhaps intended for the nose or snout. There is no tablet or single stone representing separately and by itself an entire subject, but every ornament is made up of separate stones, each of which had carved on it part of the subject, and was then set in its place in the wall. Each stone by itself is an unmeaning fractional portion, but, placed by the side of others, makes part of a whole. I have no doubt that all these ornaments have a symbolical meaning; that each stone is part of a history, allegory, or fable.

The rear elevation of the Casa del Gobernador is a solid wall, without any doorways or openings of any kind. Like the front, above the cornice it was ornamented throughout its whole length with sculptured stone. The subjects, however, were less complicated, and the sculpture less gorgeous and elaborate. On this side, too, a part of the façade has fallen. The two ends are thirty-nine feet each. The southern end has but one doorway, and of this, too, the sculptured subjects were more simple. The roof is flat, and had been covered with cement; but the whole is now overgrown with grass and bushes.

Such is the exterior of the Casa del Gobernador. Mr. Catherwood made minute architectural drawings of the whole, and has in his possession the materials for erecting a building exactly like it. He made all his drawings with the camera lucida, for the purpose of obtaining the utmost accuracy of proportion and detail. Besides which,

we had with us a Daguerreotype apparatus, the best that could be
procured in New-York. Immediately on our arrival at Uxmal, Mr.
Catherwood began taking views; but the results were not sufficiently
perfect to suit his ideas. At times the projecting cornices and ornaments threw parts of the subject in shade, while others were in broad
sunshine; so that, while parts were brought out well, other parts required pencil drawings to supply their defects. They gave a general
idea of the character of the buildings, but would not do to put into
the hands of the engraver without copying the views on paper, and in-
troducing the defective parts, which would require more labour than
that of making at once complete original drawings. He therefore completed everything with his pencil and camera lucida, while Doctor
Cabot and myself took up the Daguerreotype. In order to ensure the
utmost accuracy, the Daguerreotype views were placed with the drawings in the hands of the engravers.

   The Casa del Gobernador has eleven doorways in front and one

20. Southeast corner of the
House of the Governor,
Uxmal (Thompson, circa
1888–89)

at each end. The doors are all gone, and the wooden lintels over them have fallen. The interior is divided longitudinally by a wall into two corridors, and these again, by cross walls or partitions, into oblong rooms. Every pair of these rooms, the front and back, communicate by a doorway exactly opposite a corresponding doorway in front. The principal apartments in the centre, with three doorways opening upon the terrace, are sixty feet long. In these two we took up our abode.

The walls are constructed of square, smooth blocks of stone, and on each side of the doorway are the remains of stone rings fixed in the walls with shafts, which no doubt had some connexion with the support of the doors. The floors were of cement, in some places hard, but, by long exposure, broken, and now crumbling under the feet.

The ceiling forms a triangular arch without the keystone. The support is made by stones overlapping, and bevilled so as to present a smooth surface, and within about a foot of the point of contact covered by a layer of flat stones. Across the arch were beams of wood, the ends built in the wall on each side, which had probably been used for the support of the arch while the building was in progress.

In working out the plan, it was found that the back wall was nine feet thick, nearly equal to the width of the front apartment. Such thickness was not necessary for the support of the building, and, supposing it might contain some hidden passages, we determined to make a breach through the wall, and to do this in the centre apartment. I felt some repugnance to this work of demolition, but one stone had already been picked out by an Indian to serve for mashing maize upon; and as this was likely to be done at any time when another might be wanted, I got over my scruples.

Over the cavity left in the mortar by the removal of the stone were two conspicuous marks, which afterward stared us in the face in all the ruined buildings of the country. They were the prints of a red hand with the thumb and fingers extended, not drawn or painted, but stamped by the living hand, the pressure of the palm upon the stone. He who made it had stood before it alive as we did, and pressed his hand, moistened with red paint, hard against the stone. The seams and creases of the palm were clear and distinct in the impression. There was something lifelike about it that waked exciting thoughts, and almost presented the images of the departed inhabitants hovering about the building. And there was one striking feature about these hands; they were exceedingly small. Either of our own spread over and completely hid them. This was interesting from the fact that we had ourselves remarked, and heard remarked by others, the smallness

of the hands and feet as a striking feature in the physical conformation of the Indians at the present day.

The stones with this red hand upon them were the first that fell
as we commenced our breach into the wall. There were two crowbars
on the hacienda, and working nearly two days, the Indians made a
hole between six and seven feet deep, but throughout the wall was
solid, and consisted of large stones imbedded in mortar, almost as
hard as rock. The reason of this immense back wall, where everything else had a certain degree of fitness and conformity, we did not
discover, and we had this huge hole staring us reproachfully in the
face during all the remainder of our residence.

In the south end apartment, we found the sculptured beam of
hieroglyphics which had so much interested us on our former visit. In
some of the inner apartments the lintels were still in their places over
the doorways, and some were lying on the floor sound and solid,
which better condition was no doubt owing to their being more sheltered than those over the outer doorway. This was the only sculptured
beam in Uxmal, and at that time it was the only piece of carved
wood we had seen. We considered it interesting, as indicating a degree of proficiency in an art of which, in all our previous explorations, we had not discovered any evidence, except, perhaps, at Ocos-
ingo, where we found a beam, not carved, but which had evidently
been reduced to shape by sharp instruments of metal. This time I determined not to let the precious beam escape me. It was ten feet long,
one foot nine inches broad, and ten inches thick, of Sapote wood,
enormously heavy and unwieldy. To keep the sculptured side from being chafed and broken, I had it covered with hemp bagging, and
stuffed with dry grass. It left Uxmal on the shoulders of ten Indians,
after many vicissitudes reached this city uninjured, and was deposited
in Mr. Catherwood's panorama.

On the burning of that building, this part of Uxmal was consumed, and with it other beams afterward discovered, much more curious and interesting; as also the whole collection of vases, figures,
idols, and other relics gathered upon this journey. The collecting,
packing, and transporting of these things had given me more trouble
and annoyance than any other circumstance in our journey, and their
loss cannot be replaced. Being first on the ground, I selected only
those objects which were most curious and valuable. If I were to go
over the whole ground again, I could not find others equal to them. I
had the melancholy satisfaction of seeing their ashes exactly as the
fire had left them.

Next to the great building of the Casa del Gobernador are the three great terraces which hold it aloft, and give it its grandeur of position; all of them artificial, and built up from the level of the plain. They were all supported by substantial stone walls; that of the second terrace is still in a good state of preservation, and at the corners the stones which support it are still in their places, with their outer surfaces rounded, instead of presenting sharp angles.

Near the centre of the platform of the second terrace is a square enclosure in which stands a large round stone, measuring eight feet above the ground and five feet in diameter. This stone is striking for its uncouth and irregular proportions, and wants conformity with the regularity and symmetry of all around. From its conspicuous position, it doubtless had some important use, and, in connexion with other monuments found at this place, induces the belief that it was connected with the ceremonial rites of an ancient worship known to have existed among all Eastern nations. The Indians call this stone the Picote, or whipping-post.

Beyond this was a rude circular mound, about six feet high. We

21. Catherwood map of Uxmal

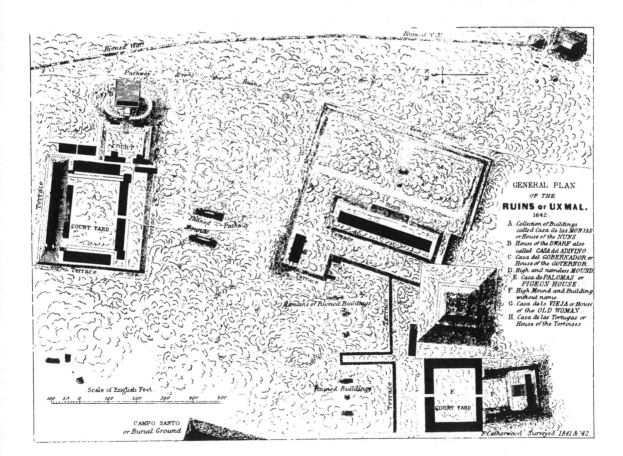

GENERAL PLAN
OF THE
RUINS OF UXMAL.
1842.

A. Collection of Buildings called Casa de las MONJAS or House of the NUNS.
B. House of the DWARF also called CASA del ADIVINO.
C. Casa del GOBERNADOR or House of the GOVERNOR.
D. High and nameless MOUND.
E. Casa de PALOMAS or PIGEON HOUSE.
F. High Mound and Building without name.
G. Casa de la VIEJA or House of the OLD WOMAN.
H. Casa de las Tortugas or House of the Tortoises.

Scale of English Feet.
100 50 0   100   200   300   400   500

CAMPO SANTO
or Burial Ground

F. Catherwood Surveyed 1841 & '42.

had used it as a position from which to take a Daguerreotype view of the front of the building, and, at the instance of the Cura Carillo, we determined to open it. On digging down to the depth of three or four feet, a sculptured monument was discovered. It is carved out of a single block of stone, and seems to represent a double-headed cat or lynx. The sculpture is rude. It was too heavy to carry away. We had it raised to the side of the mound for Mr. Catherwood to draw, and probably it remains there still.

Why this monument had been consigned to the strange place in which it was discovered we were at a loss to conjecture. This could never have been its original destination. It had been formally and deliberately buried. In my opinion, there is but one way of accounting for it. It had been one of the many idols worshipped by the people of Uxmal; and the probability is, that when the inhabitants abandoned the city they buried it, that it might not be desecrated. Or else the Spaniards, when they drove out the inhabitants and depopulated the city, in order to destroy all the reverential feelings of the Indians toward it, followed the example of Cortez at Cholula, and threw down and buried the idols.

CASA DE LAS TORTUGAS

There remains to be noticed one important building on the grand platform of the second terrace. It stands at the northwest corner, and is

22. Modern view of the two-headed jaguar throne that Stephens discovered near the House of the Governor, Uxmal

called the Casa de las Tortugas, or the House of the Turtles, which name was given to it by a neighbouring cura, from a row of turtles which goes round the cornice.

This building contrasts strikingly with the Casa del Gobernador. It wants the rich and gorgeous decoration of the former, but is distinguished for its beauty of proportions, and its chasteness and simplicity of ornament. Throughout there is nothing that borders on the unintelligible or grotesque, nothing that can shock a fastidious architectural taste. Unhappily, it is fast going to decay. On our first visit Mr. Catherwood and myself climbed to the roof, and selected it as a good position from which to make a panoramic sketch of the whole field of ruins. It was then trembling and tottering, and within the year the whole of the centre part had fallen in. In front the centre of the wall is gone, and in the rear the wooden lintel, pressed down and broken in two, still supports the superincumbent mass, but it gave us a nervous feeling to pass under it. The interior is filled up with the ruins of the fallen roof.

This building has no communication, by steps or any visible means, with the Casa del Gobernador, nor were there any steps leading to the terrace below. It stands isolated and alone, seeming to mourn over its own desolate and ruinous condition. With a few more returns of the rainy season it will be a mass of ruins, and perhaps on

23. Modern view of the ball court (foreground), Nunnery Quadrangle, and the Pyramid of the Magician, Uxmal

the whole continent of America there will be no such monument of the purity and simplicity of aboriginal art.

Descending from the Casa del Gobernador, and on a line with the doorway of the Casa de las Monjas are two ruined edifices facing each other, and seventy feet apart. Each appear to have been exactly alike in plan and ornament. The sides facing each other were embellished with sculpture, and there remain on both the fragments of entwined colossal serpents, which ran the whole length of the walls.

In the centre of each façade, at points directly opposite each other, are the fragments of a great stone ring. Each of these rings was four feet in diameter, and secured in the wall by a stone tenon of corresponding dimensions. They appear to have been broken wilfully. The part nearest the stem still projects from the wall, and the outer surface is covered with sculptured characters. We made excavations among the ruins along the base of the walls, in hope of discovering the missing parts of these rings, but without success.

These structures have no doorways or openings of any kind, either on the sides or at the ends. In the belief that they must have interior chambers, we made a breach in the wall of the one on the east to the depth of ten feet, but we found only rough stones, hanging so loosely together as to make it dangerous for the Indians to work in the holes, and they were obliged to discontinue.

This excavation, however, carried us through nearly one third of the structure, and satisfied us that these great parallel edifices did not contain any interior apartments, but that each consisted merely of four great walls, filled up with a solid mass of stones. It was our opinion that they had been built expressly with reference to the two great rings facing each other in the façades, and that the space between was intended for the celebration of some public games, in which opinion we were afterward confirmed.

CASA DE LAS MONJAS

Continuing on in the same direction, we reach the front of the House of the Nuns. This building is quadrangular, with a courtyard in the centre. It stands on the highest of three terraces. The front is two hundred and seventy-nine feet long, and above the cornice, from one end to the other, it is ornamented with sculpture. In the centre is a gateway spanned by the triangular arch, and leading to the courtyard. On each side of this gateway are four doorways with wooden lintels, opening to apartments having no communication with each other.

[The other] three ranges of buildings [that enclose] the quad-

24. Façade of the West Building, Nunnery Quadrangle, Uxmal (Thompson, circa 1888–89)

rangle have no doorways outside. The exterior of each is a dead wall, and above the cornice all are ornamented with the same rich and elaborate sculpture, [including] two rude, naked figures, which have been considered as indicating the existence of that same Eastern worship before referred to among the people of Uxmal.

Passing through the arched gateway, we enter a noble courtyard, with four great façades looking down upon it, each ornamented from one end to the other with the richest and most intricate carving known in the art of the builders of Uxmal; presenting a scene surpassing any that is now to be seen among its ruins. At the time of our first entrance it was overgrown with bushes and grass, quails started up from under our feet, and, with a whirring flight, passed over the tops of the buildings.

Among my many causes of regret for the small scale on which I am obliged to present these drawings, none is stronger than the consequent inability to present the four great façades fronting this courtyard. There is but one alleviating circumstance; which is, that the side most richly ornamented is so ruined that, under any circumstances, it could not be presented entire.

The façade on the left of the visiter entering the courtyard is distinguished by two colossal serpents entwined, running through and encompassing nearly all the ornaments throughout its whole length. The façade toward the north end of the building [has] the tail of one serpent held up nearly over the head of the other, and has an ornament upon it like a turban, with a plume of feathers. The marks on the extremity of the tail are probably intended to indicate a rattlesnake, with which species of serpent the country abounds. The lower serpent has its monstrous jaws wide open, and within them is a human head, the face of which is distinctly visible on the stone. From the ruin to which all was hurrying, Don Simon cared only to preserve this serpent's head. He said that we might tear out and carry away every other ornament, but this he intended to build into the wall of a house in Merida as a memorial of Uxmal.

Don Simon told us that in 1835 the whole front stood, and the two serpents were seen encircling every ornament in the building. In its ruins it presents a lively idea of the "large and very well constructed buildings of lime and stone" which Bernal Dias saw on landing at Campeachy, "with figures of serpents and of idols painted on the walls."

At the end of the courtyard, and fronting the gate of entrance, is the façade of a lofty building, standing on a terrace twenty feet high. The ascent is by a grand but ruined staircase, flanked on each side by a building with sculptured front, and having three doorways, each leading to apartments. The building has thirteen doorways, over each of which rose a perpendicular wall. These lofty structures were no doubt erected to give grandeur and effect to the building, and at a distance they appear to be turrets, but only four of them now remain. The whole great façade, including the turrets, is crowded with compli-

93 *Nunnery Quadrangle*

25. Modern view of feathered serpent sculpture on façade of the West Building, Nunnery Quadrangle, Uxmal

cated and elaborate sculpture, among which are human figures rudely executed: two are represented as playing on musical instruments, one being not unlike a small harp, and the other in the nature of a guitar; a third is in a sitting posture, with his hands across his breast, and tied by cords, the ends of which pass over his shoulders. Of the rest there is nothing which stands out distinct and intelligible like the serpent. The whole, loaded as it is with ornament, conveys the idea of vastness and magnificence rather than that of taste and refinement.

This building has one curious feature. It is erected over, and completely encloses, a smaller one of older date. The doorways, walls, and wooden lintels of the latter are all seen, and where the outer building is fallen, the ornamented cornice of the inner one is visible.

From the platform of the steps of this building, looking across the courtyard, a grand view presents itself [see Fig. 10], embracing all the principal buildings that now tower above the plain, except the House of the Dwarf. In the foreground is the inner façade of the front range of the Monjas, with a portion of the range on each side of the courtyard. To the left, in the distance, appears the Casa de la Vieja, or of the Old Woman, and, rising grandly above the front of the Monjas, are the House of the Turtles, that of the Governor, and the Casa de Palomos, or the House of the Pigeons.

The last of the four sides of the courtyard, standing on the right of the entrance, is the most entire of any, and, in fact, wants but little more than its wooden lintels, and some stones which have been

26. Façade of the North Structure, Nunnery Quadrangle, Uxmal (Charnay, 1860)

picked out of the façade below the cornice, to make it perfect [see Fig. 17]. It is, too, the most chaste and simple in design and ornament, and it was always refreshing to turn from the gorgeous and elaborate masses on the other façades to this curious and pleasing combination.

The ornament over the centre doorway is the most important, the most complicated and elaborate, and of that marked and peculiar style which characterizes the highest efforts of these ancient builders. The ornaments over the other doorways are less striking, more simple, and more pleasing. In all of them there is in the centre a masked face with the tongue hanging out, surmounted by an elaborate headdress; between the horizontal bars is a range of diamond-shaped ornaments, in which the remains of red paint are still distinctly visible, and at each end of these bars is a serpent's head, with the mouth wide open.

95   *East Structure, Nunnery Quadrangle*

[On] the southeast corner of this building, each side is a succession of compartments, alternately plain and presenting the form of diamond lattice-work. In both there is an agreeable succession of plain and ornamented, and, in fact, it would be difficult, in arranging four sides facing a courtyard, to have more variety, and at the same time more harmony of ornament. All these façades were painted. The traces of the colour are still visible, and the reader may imagine what the effect must have been when all this building was entire. According to its supposed design, in its now desolate doorways stood noble Maya maidens, like the vestal virgins of the Romans, to cherish and keep alive the sacred fire burning in the temples.

In the range last presented, there is one suite different from all the rest. The entrance to this suite is by the centre and principal doorway. It consists of two parallel chambers; at each end of both chambers is a doorway communicating with other chambers. The doorways of all these are ornamented with sculpture, and they are the only ornaments found in the interior of any buildings in Uxmal. The whole suite consists of six rooms; and there is a convenience in the arrangements not unsuited to the habits of what we call civilized life. Opening as they do upon this noble courtyard, in the dry season, they would be by far the most comfortable residence for any future explorer of the ruins of Uxmal. Every time I went to them I regretted that we could not avail ourselves of the facilities they offered.

With these few words I take leave of the Casa de las Monjas, remarking only that in the centre is the fragment of a large stone like that on the terrace of the Casa del Gobernador, called the Picote, and also that, induced by the account of Waldeck that the whole was once paved with sculptured turtles, I passed a morning digging all over the courtyard below the slight accumulation of earth, and found nothing of the kind. The substratum consisted of rude stones, no doubt once serving as a foundation for a floor of cement, which, from long exposure to the rainy seasons, has now entirely disappeared.

At the back of the last-mentioned range of the Monjas is another, or rather there are several ranges of buildings, standing lower than the House of the Nuns, in irregular order, and much ruined. To the first portion of these we gave the name of the House of the Birds, from the circumstance of its being ornamented on the exterior with representations of feathers and birds rudely sculptured. The remaining portion consists of some very large rooms, among which are two fifty-three feet long, fourteen wide, and about twenty high, being the largest, or at least the widest in Uxmal. In one of them are the remains of painting well preserved, and in the other is an arch, which approaches nearer to the principle of the keystone than any we had yet met with in our whole exploration of ruins. It is very similar to the earliest arches, if they may be so called, of the Etruscans and Greeks, as seen at Arpino in the kingdom of Naples, and Tiryns in Greece.

CASA DEL ADIVINO

From this range of buildings we descend to the House of the Dwarf, also known by the name of the House of the Diviner, from its overlooking the whole city, and enabling its occupant to be cognizant of all that was passing around him. The courtyard of this building is bounded by ranges of mounds, now covered with a rank growth of herbage, but which, perhaps, once formed ranges of buildings. In the centre is a large circular stone, like those seen in the other courtyards.

The base of this building is so ruined and encumbered with fallen stones that it is difficult to ascertain its precise dimensions. Its height is eighty-eight feet, and to the top of the building it is one hundred and five feet. Though diminishing as it rises, its shape is not exactly pyramidal, but its ends are rounded. It is encased with stone, and apparently solid from the plain.

A great part of the front has fallen, and now lies a mass of ruins at the foot of the mound. Along the base, about twenty feet up the mound, and probably once reached by a staircase, now ruined, is a range of curious apartments, nearly choked up with rubbish, and with the sapote beams still in their places over the door.

At the height of sixty feet is a solid projecting platform, on

which stands a building loaded with ornaments more rich, elaborate, and carefully executed, than those of any other edifice in Uxmal [see cover image]. A great doorway opens upon the platform. The sapote beams are still in their places, and the interior is divided into two apartments. Both are entirely plain, without ornament of any kind, and have no communication with any part of the mound.

The steps or other means of communication with this building are all gone, and at the time of our visit we were at a loss to know how it had been reached. From what we saw afterward, we are induced to believe that a grand staircase upon a different plan from any yet met with, and supported by a triangular arch, led from the ground to the door of the building, which, if still in existence, would give extraordinary grandeur to this great mound.

The crowning structure is a long and narrow building, measuring seventy-two feet in front, and but twelve feet deep. The front is much ruined, but even in its decay presents the most elegant and tasteful arrangement of ornaments to be seen in Uxmal. The emblems of life and death appear on the wall in close juxta position, confirming the belief in the existence of that worship practised by the Egyptians and all other Eastern nations, and before referred to as prevalent among the people of Uxmal.

The interior is divided into three apartments. They have no communication with each other; two have their doors opening to the east and one to the west. A narrow platform five feet wide projects from

27. Modern view of the west side of the Pyramid of the Magician, Uxmal

all the four sides of the building. The northern end is decayed, and part of the eastern front, and to this front ascends a grand staircase.

The steps are very narrow, and the staircase steep; and after we had cleared away the trees, and there were no branches to assist us in climbing, the ascent and descent were difficult and dangerous. The padre Cogolludo says that he once ascended these steps, and "that when he attempted to descend he repented; his sight failed him, and he was in some danger." He adds, that in the apartments of the building, which he calls "small chapels," were the "idols," and that there they made sacrifices of men, women, and children. Beyond doubt this lofty building was a great Teocalis, "El grande de los Kues," the great temple of idols worshipped by the people of Uxmal, consecrated by their most mysterious rites, the holiest of their holy places. "The High Priest had in his Hand a large, broad, and sharp Knife made of Flint. Another Priest carried a wooden collar wrought like a snake. The persons to be sacrificed were conducted one by one up the Steps, stark naked, and as soon as laid on the Stone, had the Collar put upon their Necks, and the four priests took hold of the hands and feet. Then the high Priest with wonderful Dexterity ripped up the Breast, tore out the Heart, reeking, with his Hands, and showed it to the Sun, offering him the Heart and Steam that came from it. Then he turned to the Idol, and threw it in his face, which done, he kicked the body down the steps, and it never stopped till it came to the bottom, because they were *very upright*." And "one who had been a Priest, and had been converted, said that when they tore out the Heart of the wretched Person sacrificed, it did beat so strongly that he took it up from the Ground three or four times till it cooled by Degrees, and then he threw the Body, still moving, down the Steps." In all the long catalogue of superstitious rites that darkens the page of man's history, I cannot imagine a picture more horribly exciting than that of the Indian priest, with his white dress and long hair clotted with gore, performing his murderous sacrifices at this lofty height, in full view of the people throughout the whole extent of the city.

CASA DE LAS PALOMAS

From the top of this mound we pass over the Casa del Gobernador to the grand structure marked on the general plan as the Casa de Palomos, or the House of the Pigeons. The front is much ruined, the apartments are filled, and along the centre of the roof, running longitudinally, is a range of structures built in a pyramidal form, like the fronts of some of the old Dutch houses that still remain among us, but grander and more massive. These are nine in number, built of stone, about three feet thick, and have small oblong openings through them. These openings give them somewhat the appearance of pigeon-houses, and from this the name of the building is derived. All had once been covered with figures and ornaments in stucco, portions of which still remain.

In the centre of this building is an archway ten feet wide, which leads into a courtyard. In the centre of the courtyard, thrown down, is the same large stone so often mentioned. On the right is a range of ruined buildings, on the left a similar range, and rising behind it [a] high mound. In front, at the end of the courtyard, is a range of ruined buildings, with another archway in the centre. Crossing the courtyard, and passing through this archway, we ascend a flight of steps, now ruined, and reach another courtyard. On each side of this courtyard, too, is a range of ruined buildings, and at the other end is a great Teocalis. A broad staircase leads to the top, on which stands a long narrow building divided into three apartments.

99   *House of the Pigeons*

28. Catherwood drawing of the House of the Pigeons (or Dovecote), Uxmal

29. House of the Pigeons, Uxmal (circa 1900)

There was a mournful interest about this great pile of ruins. Entering under the great archway, crossing two noble courtyards, with ruined buildings on each side, and ascending the great staircase to the building on the top, gave a stronger impression of departed greatness than anything else in this desolate city. It commanded a view of every other building, and stood apart in lonely grandeur, seldom disturbed by human footsteps. On going up to it once Mr. Catherwood started a deer, and at another time a wild hog.

At the northeast angle of this building is a vast range of high, ruined terraces, facing east and west, and called the Campo Santo. On one of these is a building of two stories, with some remains of sculpture, and in a deep and overgrown valley at the foot, the Indians say, was the burial-place of this ancient city. Though searching for it ourselves, and offering a reward to them for the discovery, we never found in it a sepulchre.

Besides these there was the Casa de la Vieja, or the House of the Old Woman, standing in ruins. Once, when the wind was high, I saw the remains of the front wall bending before its force. It is five hundred feet from the Casa del Gobernador, and has its name from a mutilated statue of an old woman lying before it.

Near by are other monuments lying on the ground, overgrown and half buried, which were pointed out to us by the Indians on our first visit. North of this there is a circular mound of ruins, probably of a circular building like that of Mayapan. A wall which was said to encompass the city is laid down on the plan so far as it can be traced. Beyond this, for a great distance in every direction, the ground is strewed with ruins. I might extend this brief description indefinitely, but I have compressed it within the smallest possible limits. We made plans of every building and drawings of every sculptured stone, and this place alone might furnish materials for larger volumes than these. But I have so many and such vast remains to present that I am obliged to avoid details as much as possible. I trust that what I have done will give the reader some definite idea of the ruins of Uxmal. Perhaps, as we did, he will imagine the scene that must have been presented when all these buildings were entire, occupied by people in costumes strange and fanciful as the ornaments on their buildings, and possessing all those minor arts which must have been coexistent with architecture and sculpture, and which the imperishable stone has survived.

The historic light which beamed upon us at Merida and Mayapan does not reach this place. It is not mentioned in any record of the conquest. The cloud again gathers, but even through it a star appears. The padre Cogolludo says, that on the memorable occasion when his sight failed as he was going down the steps of the great Teocalis, he found in one of the apartments, or, as he calls it, one of the chapels, offerings of cacao and marks of copal, used by the Indians as incense, *burned there but a short time before; an evidence, he says, of some superstition or idolatry recently committed by the Indians of that place.* He piously adds, "God help those poor Indians, for the devil deceives them very easily."

While in Merida I procured from Don Simon Peon the title papers to this estate. They were truly a formidable pile, and, unfortunately, a great portion of them was in the Maya language. But there was one folio volume in Spanish, and in this was the first formal conveyance ever made of these lands by the Spanish government. It bears date the twelfth day of May, 1673, and is entitled a testimonial of royal favour made to the Regidor Don Lorenzo de Evia, of four leagues of land from the buildings of Uxmal to the south, one to the east, another to the west, and another to the north, for his distinguished merits and services therein expressed. The preamble sets forth that the regidor had a wife and children whom it was necessary for him to maintain in a manner conforming to his office, and that he wished to stock the said places and meadows with horned cattle, and praying a grant of them for that purpose in the name of his majesty, since no injury could result to any third person, but, "*on the contrary, very great service* to God our Lord, *because with that establishment it would prevent the Indians in those places from worshipping the devil in the ancient buildings which are there, having in them their idols, to which they burn copal, and performing other detestable sacrifices, as they are doing every day notoriously and publicly.*"

Following this is a later instrument, dated the third of December, 1687, the preamble of which recites the petition of the Captain Lorenzo de Evia, setting forth the grant above referred to, and that an Indian named Juan Can had importuned him with a claim of right to the said lands on account of his being a descendant of the ancient Indians, to whom they belonged. The Indian had exhibited some confused papers and maps, and although it was not possible for him to justify the right that he claimed, to avoid litigation, Don Lorenzo de Evia agreed to give him seventy-four dollars for the price and value of the said land. The petition introduces the deed of consent, or quitclaim, of Juan Can, executed with all the formalities required in the case of Indians, and prays a confirmation of his former grant, and to be put in real and corporeal possession. The instrument confirms the former grant, and prescribes the formal mode of obtaining possession.

Under the deed of confirmation appears the deed of livery of seisin, beginning, "In the place called the edifices of Uxmal and its lands, the third day of the month of January, 1688," &c., &c., and concluding with these words: "In virtue of the power and authority which by the same title is given to me by the said governor, complying with its terms, I took by the hand the said Lorenzo de Evia, and he walked with me all over Uxmal and its buildings, *opened and shut some doors* that had several rooms, cut within the space some trees, picked up fallen stones and threw them down, drew water from one of the aguadas of the said place of Uxmal, and performed other acts of possession."

The reader will perceive that we have here two distinct, independent witnesses testifying that, one hundred and forty years after the foundation of Merida, the buildings of Uxmal were regarded with reverence by the Indians; that they formed the nucleus of a dispersed and scattered population, and were resorted to for the observance of religious rites at a distance from the eyes of the Spaniards. Cogolludo saw in the House of the Dwarf the "marks of copal recently burned," "the evidence of some idolatry recently committed"; and the private title papers of Don Simon, never intended to illustrate any point in history, besides showing incidentally that it was the policy of the government, and "doing God service," to break up the Indian customs, and drive the natives away from their consecrated buildings, are proofs, which would be good evidence in a court of law, that the Indians were, at the time referred to, openly and notoriously worshipping El Demonio, and performing other detestable sacrifices in these ancient buildings.

Can it be supposed that edifices in which they were thus worshipping, and to which they were clinging with such tenacity as to require to be driven away, were the buildings of another race, or did they cling to them because they were adapted to the forms and ceremonies received from their fathers, and because they were the same in which their fathers had worshipped? In my mind there is but little question as to the fair interpretation to be put upon these acts, and I may add that, according to the deed of the notary, but one hundred and fifty-four years ago the ruined buildings of Uxmal had "doors" which could be "opened" and "shut."

CHAPTER SEVEN

Journey to Kabáh

hile working the camera under a blazing sun in the courtyard of the Monjas, I received a note from Mr. Catherwood advising me that he had a chill and was in bed. Presently a heavy rain came down. I took refuge in a damp apartment, where I was obliged to remain so long that I became perfectly chilled. On my return, I had a severe relapse, and in the evening Dr. Cabot, depressed by the state of things, and out of pure sympathy, joined us. Our servants went away, we were all three pinned to our beds together, and determined forthwith to leave Uxmal.

[Two days later,] as we descended the steps from the Casa del Gobernador, Mr. C. suggested that it was Newyear's Day. This fact called up scenes strikingly contrasted with our own miserable condition, and for the moment we would have been glad to be at home. Our cochés were in readiness at the foot of the terrace, and we crawled in. The Indians raised us upon their shoulders, and we were in motion from Uxmal. All the interest we had felt in the place was gone, and we only wanted to get away. Silent and desolate as we found them, we left the ruins, again to be overgrown with trees, to crumble and fall, and perhaps to become, like others scattered over the country, mere shapeless and nameless mounds.

Notwithstanding the comparatively easy movement of the coché, both Mr. C. and I suffered excessively, for, being made of poles hastily tied together, the vehicle yielded under the irregular steps of the carriers. The next day, near dark, we reached the foot of the sierra, and, as we ascended, the clouds threatened rain. On top the rain came on, and the Indians hurried down as fast as the darkness and the ruggedness of the road would permit. I had great confidence in their sureness of foot, when all at once I felt the coché going over, and pinned in as I was, unable to help myself, with a frightful crash it came down on its side. My fear was that it would go over a precipice. But the Indians on the upper side held on, and I got out with considerable celerity. The rain was pouring, and it was so dark that I could see nothing. My shoulder and side were bruised, but, fortunately, none of the Indians were missing. They all gathered round, apparently more frightened than I was hurt. We righted the coché, arranged things as well as we could, and in due season I was set down at the door of the convent of Ticul.

The change which two weeks had made in the cura's appearance was appalling. Naturally thin, his agonizing pains had frightfully reduced him, and as he lay extended on a cot with a sheet over him, he seemed more dead than living. He was barely able, by the feeble pressure of his shrunken hand, to show that he appreciated our visit, and to say that he had never expected to see us again. The happy faces of those around him spoke more than words. It was actually rejoicing as over one snatched from the grave.

The next morning we visited him again. His sunken eyes lighted up as he inquired about our excavations at Uxmal, and a smile played upon his lips as he alluded to the superstition of the Indians about digging up the bones in San Francisco. Our visit seemed to give him so much satisfaction, that, though we could not talk with him, we remained at the house nearly all day, and the next day we returned to Nohcacab on horseback. Our visit to Ticul had recruited us greatly, and we determined immediately to resume our occupations.

On leaving Uxmal we had directed our steps toward Nohcacab, on account of the ruins which we had heard of as existing in that neighbourhood; and, after ascertaining their position, we considered that they could be visited to the best advantage by making this place our head-quarters. It is ascertained by historical accounts, that at the time of the conquest an Indian town existed in this immediate neighbourhood, bearing the name of Nohcacab. This name is compounded

30. *Page 104:* Corbelled arch on east façade of the House of the Governor, Uxmal (Thompson, circa 1888–89)

of three Maya words, signifying literally the great place of good land. From the numerous and extraordinary ruins scattered around, there is reason to believe that it was the heart of a rich, and what was once an immensely populous country. In the suburbs are numerous and large mounds, grand enough to excite astonishment, but even more fallen and overgrown than those of San Francisco, and, in fact, almost inaccessible.

The village stands in the same relative position to these ruins that Ticul does to the ruins of San Francisco, and, like that, in my opinion it stands on the offskirts of the old Indian town. Rather it occupies part of the very site, for in the village itself are the remains of mounds exactly like those in the suburbs. In making excavations in the plaza, vases and vessels of pottery are continually brought to light, and in the street wall of [a] house is a sculptured head dug up fifteen years ago.

The village does not lie on the way to any place of general resort, and is not worth stopping at on its own account. It was the most backward and thoroughly Indian of any village we had visited. Merida was too far off for the Indians to think of; Ticul was their capital. Everything that was deficient in the village they told us was to be had at Ticul. The sexton, who went over once a week for the holy wafer, was always charged with some errand for us.

The first place which we proposed visiting was the ruins of Xcoch. Xcoch was but a league distant, and, besides the ruins of buildings, it contained an ancient poso, or well, of mysterious and marvellous reputation, the fame of which was in everybody's mouth. This well was said to be a vast subterraneous structure, adorned with sculptured figures, an immense table of polished stone, and a plaza with columns supporting a vaulted roof. It was said to have a subterraneous road, which led to the village of Mani, twenty-seven miles distant.

Notwithstanding this wondrous reputation, and although within three miles of Nohcacab, the intelligence we received was so vague and uncertain that we were at a loss how to make our arrangements for exploring the well. Not a white man in the place had ever entered it, though several had looked in at the mouth, who said that the wind had taken away their breath, and they had not ventured to go in. Its fame rested entirely upon the accounts of the Indians, which, coming to us through interpreters, were very confused. Two men were brought to us who were considered most familiar with the place. They said that it would be impossible to enter it except by employing several men one or two days in making ladders, and, at all events, they said it would be useless to attempt the descent after the sun had crossed the meridian. To this all our friends and counsellors, who knew nothing about it, assented. Knowing, however, their dilatory manner of doing business, we engaged them to be on the ground at daylight. In the mean time we got together all the spare ropes in the village, and at eight o'clock the next morning we set out.

For a league we followed the camino real, at which distance we saw a little opening, where one of our Indians was waiting for us. Following him by a narrow path, we again found ourselves among ruins, and soon reached the foot of the high mound which towered above the plain, itself conspicuous from the House of the Dwarf at Uxmal. The ground in this neighbourhood was open, and there were the remains of several buildings, but all prostrate and in utter ruin.

The great cerro stands alone, the only one that now rises above the plain. The sides are all fallen, though in some places the remains of steps are visible. On the south side about half way up, there is a large tree, which facilitates the ascent to the top. One corner of a building is all that is left; the rest of the top is level and overgrown with grass. The view commanded an immense wooded plain, and, rising above it, toward the southeast the great church of Nohcacab, and on the west the ruined buildings of Uxmal.

Returning, we entered a thick grove, in which we dismounted and tied our horses. It was the finest grove we had seen in the country, and within it was a great circular cavity or opening in the earth, twenty feet deep, with trees and bushes growing out of the bottom and sides, and rising above the level of the plain. It was a wild-looking place, and had a fanciful, mysterious, and almost fearful appearance; for while in the grove all was close and sultry, and without a breath of air, and every leaf was still, within this cavity the branches and leaves were violently agitated, as if shaken by an invisible hand.

This cavity was the entrance to the poso, or well. Its appearance was wild enough to bear out the wildest accounts we had heard of it. We descended to the bottom. At one corner was a rude natural opening in a great mass of limestone rock, low and narrow, through which rushed constantly a powerful current of wind, agitating the branches and leaves. This was the mouth of the well, and on our first attempting to enter it the rush of wind was so strong that it made us fall back gasping for breath, confirming the accounts we had heard in Nohcacab. Our Indians had for torches long strips of the castor-oil plant, which the wind only ignited more thoroughly. With these they led the way, other Indians coming after us with coils of rope.

The entrance was so low that we were obliged to crawl on our hands and feet, and descended at an angle. The wind rushed through this passage with such force that we could scarcely breathe. As we all had in us the seeds of fever and ague, we very much doubted the propriety of going on, but curiosity was stronger than discretion, and we proceeded. In the floor of the passage was a single track, worn three inches deep by long-continued treading of feet. The roof was incrusted with a coat of smoke from the flaring torches. The labour of crawling through this passage with the body bent, against the rush of cold air, made a rather severe beginning, and, probably, if we had undertaken the enterprise alone we should have turned back.

At [a] distance, the passage enlarged to an irregular cavern. We no longer felt the rush of cold wind, and the temperature was sensibly warmer. The sides and roof were of rough, broken stone, and through the centre ran the same worn path. From this passage others branched off to the right and left, and in passing along it, at one place the Indians held their torches down to a block of sculptured stone. We had already satisfied ourselves that the cave or passage, whatever it might lead to, was the work of nature, and had given up all expectation of seeing the great monuments of art which had been described to us. But the sight of this block encouraged us with the hope that the accounts might have some foundation. Very soon, however, our hopes on this head were materially abated, if not destroyed, by reaching what the Indians had described as a mesa, or table. This had been a great item in all the accounts, and was described as made by hand and highly polished. It was simply a huge block of rude stone, the top of which happened to be smooth, but entirely in a state of nature. Beyond this we passed into a large opening of an irregular circular form, being what had been described to us as a plaza. Here the Indians stopped and flared their torches. It was a great vaulted chamber of stone, with a high roof supported by enormous stalactite pillars, which were what the Indians had called the columns. Though entirely different from what we had expected, the effect under the torchlight, and heightened by the wild figures of the Indians, was grand, and almost repaid us for all our trouble. This plaza lay at one side of the regular path, and we remained in it some minutes to refresh ourselves, for the closeness of the passage and the heat and smoke were becoming almost intolerable.

Farther on we climbed up a high, broken piece of rock, and descended again by a low, narrow opening, through which we were obliged to crawl, and which was so hot that we were panting with exhaustion and thirst. This brought us to a rugged, perpendicular hole, four feet in diameter, with steps barely large enough for a foothold, worn in the rock. We descended with some difficulty, and at the foot came out upon a ledge of rock, which ran up on the right to a great height. On the left was a deep, yawning chasm. A few rude logs were laid along the edge of this chasm, which, with a pole for a railing, served as a bridge, and, with the torchlight thrown into the abyss below, made a wild crossing-place. The passage then turned to the right, contracting to about three feet in height, and descending rapidly. We were again obliged to betake ourselves to crawling, and again the heat became insufferable. Indeed, we went on with some apprehensions. To faint in one of those narrow passages would be almost to die there.

This passage continued fifty feet, when it doubled on itself, still rapidly descending. It then enlarged to a rather spacious cavern, and took a southwest direction, after which there was another perpendicular hole, leading, by means of a rude and rickety ladder, to a steep, low, crooked, and crawling passage, descending until it opened into a large broken chamber, at one end of which was a basin of water.

The sight of it was more welcome to us than gold or rubies. We were dripping with sweat, black with smoke, and perishing with thirst. It lay before us clear and inviting, but completely out of reach. The basin was so deep that we could not reach the water with our hands, and we had no vessel of any kind to dip it out with. In our entire ignorance of the character of the place, we had not made any provision, and the Indians had only brought what they were told to bring. I crawled down on one side, and dipped up a little with one hand. But it was a scanty supply, and with this water before us we were compelled to go away with our thirst unsatisfied. Fortunately, however, after crawling back through the first narrow passage, we found some fragments of a broken water-jar, with which the Indians returned and brought us enough to cool our tongues.

In going down we had scarcely noticed anything except the wild path before us. Having now some knowledge of the place, the labor was not so great, and we inquired for the passage which the Indians had told us led to Mani. On reaching it, we turned off, and, after following it a short distance, found it completely stopped by a natural closing of the rock. Although all said the passage led to Mani, we were satisfied that the Indians had never attempted to explore it. It did not lead to the water, nor out of the cave, and our guides had never entered it before. We advised them for the future to omit this and some other particulars in their stories about the well; but probably the next travellers will hear the same accounts that we did.

As we advanced, we remained a little while in the cooler atmosphere before exposing ourselves to the rush of cold air toward the mouth, and in an hour and a half from the time of entering, we emerged into the outer air.

As a mere cave, this was extraordinary; but as a well for an ancient city, it was past belief, except for the proofs under our own eyes. Around it were the ruins of a city without any other visible means of supply. The Indians say that it was not discovered by them; it was used by their fathers. They did not know when it began to be used. They ascribe it to that remote people whom they refer to as the antiguos. A strong circumstance to induce the belief that it was once used by the inhabitants of a populous city is the deep track worn in the rock. For ages the region around has been desolate, or occupied only by a few Indians during the time of working in the milpas. Their straggling footsteps would never have made that deep track. It could only have been made by the constant and long-continued tread of thousands. It must have been made by the population of a city.

The next day we set out for another ruined city. It lay on the road to Uxmal, and was known by the name Nohpat. At the distance of a league we turned off from the main road, and, following a narrow milpa path, in fifteen minutes reached the field of ruins. One mound rose high above the rest, holding aloft a ruined building. We dismounted and tied our horses. The mound with the building upon it had separated and fallen apart, and while one side still supported part of the edifice, the other presented the appearance of a mountain slide.

Our guide told us that the separation had happened only with the floods of the last rainy season. We ascended on the fallen side, and found a gigantic staircase, overgrown, but with the great stone steps still in their places. The ruined building consisted of a single corridor. With the ruins of Nohpat at our feet, we looked out upon a great desolate plain, studded with overgrown mounds, of which we took the bearings and names as known to the Indians. Toward the west by north, startling by the grandeur of the buildings and their height above the plain, with no decay visible, and at this distance seeming perfect as a living city, were the ruins of Uxmal. Fronting us was the great Casa del Gobernador, apparently so near that we almost looked into its open doors, and could have distinguished a man moving on the terrace; and yet, for the first two weeks of our residence at Uxmal, we did not know of the existence of this place.

Descending the mound, we rose upon an elevated platform, in the centre of which was a huge and rude round stone, like that called the picote in the courtyards at Uxmal. At the base of the steps was a large flat stone, having sculptured upon it a colossal human figure in bas-relief. The stone lies on its back, broken in two in the middle. Probably it once stood erect at the base of the steps, but, thrown down and broken, has lain for ages with its face to the sky, exposed to the floods of the rainy season. The sculpture is rude and worn, and the lines were difficult to make out. The Indians said that it was the figure of a king of the antiguos, and no doubt it was intended as a portrait of some lord or cacique.

At a short distance to the southeast of the courtyard was another platform or terrace, on two sides of which were ranges of buildings. One of them had two stories, and trees growing out of the walls and on the top, forming the most picturesque ruins we had seen in the country. As we approached it Doctor Cabot was climbing up a tree at the corner to get on the roof in pursuit of a bird, and, in doing so, started a gigantic lizard, which went bounding among the trees and along the cornice till he buried himself in a large fissure in the front.

Leaving this neighbourhood, and passing by many ruined buildings and mounds, we reached an open place, forming the most curious and interesting part of this field of ruins. It was in the vicinity of three mounds. In the open space were some sculptured monuments, shattered, fallen, some of them half buried. Strange heads and bodies lay broken and scattered, so that at first we did not discover their connexion. But, by examining carefully, we found two fragments, which, from the shape of the broken surfaces, seemed to be parts of one block, one of them representing a huge head, and the other a huger body. The latter we set up in its proper position, and with some difficulty, by means of poles, and ropes which the Indians took from their sandals, we got the other part on the top, and fitted in its place. It was a solid block of stone, and represents a human figure in a crouching posture, with the face, having a hideous expression, turned over the shoulder, almost behind. The headdress is a representation of the head of a wild beast, the ears, eyes, teeth, and jaws being easily distinguishable. The sculpture is rude, and the whole appearance uncouth and ugly. Probably it was one of the idols worshipped by the people of this ancient city.

There were others of the same general character, of which the sculpture was more defaced and worn. Besides these, there were monuments of a different character, half buried, and dispersed without apparent order. After some examination, we made out what we considered the arrangement in which they had stood, and had them set up.

Each stone is two feet three inches high. The subject is the skull and cross-bones. The sculpture is in bas-relief, and the carving good, and still clear and distinct. Probably this was the holy place of the city, where the idols or deities were presented to the people with the emblems of death around them.

The ruins lie on the common lands of the village of Nohcacab, at least so say the alcaldes of that place. Don Simon Peon claims that they are within the old boundaries of the hacienda of Uxmal, and the settling of the question is not worth the expense of a survey. The name Nohpat is compounded of two Maya words, which signify a great lord or señor. This is all the information I was able to collect about this ancient city. If we had met with it on our former journey we should have planted ourselves, and given it a thorough exploration. The mounds and vestiges of buildings were perhaps as numerous as those of Uxmal, but they were all ruined.

The day was like the finest of October at home, and, as a relief from the heat of the sun, there was a constant and refreshing breeze. The country was open, or studded with trees barely enough to adorn the landscape, and give picturesque beauty to the ruins. It was cut up by numerous paths, and covered with grass like a fine piece of up-

113   *Approach to Kabáh*

31. Catherwood view of the front of Casa No. 2 (Palace), Kabáh

land at home, and for the first and only time in the country we found pleasure in a mere ramble over fields. Bernaldo came out from the village with a loaded Indian at the precise moment when we wanted dinner, and altogether it was one of the most agreeable and satisfactory days that we passed among the relics of the antiguos.

The next day we set out for the ruins of Kabah. Our direction was south, on the camino real to Bolonchen. The descent from the great rocky table was rough, broken, and precipitous. We passed through a long street having on each side thatched huts, occupied exclusively by Indians. Beyond, the road was stony, bordered on both sides by scrubby trees and bushes. As we advanced we passed through an open country, adorned with large forest trees. At the distance of two leagues we turned off, and very soon found ourselves among trees, bushes, and a thick, overgrown foliage. Beyond we saw through an opening a lofty mound, overgrown, and having upon it the ruins of a building like the House of the Dwarf, towering above every other object, and proclaiming the site of another lost and deserted city. Moving on, we had a glimpse of a great stone edifice, with its front apparently entire. We had hardly expressed our admiration before we saw another, and at a few horses' length a third. Three great buildings at once, with façades which, at that distance, and by the imperfect glimpses we had of them, showed no imperfection, and seemed entire.

114 CHAPTER
     SEVEN

32. Modern view of the Palace, Kabáh

Our guides cut a path for us, and with great difficulty we went on till we found ourselves at the foot of an overgrown terrace in front of the nearest building. Here we stopped; the Indians cleared a place for our horses. Before us was a building with its walls entire, its front more fallen, but the remains showing that it had once been more richly decorated than any at Uxmal. We ranged through every apartment. Then we descended the back terrace, and rose upon a high mound, having a great stone staircase different from anything we had seen, and, groping our way among the trees, passed on to the next. The third presented a façade almost entire.

Since we first set out in search of ruins we had not been taken so much by surprise. During the whole time of our residence at Uxmal, and until my forced visit to Ticul, and fortunate intimacy with the cura Carillo, I had not even heard of the existence of such a place. It was absolutely unknown. The Indians who guided us to these buildings, of all the rest seemed as ignorant as ourselves. They told us, in fact, that these were all. But we could not believe them. We felt confident that more lay buried in the woods, and, tempted by the variety and novelty of what we saw, we determined not to go away until we had discovered all. Since we began at Nohcacab, we had "done up" a city a day, but we had now a great field of labour before us, and we saw at once that it was to be attended with many difficulties.

There was no rancho, and no habitation of any kind nearer than the village. The buildings themselves offered good shelter; with clearings they could be made extremely agreeable. It was advisable again to take up our abode among the ruins; but this arrangement was not without its dangers. The season of El Norte seemed to have no end; every day there was rain. The foliage was so thick that the hot sun could not dry the moisture before another rain came, and the whole country was enveloped in a damp, unwholesome atmosphere. Besides, unluckily for us, it was a season of great abundance in the village. The corn crop had been good; the Indians had plenty to eat, and did not care to work. Already we had found difficulty in hiring them. It would require constant urging and our continual presence to secure them from day to day. As to getting them to remain with us, it was out of the question. We determined, therefore, to continue our residence at the convent, and go out to the ruins every day.

CHAPTER EIGHT

Kabáh

All the ruins scattered about the country are known to the Indians under the general name of "Xlap-pahk," which means "old walls." The information we obtained was in general so confused that we were unable to form any idea of the extent or character of the ruins. To some I made preliminary visits; those from which I expected most turned out not worth the trouble of going to, while others, from which I expected but little, proved extremely interesting. Almost every evening, on returning to the convent, the padrecito hurried into our room, with the greeting, "Buenas noticias! Otras ruinas!" "Good news! More ruins!" At one time these noticias came in so fast that I sent Albino on a two days' excursion to "do" some preliminary visits, who returned with a report justifying my opinion of his judgment, and a bruised leg from climbing over a mound, which disabled him for some days.

Chichen was the only place we heard of in Merida, and the only place we knew of with absolute certainty before we embarked for Yucatan; but we found that a vast field of research lay between us and it, and, not to delay the reader, I proceed at once to the ruins of Kabah. The plan of the buildings of

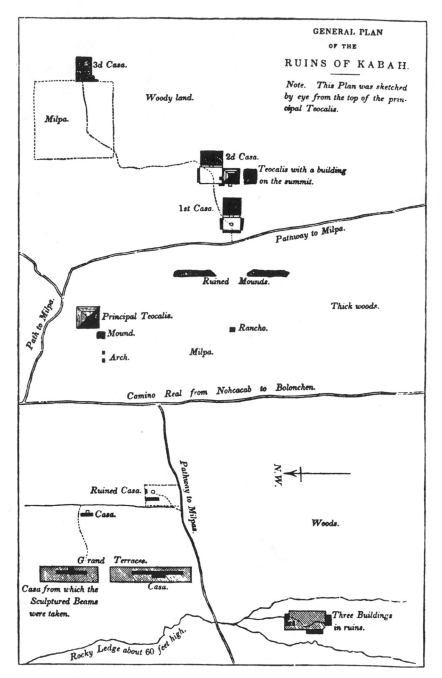

GENERAL PLAN
OF THE
RUINS OF KABAH.

Note.   This Plan was sketched
by eye from the top of the principal Teocalis.

3d Casa.

Woody land.

Milpa.

2d Casa.

Teocalis with a building
on the summit.

1st Casa.

Pathway to Milpa.

Ruined   Mounds.

Thick woods.

Principal Teocalis.

Mound.

Rancho.

Arch.

Milpa.

Camino   Real   from   Nohcacab   to   Bolonchen.

Pathway to Milpas.

Path to Milpa.

Ruined Casa.

Casa.

N.W.

Woods.

Grand   Terraces.

Casa from which the
Sculptured Beams
were taken.

Casa.

Three Buildings
in ruins.

Rocky Ledge about 60 feet high.

33. *Page 116:* Modern
view of Chaac masks lying
reassembled at the base of
the façade of the Codz
Poop (Palace of the
Masks), Kabáh

this city is not made from actual measurements, for this would have required clearings which would have been impossible to make. The bearings were taken with the compass from the top of the great teocalis, and the distances are laid down according to our best judgment with the eye.

Following a path toward the field of ruins, the teocalis is the first object that meets his eye, grand, picturesque, ruined, and covered with trees, like the House of the Dwarf at Uxmal, towering above every other object on the plain. The steps are all fallen, and the sides present a surface of loose stones, difficult to climb, except on one side, where the ascent is rendered practicable by the aid of trees. I ascended it for the first time toward evening, when the sun was about setting, and the ruined buildings were casting lengthened shadows over the plain. At the north, south, and east the view was bounded by a range of hills. In part of the field of ruins was a clearing, in which stood a deserted rancho. The only indication that we were in the vicinity of man was the distant church in the village of Nohcacab.

Leaving this mound, again taking the milpa path, we reach the foot of a terrace which is overgrown with trees. Ascending this, we stand on a platform facing [another] building. On the right is a high range of structures, ruined and overgrown with trees, with an im-

119   *Palace of the Masks*

34. *Opposite:* Catherwood map of Kabáh

35. *Below:* Stephens' Casa No. 1 (Codz Poop, or Palace of the Masks), Kabáh (Thompson, circa 1890)

mense back wall built on the outer line of the platform, perpendicular to the bottom of the terrace. On the left is another range of ruined buildings, and in the centre of the platform is a stone enclosure, like that surrounding the picote at Uxmal. But the layer of stones around the base was sculptured, and, on examination, we found a continuous line of hieroglyphics. In the centre of the platform is a range of stone steps leading to an upper terrace, on which stands the building. The moment we saw this building we were struck with the extraordinary richness and ornament of its façade. In all the buildings of Uxmal, up to the cornice which runs over the doorway the façades are of plain stone. This was ornamented from the very foundation, two layers under the lower cornice, to the top. A great part of this façade has fallen. Toward the north end, however, a portion of about twenty-five feet remains, which shows the gorgeousness of decoration with which this façade was once adorned.

The ornaments are of the same character with those at Uxmal, alike complicated and incomprehensible. Every part of the façade was ornamented with sculpture, even to the portion now buried un-

36. Modern view of hieroglyphic inscriptions found on the altar in front of Casa No. 1, Kabáh

37. Left end of the façade of the Codz Poop, Kabáh (Charnay, 1882)

der the lower cornice. The whole must have presented a greater appearance of richness than any building at Uxmal. The cornice running over the doorways, tried by the severest rules of art recognised among us, would embellish the architecture of any known era. Amid a mass of barbarism it stands as an offering by American builders worthy of the acceptance of a polished people.

The lintels of the doorways were of wood; these are all fallen, and of all the ornaments which decorated them not one now remains. No doubt they corresponded in beauty of sculpture with the rest of the façade. The whole now lies a mass of rubbish and ruin at the foot of the wall.

On the top is a structure which, seen indistinctly through the trees, had the appearance of a second story. There was no staircase or other visible means of communication, but in the rear the wall and roof had fallen, and made in some places high mounds reaching nearly to the top. Climbing up these tottering fabrics was not free from danger. Parts which appeared substantial had not the security of buildings constructed according to true principles of art. The disorderly masses seemed held up by an invisible hand. While we were clearing off the trees upon the roof, a shower came up suddenly, and, as we were hurrying to descend and take refuge in one of the apartments below, a stone on the edge of the cornice gave way and carried me down with it. By great good fortune, underneath was a mound of ruins which reached nearly to the roof, and saved me from a fall that would have been most serious, if not fatal. The expression on the face of an Indian attendant as he saw me going was probably a faint reflection of my own.

The structure on the top of this building extends the whole length of the edifice. In many places it has fallen, but we were now more struck than when at a distance with its general resemblance to the ruined structures on the top of some of the buildings at Palenque. The latter were stuccoed; this was of cut stone, more chaste and simple. It could not have been intended for any use as part of the edifice. The only purpose we could ascribe to it was that of *ornament,* as it improved the appearance of the building seen from a distance, and set it off with great effect on near approach.

At Uxmal there was no variety; the interiors of all the apartments were the same. Here we were presented with a scene entirely new. The interior of this apartment consists of two parallel chambers communicating by a door in the centre. The inner room is raised higher than the front, and the ascent is by two stone steps carved out of a single block of stone, the lower one being in the form of a scroll. The sides of the steps are ornamented with sculpture, as is also the wall under the doorway. The whole design is graceful and pretty, and the effect is extremely good. Here, on the first day of our arrival, we spread out our provisions, and ate to the memory of the former tenant. His own domains could not furnish us with water, and we were supplied from the wells of Nohcacab.

The whole edifice formed a square. It covered nearly as many square feet as the Casa del Gobernador, and probably, from its lavishness of ornament, contained more sculptured stone. The rest of the building, however, was in a much more ruinous condition. At both ends the wall had fallen, and the whole of the other front, with

the roof, and the ruins filled up the apartments so that it was extremely difficult to make out the plan.

The terrace is overgrown with trees, called the alamo, or elm, the leaves of which, with those of the ramon, form in that country the principal fodder for horses. Springing up beside the front wall, its shoots and branches unsettled and overturned the wall, and still grew, carrying up large stones fast locked in their embraces, which they now hold aloft in the air. At the same time, its roots have girded the foundation wall, and form the only support of what is left. No sketch can convey a true idea of the ruthless gripe in which these gnarled and twisted roots encircle sculptured stones.

To many of these structures the Indians have given names stupid, senseless, and unmeaning, having no reference to history or tradition. This one they call Xcocpoop, which means a straw hat doubled up; the name having reference to the crushed and flattened condition of the façade and the prostration of the rear wall of the building.

38. Step fashioned from the coiled snout of a Chaac mask, found inside Stephens' Casa No. 1, Kabáh (Charnay, 1882)

Descending the corner of the back terrace, rises a broken and overgrown mound, on which stands a ruined building, called by the Indians the cocina, or kitchen, because, as they said, it had chimneys to let out smoke. According to their accounts, it must have contained something curious; and it was peculiarly unfortunate that we had not reached it one year sooner, for then it stood entire. During the last rainy season some muleteers from Merida, scouring the country in search of maize, were overtaken by the afternoon's rain, and took shelter under its roof, turning their mules out to graze among the ruins. During the night the building fell, but, fortunately, the muleteers escaped unhurt. Leaving their mules behind them, in the darkness and rain [they] made their way to Nohcacab, reporting that El Demonio was among the ruins of Kabah.

On the left of this mound is a staircase leading down to the area of Casa No. 2, and on the right is a grand and majestic pile of buildings, having no name assigned to it, and which, perhaps, when entire, was the most imposing structure at Kabah [see Figs. 31 and 32]. It consisted of three distinct stories or ranges, one on the roof of the other, the second smaller than the first, and the third smaller than the second. Along the base on all four of the sides was a continuous range of apartments, with the doorways supported by pillars, and on the side fronting the rear of Casa No. 1 was another new and interesting feature.

This was a gigantic stone staircase, rising to the roof, on which stood the second range of apartments. This staircase was not a solid mass, resting against the wall of the mound, but was supported by the half of a triangular arch springing from the ground, and resting against the wall so as to leave a passage under the staircase. This staircase was interesting not only for its own grandeur and the novelty of its construction, but as explaining what had before been unintelligible in regard to the principal staircase in the House of the Dwarf at Uxmal. The steps of this staircase are nearly all fallen, and the ascent is as on an inclined plane. The buildings on the top are ruined, and many of the doorways so encumbered that there was barely room to crawl into them. On one occasion, while clearing around this so as to make a plan, rain came on, and I was obliged to crawl into one with all the Indians, and remain in the dark, breathing a damp and unwholesome atmosphere, pent up and almost stifled, for more than an hour.

The doorways of the ranges on the north side of this mound opened upon the area of Casa No. 2. The platform had been planted with corn, and required little clearing. The edifice stands upon an upper terrace. Running the whole length is a range of apartments, with their doors opening upon the area. The front wall and the roof of this range have nearly all fallen.

A ruined staircase rises to the roof of this range, which forms the platform in front of the principal building. This staircase is supported by the half of a triangular arch, precisely like the other already mentioned. The whole front was ornamented with sculpture, and the ornaments best preserved are over the doorway of the centre apartment.

The principal building has pillars in two of its doorways. For the first time, we met with pillars used legitimately as a support, and they added greatly to the interest which the other novelties here disclosed to us presented. These pillars, however, were but six feet high, rude and unpolished, with square blocks of stone for capitals and pedestals. They wanted the architectural majesty and grandeur which in other styles is always connected with the presence of pillars, but they were not out of proportion, and, in fact, were adapted to the lowness of the building. The lintels over the doors are of stone.

Leaving this building, and crossing an overgrown and wooded plain, we reach the terrace of Casa No. 3. The platform of this ter-

125 *Building of the Columns*

39. Catherwood drawing of Stephens' Casa No. 3 (Building of the Columns), Kabáh

race, too, had been planted with corn, and was easily cleared. The front of the edifice was so beautifully shrouded by trees that it was painful to be obliged to disturb them, and we spared every branch that did not obstruct the view. While Mr. Catherwood was making his drawing, rain came on, and, as he might not be able to get his camera lucida in position again, he continued his work, with the protection of an India-rubber cloak and an Indian holding an umbrella over the stand. The rain was of that sudden and violent character often met with in tropical climates, and in a few minutes flooded the whole ground. This building is called by the Indians la Casa de la Justicia. There are five apartments, all perfectly plain. The front is plain, except the pillars in the wall between the doorways.

Besides these, there are on this side of the camino real the remains of other buildings, all in a ruinous condition. There is one monument, perhaps more curious and interesting than any that has been presented. It is a lonely arch, of the same form with all the rest, having a span of fourteen feet. It stands on a ruined mound, disconnected from every other structure, in solitary grandeur. Darkness rests upon its history, but in that desolation and solitude, among the ruins around, it stood like the proud memorial of a Roman triumph. Perhaps, like the arch of Titus, which at this day spans the Sacred Way at Rome, it was erected to commemorate a victory over enemies.

These were all the principal remains on this side of the camino real. They were all to which our Indian guides conducted us, and, excepting two mentioned hereafter, they were all of which any knowledge existed. But on the other side of the camino real, shrouded by trees, were the trembling and tottering skeletons of buildings which had once been grander than these. Following the camino real to a point [near] the triumphal arch, there is a narrow path which leads to two buildings enclosed by a fence for a milpa. They are small, and but little ornamented. They stand at right angles to each other, and in front of them is a patio, in which is a large broken orifice, like the mouth of a cave, with a tree growing near the edge of it.

My first visit to this place was marked by a brilliant exploit on the part of my horse. On dismounting, Mr. Catherwood found shade for his horse, Doctor Cabot got his into one of the buildings, and I tied mine to this tree, giving him fifteen or twenty feet of halter as a range for pasture. Here we left them, but on our return in the evening my horse was missing, and, as we supposed, stolen; but before we reached the tree I saw the halter still attached to it, and knew that an Indian would be much more likely to steal the halter and leave the horse than *vice versa*. The halter was drawn down into the mouth of

40. *Opposite:* Ruined arch (since restored), Kabáh (Thompson, circa 1890)

the cave, and looking over the edge, I saw the horse hanging at the other end, with just rope enough, by stretching his head and neck, to keep a foothold at one side of the cave. One of his sides was scratched and grimed with dirt, and it seemed as if every bone in his body must be broken. On getting him out we found that, except some scarifications of the skin, he was not at all hurt. In fact, he never moved better than on our return to the village.

Striking directly from these buildings in a westerly direction through a thick piece of woods, and passing a small ruined building with a staircase leading to the roof, we reached a great terrace. Besides being overgrown with trees, this terrace was covered with thornbushes, and the maguey plant, or Agave Americana, with points as sharp as needles, which made it impossible to move without cutting the way at every step.

Two buildings stood upon this overgrown terrace, the first having seven doorways in front, all opening to apartments. In the rear were other apartments, with doorways opening upon a courtyard, and from the centre a range of buildings ran at right angles, terminating in a large ruined mound. The wall of the whole of this great pile had been more ornamented than either of the buildings before presented except the first, but, unfortunately, it was more dilapidated. The doorways had wooden lintels, most of which have fallen.

To the north of this building is another with double corridors, and a gigantic staircase leading to the roof, on which are the ruins of another building. The doors of two centre apartments open under the arch of this great staircase. We again found the prints of the red hand; not two or three, as in other places. The whole wall was covered with them, bright and distinct as if newly made.

All the lintels over the doorways are of wood, and all are still in their places, mostly sound and solid. The doorways were encumbered with rubbish and ruins. That nearest the staircase was filled up to within three feet of the lintel. Crawling under on his back, to measure the apartment, Mr. Catherwood's eye was arrested by a sculptured lintel, which, on examination, he considered the most interesting memorial we had found in Yucatan. On my return that day from a visit to three more ruined cities entirely unknown before, he claimed this lintel as equal in interest and value to all of them together. The next day I saw them, and determined immediately to carry them home with me. But this was no easy matter. Our operations created much discussion in the village. The general belief was that we were searching for gold. No one could believe that we were expending money in such a business without being sure of getting it back again; and I was afraid to have it known that there was anything worth carrying away. We procured a good set of men, and went down with crowbars for the purpose of working them out of the wall. Doctor Cabot, who had been confined to the village for several days by illness, turned out on this great occasion.

The lintel consisted of two beams, the outer one split in two lengthwise. They lapped over the doorway about a foot at each end, and were as firmly secured as any stones in the building. Fortunately, we had two crowbars. The doorway being filled up with earth both inside and out, the men were enabled to stand above the beam, and use the crowbars to advantage. They began inside, and in about two hours cleared the lintel directly over the doorway, but the ends were still firmly secured. The beams were about ten feet long, and to keep the whole wall from falling and crushing them, it was necessary to knock away the stones over the centre, and make an arch in proportion to the base. The wall was four feet thick over the doorway, increasing in thickness with the receding of the inner arch. The whole was a solid mass, the mortar being nearly as hard as the stone. As the breach was enlarged it became dangerous to stand near it. The crowbar had to be thrown aside, and the men cut down small trees, which they used as a sort of battering-ram.

To save the beams, we constructed an inclined plane three feet above them, resting against the inner wall, which caught the stones and carried them off. As the breach increased it became really dangerous to work under it, and one of the men refused to do so any longer. The beams were almost within my grasp, but if the ragged mass above should fall, it would certainly bury the beams and the men too, either of which would be disagreeable. Fortunately, we had the best set of assistants that ever came out to us from Nohcacab. At length, having broken a rude arch almost to the roof, the inner beam was got out uninjured. With great labour, anxiety, and good fortune, the whole three at length lay before us. We did no more work that day; we had hardly changed our positions, but, from the excitement and anxiety, it was one of the most trying times we had in the country.

This lintel [consists of] three pieces of wood, but originally only two, that on which the figure is carved being split through the middle. The top was worm-eaten and decayed, probably from the trickling of water, which, following some channel in the ornaments, touched only this part. The subject is a human figure standing upon a serpent. The face was obliterated, the headdress was a plume of feathers, and the general character of the figure and ornaments was the same with that of the figures found on the walls at Palenque. It was

41. Wooden lintel removed
from Kabáh by Stephens
and destroyed by fire at
Catherwood's Panorama in
New York City in July
1842

the first subject we had discovered bearing such a striking resemblance in details, and connecting so closely together the builders of these distant cities.

But the great interest of this lintel was the carving. The lines were clear and distinct, indicating great skill and proficiency in the art of carving on wood. When we had finished our whole exploration, we were satisfied that these were the most interesting specimens the country afforded. I had the sculptured sides packed in dry grass and covered with hemp bagging, and intended to pass them through the village without stopping. But the Indians left them two days on the ground exposed to heavy rain, and I was obliged to have them brought to the convent, where the grass was taken out and dried. The first morning one or two hundred Indians came up in a body to look at them. It was several days before I could get them away. To my great relief, they at length left the village on the shoulders of Indians, and I brought them with me safely to this city. The reader anticipates my conclusion, and if he have but a shade of sympathy with the writer, he mourns over the melancholy fate that overtook them but a short time after their arrival.

The accidental discovery of these sculptured beams induced us to be more careful than ever in our examination of every part of the building. The lintel over the corresponding doorway on the other side of the staircase was still in its place, and in good condition, but perfectly plain. There was no other sculptured lintel among all the ruins of Kabah. Why this particular doorway was so distinguished it is impossible to say. The character of this sculpture added to the interest and wonder of all that was connected with the exploration of these American ruins. There is no account of the existence of iron or steel among the aborigines on this continent. The general and well-grounded belief is, that the inhabitants had no knowledge whatever of these metals. How, then, could they carve wood of the hardest kind?

Bernal Dias, in his account of the first voyage of the Spaniards along the coast of Guacaulco, in the Empire of Mexico, says, "It was a Custom of the Indians of this Province *invariably* to carry small Hatchets of Copper, very bright, and the wooden Handles of which were highly painted, as intended both for Defence and Ornament. These were supposed by us to be Gold, and were, of Course, eagerly purchased, *insomuch that within three days we had amongst us procured above six hundred,* and were, while under the Mistake, as well pleased with our Bargain as the Indians with their green Beads." In my opinion, the carving of these beams was done with the copper instruments known to have existed among the aboriginal inhabitants, and it is not necessary to suppose, without and even against all evidence, that at some remote period of time the use of iron and steel was known on this continent, and that the knowledge had become lost among the latter inhabitants.

From the great terrace a large structure is seen at a distance through the trees. I set out with an Indian to examine it. Descending among the trees, we soon lost sight of it entirely, but, pursuing the direction, the Indian cutting a way with his machete, we came upon a building, which I discovered was not the one we were in search of. The walls were cracked, and all along the base the ground was strewed with sculptured stones, the carving of which was equal to any we had seen. Before reaching the door I crawled through a fissure in the wall into an apartment, at one end of which, in the arch, I saw an enormous hornet's nest; and in turning to take a hasty leave, saw at the opposite end a large ornament in stucco, having also a hornet's nest attached to it, painted, the colours still bright and vivid, and surprising me as much as the sculptured beams. A great part had fallen, and it had the appearance of having been wantonly destroyed. The ornament appears to represent two large eagles facing each other; on each side are seen drooping plumes of feathers. The opposite end of the arch, where hung the hornet's nest, had marks of stucco in the same form, and probably once contained a corresponding ornament.

Beyond this was the great building which we had set out to find. The front was still standing, in some places, particularly on the corner, richly ornamented. But the back was a heap of ruins. In the centre was a gigantic staircase leading to the top, on which there was another building with two ranges of apartments, the outer one fallen, the inner one entire.

In descending on the other side over a mass of ruins, I found a deep hole, which apparently led into a cave. Crawling down, I found that it conducted to the buried door of a chamber on a new and curious plan. It had a raised platform, and in each of the inner corners was a rounded vacant place, about large enough for a man to stand in. Part of the back wall was covered with prints of the red hand. They seemed so fresh, and the seams and creases were so distinct, that I made several attempts with the machete to get one print off entire, but the plaster was so hard that every effort failed.

Beyond this was another building, so unpretending in its appearance compared with the first that I should hardly have noticed it. This building had but one doorway, which was nearly choked up. Passing into it I noticed sculptured on the jambs, nearly buried, a protruding corner of a plume of feathers. This I immediately supposed to be a headdress, and that below was a sculptured human figure. I found on the opposite jamb a corresponding stone, but entirely buried. The top stone of both was missing, but I found them near by, and determined immediately to excavate the parts that were buried, and carry the whole away. But it was a more difficult business than getting out the beams. A solid mound of earth descended from the outside to the back wall of the apartment, choking the doorway to within a few feet of the top. To clear the whole doorway was out of the question, for the Indians had only their hands with which to scoop out the accumulated mass. The only way was to dig down beside each stone, then separate it from the wall with the crowbar, and

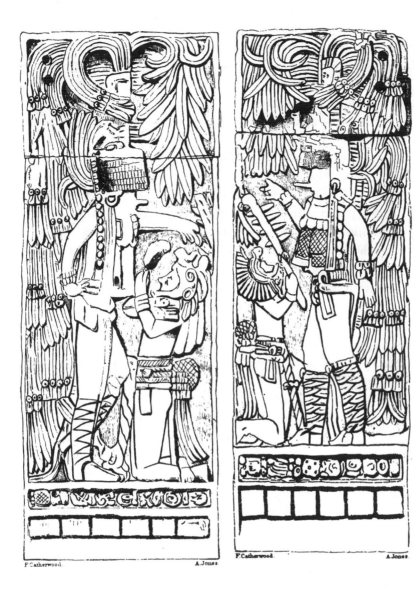

F. Catherwood.   A. Jones.   F. Catherwood.   A. Jones.

pry it out. I was engaged in this work two entire days, and on the second the Indians wanted to abandon it. They had dug down nearly to the bottom, and one man in the hole refused to work any longer. To keep them together and not lose another day, I was obliged to labour myself. Late in the afternoon we got out the stones, lifted them over the mound, and set them up against the back wall.

Each consists of two separate stones [with] two figures, one standing, and the other kneeling before him. [In one,] a weapon [is] in the hands of the kneeling figure. Both have unnatural and grotesque faces, probably containing some symbolical meaning. The

42. Stone doorjambs removed from Kabáh by Stephens, now in the collection of the American Museum of Natural History, New York

headdress is a lofty plume of feathers, falling to the heels of the standing figure. Under his feet is a row of hieroglyphics. Herrera says the Indians had "Swords made of Wood, having a Gutter in the fore Part, in which were sharp-edged Flints, strongly fixed with a sort of Bitumen and Thread." The same weapon is described in every account of the aboriginal weapons. It is seen in every museum of Indian curiosities, and it is in use at this day among the Indians of the South Sea Islands. The sword borne by [this] figure is precisely of the kind described by Herrera. I was not searching for testimony to establish any opinion or theory. There was interest enough in exploring these ruins without attempting to do so, and this witness rose unbidden.

In lifting these stones out of the holes and setting them up against the walls, I had been obliged to assist myself. Almost the moment it was finished I found that the fatigue and excitement had been too much for me. My bones ached; a chill crept over me. I looked around for a soft stone to lie down upon; but the place was cold and damp, and rain was threatening. I saddled my horse, and when I mounted I could barely keep my seat. My horse seemed to know my condition and went on a slow walk, nibbling at every bush. The fever came on, and I was obliged to dismount and lie down under a bush. But the garrapatas drove me away.

This was my last visit to Kabah. Doubtless more ruins lie buried in the woods, and the next visiter, beginning where we left off, will push his investigations much farther. We were groping in the dark. Since the hour of their desolation and we came upon them, these buildings had remained unknown. Except the cura Carillo, who informed us of them, perhaps no white man had wandered through their silent chambers. We were the first to throw open the portals of their grave, and they are now for the first time presented to the public.

But I can do little more than state the naked fact of their existence. The cloud which hangs over their history is much darker than that resting over the ruins of Uxmal. Perhaps they have been known to the Indians from time immemorial. But until the opening of the camino real to Bolonchen they were utterly unknown to the white inhabitants. This road passed through the ancient city, and discovered the great buildings, overgrown, and in some places towering above the tops of the trees. The discovery, however, created not the slightest sensation; the intelligence of it had never reached the capital. Though the great edifices were visible to all who passed along the road, not a white man in the village had ever turned aside to look at them, except the padrecito, who, on the first day of our visit, rode in, but without dismounting, in order to make a report to us. The Indians say of them, as of all the other ruins, that they are the works of the anti-guos. The traditionary character of the city is that of a great place, su-perior to the other Xlap-pahk scattered over the country, coequal and coexistent with Uxmal. And there is a tradition of a great paved way, made of pure white stone, called in the Maya language Sacbé, leading from Kabah to Uxmal, on which the lords of those places sent mes-sengers to and fro, bearing letters written on the leaves and bark of trees.

135   *Road from Kabáh
to Uxmal*

CHAPTER NINE

Sayil

e were entering a region occupied entirely by Indians. A league beyond the ruins of Kabah we reached the rancho of Chack. As we rode through, the women snatched up their children, and ran from us like startled deer. I rode up to a hut into which I saw a woman enter, and, stopping at the fence, merely from curiosity, took out a cigar, and, making use of some of the few Maya words we had picked up, asked for a light. But the door remained shut. I dismounted, and before I had tied my horse the woman rushed out and disappeared among the bushes.

On leaving this rancho we saw at a distance a high ruined building standing alone amid a great intervening growth of woods, and apparently inaccessible. Beyond, we reached the rancho of Schawill, our first stopping-place on account of the ruins in its immediate neighbourhood. This place also was inhabited exclusively by Indians, rancho being the name given to a settlement not of sufficient importance to constitute a village. The casa real was a large hut with mud walls and a thatched roof. Around the hut were large seybo trees. The casa real is erected in every rancho of Indians expressly for the reception of the cura on his occasional visits, but it is occupied also by small dealers from the villages, who sometimes find their way to these ranchos to buy up hogs, maize, and fowls. The hut, when swept out, and comparatively clear of fleas, made a large and comfortable apartment, and furnished ample swinging room for six hammocks, the number requisite for our whole retinue.

Although we had been some time in the country, we regarded this as really the beginning of our travels; and our first day's journey introduced us to some scenes that were entirely new. The Indians assembled under the arbour, where they, with great formality, offered us seats. The alcalde told us that the rancho was poor, but they would do all they could to serve us. Neither he nor any other in the place spoke a word of Spanish, and our communications were through Albino. We opened the interview by remonstrating against the charge of two reals for watering our horses, but the excuse was satisfactory enough. In the rainy season they had sources of supply in the neighbourhood. These deposites of water are very numerous; during the rainy season they are replenished as fast as they are exhausted, and at the time of our visit, owing to the long continuance of the rains, they furnished a sufficient supply for domestic use. In the dry season this source of supply failed. The people were obliged to send to the rancho of Chack, the well of which they represented as being half a mile under ground, and so steep that it was reached only by descending nine different staircases.

It seemed strange that any community should be willing to live where this article of primary necessity was so difficult to be obtained, and we asked them why they did not break up their settlement and go elsewhere. This idea seemed never to have occurred to them. They said their fathers had lived there before them, and the land around was good for milpas. In fact, they were a peculiar people, and I never before regretted so much my ignorance of the Maya language. They are under the civil jurisdiction of the village of Nohcacab, but the right of soil is their own by inheritance. They consider themselves better off than in the villages, where the people are subject to certain municipal regulations and duties, or than on the haciendas, where they would be under the control of masters.

Their community consists of a hundred labradores, or working men; their lands are held in common, and the products are shared by all. Their food is prepared at one hut, and every family sends for its portion, which explained a singular spectacle we had seen on our arrival; a procession of women and children, each carrying an earthen bowl containing a quantity of smoking hot broth, all coming down the same road, and dispersing among the different huts.

43. *Page 136:* Yucatec Maya dwelling at the village of Tabi (date unknown)

No stranger is allowed to enter their community; every member must marry within the rancho, and no such thing as a marriage out of it had ever occurred. They said it could not happen. They were in the habit of going to the villages to attend the festivals; and when we suggested a supposable case of a young man or woman falling in love with some village Indian, they said it might happen; there was no law against it; but none could *marry* out of the rancho. This was a thing so little apprehended that the punishment for it was not defined in their penal code. But being questioned, after some consultation they said that the offender, whether man or woman, would be expelled. We remarked that in their small community constant intermarriages must make them all relatives, which they said was the case since the reduction of their numbers by the cholera. It was allowable for kinsfolk to marry except in the relationship of brothers and sisters. They were very strict in attendance upon the ceremonies of the Church, and had just finished the celebration of the carnival two weeks in advance of the regular time. When we corrected their chronology, they said they could celebrate it over again.

Early in the morning we set out for the ruins of Zayi, or Salli. After proceeding a mile and a half we saw at some distance before us a great tree-covered mound, which astonished us by its vast dimensions. The woods commenced from the roadside. Our guides cut a path, and, clearing the branches overhead, we followed on horseback, dismounting at the foot of the Casa Grande. It was by this name that the Indians called the immense pile of white stone buildings, buried in the depths of a great forest. We tied our horses, and worked our way along the front. The trees were so close that we could take in but a small portion of it at once. Without waiting to explore the rest of the ground, we set the Indians at work, and in a few minutes the stillness of ages was broken by the sharp ringing of the axe and the crash of falling trees. With a strong force of Indians, we were able, in the course of the day, to lay bare the whole of the front.

The front of this building has three stories or ranges, and in the centre is a grand staircase, rising to the highest terrace. This staircase, however, is in a ruinous condition, and, in fact, a mere mound. All that part of the building on the right had fallen, and was so dilapidated that no intelligible drawing could be made of it. We did not even clear away the trees.

The lowest of the three ranges had sixteen doorways, opening into apartments of two chambers each. The whole front wall has fallen; the interiors are filled with fragments and rubbish. The ground in front was so encumbered with the branches of fallen trees, even after they had been chopped into pieces and beaten down with poles, that, at the distance necessary for making a drawing, but a small portion of the interior could be seen. The two ends of this range have each six doorways, and the rear has ten, all opening into apartments. In general they are in a ruinous condition.

The range of buildings on the second terrace had four doorways on each side of the grand staircase. Those on the left, which are all that remain, have two columns in each doorway, each column roughly made, with square capitals, like Doric, but wanting the grandeur pertaining to all known remains of this ancient order. Filling up the spaces between the doorways are four small columns curiously ornamented, close together, and sunk in the wall. Between the first and second and third and fourth doorways a small staircase leads to the terrace of the third range. The building [on] this terrace has seven doorways opening into as many apartments. The lintels over the doorways are of stone.

The exterior of the third and highest range was plain; that of the two other ranges had been elaborately ornamented. Among designs common in other places is the figure of a man supporting himself on his hands, with his legs expanded in a curious rather than delicate attitude.

The north side of the second range has a curious and unaccountable feature, called the Casa Cerrada, or closed house, having ten

44. Modern view of the Great Palace, Sayil (Stephens' Casa Grande at Zayi or Salli)

doorways, all of which are blocked up inside with stone and mortar. Like the well at Xcoch, it had a mysterious reputation. All believed that it contained hidden treasure. The first sight of these closed-up doorways gave us a strong desire to break into the closed apartments and discover the precious hoard; but on moving along we found that the Indians had been beforehand with us. In front of several were piles of stones worked out from the doorways, and under the lintels were holes, through which we were able to crawl inside. Here we found ourselves in apartments finished with walls and ceilings like all the others, but filled up (except so far as they had been emptied by the Indians) with solid masses of mortar and stone. There were ten of these apartments in all, which being thus filled up, made the whole building a solid mass. The strangest feature was that the filling up of the apartments must have been simultaneous with the erection of the buildings, for the filling-in rose above the tops of the doorways. It must have been done as the walls were built, and the ceiling must have closed over a solid mass. Why this was so constructed it was impossible to say, unless the solid mass was required for the support of

45. Second range of the Great Palace, Sayil (date unknown)

the upper terrace and building. If this was the case, it would seem to have been much easier to erect a solid structure at once, without any division into apartments.

The top of this building commanded a grand view of undulating woodlands. Toward the northwest, crowning the highest hill, was a lofty mound, covered with trees, which shrouded a building. The whole intervening space was thick wood and underbrush, and the Indians said the mound was inaccessible. I selected three of the best, and told them that we must reach it. They really did not know how to make the attempt, and set out on a continuation of the road by which we had reached the ruins, which led us rather from than to the mound. On the way we met another Indian, who turned back with us. A little beyond, he cut through the woods to another path, following which a short distance, he again struck through the woods. All cutting together, we reached the foot of a stony hill covered with the gigantic maguey, or Agave Americana, its long thorny points piercing and tearing all that touched them. Climbing up this hill with great toil, we reached the wall of a terrace, and, climbing this, found ourselves at the foot of the building.

It was in a ruinous condition, and did not repay us for the labour. Over the door was a sculptured head with a face of good expression and workmanship. In one of the apartments was a high projection running along the wall; in another a raised platform about a foot high. On the walls of this apartment was the print of the red hand. The doorway commanded an extensive view of rolling woodland, which, with its livery of deep green, ought to have conveyed a sensation of gladness, but, perhaps from its desolation and stillness, it induced a feeling of melancholy. There was but one opening in the forest, that made by us, disclosing the Casa Grande, with the figures of a few Indians still continuing their clearings on the top.

In front of the Casa Grande, also visible from the top, is another structure, strikingly different from any we had seen, more strange and inexplicable, and having at a distance the appearance of a New England factory. It stands on a terrace, and may be considered two separate structures, one above the other. The lower one resembled all the rest. In the centre was an archway running through the building. The front is fallen, and the whole so ruined that nothing but the archway appears. Along the middle of the roof, unsupported, rises a perpendicular wall to the height of thirty feet. It is of stone, about two feet thick, and has oblong openings through it, like small windows. It had been covered with stucco, which had fallen off, and left the face of

46. *Opposite:* Early twentieth-century view of the north side of Mirador Temple, Sayil

rough stone and mortar. On the other side were fragments of stuccoed figures and ornaments. Since we began our exploration of American ruins we had not met with anything more inexplicable than this great perpendicular wall. It seemed built merely to puzzle posterity.

These were the only buildings in this immediate neighbourhood which had survived the wasting of the elements; but, inquiring among the Indians, one of them undertook to guide me to another, which he said was still in good preservation. Our direction was south-southwest from the Casa Grande. At the distance of about a mile, the whole intermediate region being desolate and overgrown, we reached a terrace, the area of which far exceeded anything we had seen. From north to south, it must have been fifteen hundred feet in length, and probably was quite as much in the other direction.

On this great platform was the building of which the Indian had told us. I had it cleared, and Mr. Catherwood drew it the next day. It contains sixteen apartments, of which those in front, five in number, are best preserved. That in the centre has three doorways. It communicates by a single doorway with a back room. Along the bottom of the front room, as high as the sill of the door, is a row of small columns, thirty-eight in number, attached to the wall. In several places the great platform is strewed with ruins, and probably other buildings lie buried in the woods, but without guides or any clew whatever, we did not attempt to look for them.

Such, so far as we were able to discover them, are the ruins of Zayi, the name of which, to the time of our visit, had never been uttered among civilized men, and, but for the notoriety connected with our movements, would probably be unknown at this day in the capital of Yucatan. Our first accounts of them were from the cura Carillo, who, on the occasion of his only visit to this part of his curacy, passed a great portion of his time among them.

It was strange and almost incredible that, with these extraordinary monuments before their eyes, the Indians never bestowed upon them one passing thought. The question, who built them? never by any accident crossed their minds. The great name of Montezuma, which had gone beyond them to the Indians of Honduras, had never reached their ears, and to all our questions we received the same dull answer which first met us at Copan, "Quien sabe?" "Who knows?" They had the same superstitious feelings as the Indians of Uxmal; they believed that the ancient buildings were haunted. As in the remote region of Santa Cruz del Quiche, they said that on Good Friday of every year music was heard sounding among the ruins.

There was but one thing connected with the old city that interested them at all, and that was the subject of a well. They supposed that somewhere among these ruins, overgrown and lost, existed the fountain which had supplied the ancient inhabitants with water. Believing that by the use of our instruments its site could be discovered, they offered to cut down all the trees throughout the whole region covered by the ruins.

The next morning, while Mr. Catherwood was drawing, Dr. Cabot and myself set out to visit the [well] which we had passed in coming from the rancho of Chack. In the suburbs of the rancho we turned off by a path, which we followed for some distance on horseback, and dismounted. Our guides cut a path through the woods, and we came out upon a large field of táje, being long stems growing close together, having a yellow flower on the top, which is a favourite food for horses. The stems, tied up in bundles four inches thick, are used for torches. On one side of this field we saw the high building before referred to, and on the other side was a second not visible before. This táje was as bad as the woods to walk through, for it grew so high as to exclude every breath of air, and was not high enough to be any protection against the sun.

The building stood on the top of a stony hill, on a terrace still firm and substantial. It consisted of two stories. The upper building had a large apartment in the centre, and a smaller one on each side, much encumbered with rubbish. From one we were driven by a hornet's nest, and in another a young vulture, with a hissing noise, flapped its plumeless wings and hopped out of the door.

The terrace commanded a picturesque view of wooded hills, the Casa Grande, and the high wall. All the intermediate space was overgrown. The Indians had traversed it in all directions in the dry season, when there was no foliage to hide the view, and they said that in all this space there were no vestiges of buildings. Close together as we had found the remains of ancient habitations, it seemed hardly possible that independent cities had existed with but such a little space between, and yet it was harder to imagine that one city had embraced within its limits these distant buildings, the extreme ones being four miles apart, and that the whole intermediate region of desolation had once swarmed with a teeming and active population.

Leaving this, we toiled back to our horses, and, returning to the road, passed through the rancho, about a mile beyond which we reached the pozo, or well, the accounts of which we had heard on our first arrival. Near the mouth were some noble seybo trees, throwing their great branches far and wide, under which groups of Indians were arranging their calabashes and torches, preparing to descend. Others, just out, were wiping their sweating bodies. We noticed that there were no women, who, throughout Yucatan, are the drawers of water, and always seen around a well. We were told that no woman ever enters the well of Chack. All the water for the rancho was procured by the men, which alone indicated that the well was of an extraordinary character. We made immediate preparations to descend, reducing our dress as near as possible to that of the Indians.

Our first movement was down a hole by a perpendicular ladder, at the foot of which we were fairly entered into a great cavern. Our guides preceded us with bundles of táje lighted for torches, and we came to a second descent almost perpendicular, which we achieved by a ladder laid flat against the rock. Beyond this we moved on a short distance, still descending, when we saw our guides' torches disappearing, and reached a wild hole, which also we descended by a long rough ladder. At the foot of this the rock was damp and slippery. There was barely room enough to pass around it, and get upon another ladder down the same hole, now so small that, with the arms akimbo, the elbows almost touched on each side. At this time our Indians were out of sight. In total darkness, feeling our way by the rounds of the ladder, we cried out to them, and were answered by distant voices directly underneath. Looking down, we saw their torches like moving balls of fire, apparently at an interminable distance below us.

At the foot of this ladder there was a rude platform as a resting-place, made to enable those ascending and descending to pass each other. A group of naked Indians, panting and sweating under the load of their calabashes, were waiting till we vacated the ladder above. Even in this wild hole, with loads on their backs, straps binding their foreheads, and panting from fatigue and heat, they held down their torches, and rendered obeisance to the blood of the white man. Descending the next ladder, both above and below us were torches gleaming in the darkness. We had still another ladder to descend. The whole perpendicular depth of this hole was perhaps two hundred feet.

From the foot of this ladder there was an opening. We soon entered a low, narrow passage, through which we crawled on our hands and knees. With the toil and the smoke of the torches the heat was almost beyond endurance. The passage enlarged and again contracted, descending steeply, and so low that the shoulders almost touched the roof. This opened upon a great chasm. Beyond we came to another perpendicular hole, which we descended by steps cut in the rock. From this there was another low, crawling passage. Almost stifled with heat and smoke, we came out into a small opening, in which was a basin of water. The place was crowded with Indians filling their calabashes. They started at the sight of our smoky white faces as if El Demonio had descended among them. It was, doubtless, the first time that the feet of a white man had ever reached this well.

On returning we measured the distance. I had two Indians with long bundles of lighted sticks, who, whenever I stopped to write, either held them so far off as to be of no use, or else thrust them into my face, blinding the eyes with smoke and scorching the skin. I was dripping as if in a vapour-bath; my face and hands were black with smoke and incrusted with dirt. Large drops of sweat fell upon my book, which, with the dirt from my hands, matted the leaves together, so that my notes are almost useless. The distance, as we traversed it, with its ladders, ascents and descents, winding and crawling passages, seemed a full half league. By measurement it was not quite fifteen hundred feet. This well was the regular and only supply of a living population. The whole rancho of Chack was entirely dependant upon it, and in the dry season the rancho of Schawill, three miles distant.

We consumed a calabash of water in washing and quenching our thirst, and as we rode back to the rancho of Schawill, came to the conclusion that an admission into the community of this exclusive people was no great privilege, when it would entail upon the applicant, for six months in the year, a daily descent into this subterraneous well. We arrived at the rancho in good season. Mr. Catherwood had finished his drawing, and Bernaldo was ready with his dinner. We had nothing to detain us, ordered carriers forthwith for our luggage, and at half past two we were in the saddle again in search of ruined cities.

The reader has some idea of the caminos reales of this country, and they were all like English turnpikes compared with that upon which we entered on leaving this rancho. In fact, it was a mere path through the woods, the branches of the trees being trimmed away to a height barely sufficient to admit an Indian with a load of maize on his back. We were obliged to keep dodging the head and bending the body to avoid the branches. At times we were brought to a stand by some overhanging arm of a tree, and obliged to dismount.

At half past five we reached the rancho of Sabachshé, inhabited entirely by Indians. This rancho was distinguished by a well, the sight of which was more grateful to us than that of the best hotel to the traveller in a civilized country. We were scratched with thorns, smarting with garrapata bites, and looked forward to the refreshment of a bath. The well was built by the present owner, and formerly the inhabitants were dependant entirely upon the well at Tabi, six miles distant! Besides its real value, it presented a curious and lively spectacle. A group of Indian women was around it. It had no rope or fixtures of any kind for raising water, but across the mouth was a round beam laid upon two posts, over which the women were letting down and hoisting up little bark buckets. Every woman brought with her and carried away her own bucket and rope, the latter coiled up and laid on the top of her head, with the end hanging down behind, and the coil forming a sort of headdress.

Near the well was the hut of the alcalde, enclosed by a rude fence. Within were dogs, hogs, turkeys, and fowls, which all barked, grunted, gobbled, and cackled together as we entered. The yard was shaded by orange-trees loaded with ripe and unusually large fruit. Under one of them was a row of twenty or thirty wild boars' jaws and tusks, trophies of the chase, and memorials attesting the usefulness of the barking dogs. The noise brought the alcalde to the door, a heavy and infirm old man, apparently rich, and suffering from the high living indicated by his hogs and poultry. He received us with meekness and humility. We negotiated forthwith for the purchase of some oranges, and bought thirty for a medio, stipulating that they should all be the largest and best on the trees; after which, supporting himself by his cane, he hobbled on to the casa real, had it swept out, and assigned Indians to attend upon us.

Having made our arrangements for the next day, we went into the hut and shut the door. Some time afterward the old alcalde sent in to ask permission to go home, as he was very sleepy, which we graciously granted. By his direction, three or four Indians swung their little hammocks under the arbour, to be at hand in case we should need anything. During the night we found it extremely cold, and, with the little covering we had brought, could hardly keep ourselves comfortable.

Early in the morning we found a large gathering round the house to escort us to the ruins. In the suburbs of the rancho we turned off, and passed among the huts of the Indians, almost smothered by weeds, and having rude boxes of earth set up on posts, for vegetables to grow in out of the reach of the hogs. Crossing the fence of the last hut, we entered a thick growth of trees. As if instinctively, every Indian drew his machete. In a few minutes they cut a path to the foot of a small building, not rich in ornament, but tasteful, having some shades of difference from any we had seen, overgrown by trees, and beautifully picturesque. On one corner of the roof a vulture had built her nest, and, scared away at our approach, hovered over our heads.

All the Indians fell to work, and in a few minutes the small terrace in front was cleared. I had not expected so many Indians, and I told them that I did not need so great a number, and should only pay those whom I had engaged. When the purport of my words was explained to them, they said that made no difference and immediately set to work again. The machetes fell with a rapidity unparalleled in our experience. In half an hour space enough was cleared for Mr. Catherwood to set up his camera lucida. The same alertness was shown in preparing a place for him to stand in. Half a dozen stood ready to hold an umbrella for his protection against the sun.

The design of the building is tasteful and even elegant. It has a single doorway, opening into a chamber. Above the door is a portion of plain masonry, and over this a cornice supporting twelve small pilasters, having between them the diamond ornament, then a massive cornice, with pilasters and diamond work, surmounted by another cornice, making in all four cornices; an arrangement we had not previously met with.

While Mr. Catherwood was making his drawing, the Indians stood around under the shade of the trees, looking at him quietly and respectfully, and making observations to each other. They were a fine-looking race. Some of them, one tall old man particularly, had noble Roman faces, and they seemed to have more respectability of appearance and character than was consistent with the condition of men not wearing pantaloons. All at once an enormous iguana, or lizard, doubled the corner of the building, ran along the front, and plunged into a crevice over the door, burying his whole body, but leaving the long tail out. Among these unsophisticated people this reptile is a table delicacy, and here was a supper provided for some of them. Machetes flew out, and, cutting down a sapling with a crotch in it, they rested it against the wall, and, standing in the crotch, pulled upon the tail; but the animal held on with his feet as if a part of the building. All the Indians, one after the other, had a pull at the tail, but could not make him budge. At length two of them contrived to get hold together, and, while pulling with all their strength, the tail came off by the roots, a foot and half long in their hands. The animal was now more out of their reach than before, his whole body hidden in the wall. But he could not escape. The Indians picked away the mortar with their machetes, and enlarged the hole until they got his hind legs clear, when, griping the body above the legs, they again hauled; but, though he had only the fore legs to hold on with, they could not tear him out. They then untied the ropes of their sandals, fastening them above the hind legs. Pulling till the long body seemed parting like the tail, they at length dragged him out. They secured him by a gripe under the fore part of the body, cracked his spine, and broke the bones of his fore legs so that he could not run; pried his jaws open, fastened them apart with a sharp stick so that he could not bite, and then put him away in the shade. This refined cruelty was to avoid the necessity of killing him immediately, for if killed, in that hot climate he would soon be unfit for food. Mutilated and mangled as he was, he could be kept alive till night.

This over, we moved on to the next building, a quarter of a mile distant, completely buried in woods. It had three doorways, leading to the same number of apartments. A great part of the front had

47. Catherwood drawing of the first building explored at Sabacché

fallen. With some slight difference in the detail of ornament, the character is the same as in all the other buildings, and the general effect pleasing. Growing on the roof are two maguey plants, Agave Americana, in our latitude called the century plant, but under the hot sun of the tropics blooming every four or five years. There are four species of this plant in Yucatan: the maguey, from which is produced the pulqué, a beverage common in all the Mexican provinces, which, taken in excess, produces intoxication; the henneken, which produces

48. Late nineteeth-century view of the same building (Thompson, circa 1890)

the article known in our markets as Sisal hemp; the sabila, with which the Indian women wean children, covering the breast with the leaf, which is very bitter to the taste; and the peta, having leaves twice as large as the last, from which a very fine white hemp is made. These plants, in some or all of their varieties, were found in the neighbourhood of all the ruins, forming around them a pointed and thorny wall, which we were obliged to cut through to reach the buildings.

While Mr. C. was engaged in drawing this structure, the Indians told us of two others half a league distant. We had a good path nearly all the way, until the Indians pointed out a white object seen indistinctly through the trees, again uttering, with strong gutturals, the familiar sound of "Xlap-pahk," or old walls. The building was larger than the last. We cleared it, and left it for another, in regard to which I formed some curious expectations, for the Indians described it as *very new*. It lay on the same path, separated from us by a great field of táje. The walls were entire and very massive. Climbing up it, I found only a small building, consisting of but two apartments, the front much fallen, and the doors filled up, but no sign or token distinguishing it as *newer* or more modern. I now learned that all they meant was that it was the newest known to them, having been discovered but twelve years before, on clearing the ground for a milpa. This intelligence gave great weight to the consideration that cities may exist equal to any now known, buried in the woods, overgrown and lost, which will perhaps never be discovered.

On the walls of this desolate edifice were prints of the red hand. Often as I saw this print, it never failed to interest me. It was the stamp of the living hand; it always brought me nearer to the builders of these cities. These prints were larger than any I had seen. In several places I measured them with my own, opening the fingers to correspond with those on the wall. The Indians said it was the hand of the master of the building.

I have been advised that in Mr. Catlin's collection of Indian curiosities, made during a long residence among our North American tribes, was a tent presented to him by the chief of the powerful but now extinct race of Mandans, which exhibits, among other marks, two prints of the red hand. I have been farther advised that the red hand is seen constantly upon the buffalo robes and skins of wild animals brought in by the hunters on the Rocky Mountains, and, in fact, that it is a symbol recognised and in common use by the North American Indians of the present day. I do not mention these as facts within my own knowledge, but with the hope of attracting the attention of those who have opportunities and facilities for investigation. If true, the red hand on the tent and the buffalo robes points back from the wandering tribes in our country to the comparatively polished people who erected the great cities at the south; and its meaning can be ascertained fromm living witnesses. Through ages of intervening darkness a ray of light may be thrown back upon the now mysterious and incomprehensible characters which perplex the stranger on the walls of the desolate southern buildings.

CHAPTER TEN

Labná

Our road lay southeast, among hills, and was more picturesque than any we had seen in the country. At the distance of a mile and a half we reached a field of ruins, which, after all we had seen, created in us new feelings of astonishment. It was one of the circumstances attending our exploration of ruins in this country, that until we arrived on the ground we had no idea of what we were to meet with. The accounts of the Indians were never reliable. When they gave us reason to expect much we found but little, and, on the other hand, when we expected but little a great field presented itself. Since our arrival in the country we had not met with anything that excited us more strongly. Now we had mingled feelings of pain and pleasure; of pain, that they had not been discovered before the sentence of irretrievable ruin. At the same time it was matter of deep congratulation that, before the doom was accomplished, we were permitted to see these decaying memorials of a mysterious people. In a few years, even these will be gone; and as it has been denied that such things ever were, doubts may again arise whether they have indeed existed. So strong was this impression that we determined to fortify in every

50. Stephens' watchtower
(called the Mirador
Temple), Labná
(Thompson, circa 1890)

49. *Page 154:* Serpent
mask with human head
emerging, the southwest
corner of the east section of
the Palace, Labná
(Thompson, circa 1890)

possible way our proofs. If anything could have added to the interest
of discovering such a new field of research, it was the satisfaction of
having at our command such an effective force of Indians. No time
was lost, and they began work with a spirit corresponding to their
numbers. Many of them had small axes, and the crash of falling trees
was like the stirring noise of felling in one of our own forests.

We passed an entire day before a pyramidal mound, holding
aloft the most curious and extraordinary structure we had seen in the
country. Above the cornice of the building rises a gigantic perpendicular wall to the height of thirty feet, once ornamented with colossal
figures and other designs in stucco, now broken and in fragments,
but still presenting a curious and extraordinary appearance. Along
the top, standing out on the wall, was a row of death's heads; underneath were two lines of human figures (of which scattered arms and

legs alone remain). Over the centre doorway was a colossal figure seated, of which only a large tippet and girdle, and some other detached portions, have been preserved. Conspicuous over the head of this principal figure is a large ball, with a human figure standing up beside it, touching it with his hands, and another below it with one knee on the ground, and one hand thrown up as if in the effort to support the ball, or in the apprehension of its falling upon him. In all our labours in that country we never studied so diligently to make out from the fragments the combinations and significance of these figures and ornaments. Standing in the same position, and looking at them all together, we could not agree.

157 *Mirador Temple and Portal Arch*

Mr. Catherwood made two drawings at different hours and under a different position of the sun, and Dr. Cabot and myself worked upon it the whole day with the Daguerreotype. With the full blaze of a vertical sun upon it, the white stone glared with an intensity dazzling and painful to the eyes.

Our best view was obtained in the afternoon, when the edifice was in shade, but so broken and confused were the ornaments that a distinct representation could not be made even with the Daguerreotype. The only way to make out all the details was near approach by means of a ladder. We had all the woods to make one of, but it was difficult for the Indians to make one of the length required; and when made it would have been too heavy and cumbersome to manage on the narrow platform in front. Besides, the wall was tottering and ready to fall. One portion was already gone, and right of the centre

51. Monumental portal arch viewed from the Mirador Temple, Labná (Thompson, circa 1890)

doorway the wall is cracked and stands apart more than a foot. In a few years it must fall. Its doom is sealed. Human power cannot save it; but in its ruins it gave a grand idea of the scenes of barbaric magnificence which this country must have presented when all her cities were entire. The figures and ornaments on this wall were painted; the remains of bright colours are still visible, defying the action of the elements.

At the distance of a few hundred feet from this structure, in sight at the same time as we approached it, is an arched gateway, remarkable for its beauty of proportions and grace of ornament. On the right is a long building much fallen, which forms an angle with another building, and on the return of the wall there is a doorway more richly ornamented than any other portion of the structure. The effect of the whole combination was curious and striking.

The gateway is ten feet wide, passing through which we entered a thick forest, growing so close upon the building that we were unable to make out even its shape. On clearing away the trees, we discovered that this had been the principal front, and that these trees were growing in what had once been the courtyard [see Fig. 6]. The doors of the apartments on both sides of the gateway opened upon

52. Catherwood drawing of the portal arch from the interior courtyard, Labná

this area. Over each doorway was a square recess, in which were the remains of a rich ornament in stucco, with paint still visible, apparently intended to represent the face of the sun surrounded by its rays, probably once objects of adoration and worship, but now wilfully destroyed.

Northeast from the mound on which the great wall stands is a large building, erected on a terrace, and hidden among the trees, with its front much ruined, and having but few remains of sculptured ornaments. Still farther in the same direction, through the woods, we reach [a] magnificent building. It stands on a gigantic terrace covered with buildings. The front consisted of three distinct parts, differing in style, and perhaps erected at different times. At a distance, seen through the trees, we had no idea of its extent. We came upon it at the corner, our guide cut a path along the front wall, and stopping to look at the ornaments, and entering the apartments, the building seemed immense. The whole long façade was ornamented with sculptured stone. At the left end of the principal building, and in the angle of the corner are the huge open jaws of an alligator, or some other hideous animal, enclosing a human head [see Fig. 49].

I had been at work nearly the whole day upon the terrace, without knowing that there was another building on the top. In order to take in the whole front at one view, it was necessary to carry the clearing back some distance into the plain, and in doing this I discovered the upper structure. The growth of trees before it was almost

53. Modern view of sculptured wall, interior courtyard of the portal arch, Labná

equal to that on the terrace, or in any part of the forest. The whole had to be cleared, the trees thrown down, and dragged away. This building consists of single narrow corridors, and the façade is of plain stone, without any ornaments.

The platform in front is the roof of the building underneath, and in this platform was a circular hole, like those we had seen at Uxmal and other places, leading to subterraneous chambers. This hole had a marvellous reputation; and yet the Indians never mentioned it until I climbed up to examine the upper building. They said it was the abode of *el dueno de la casa,* or the owner of the building. I immediately proposed to descend, but the old Indian begged me not to do so, and said apprehensively to the others, "Who knows but that he will meet with the owner?" I immediately sent for rope, lantern, and matches. Absurd as it may seem, as I looked upon the wild figures and earnest faces of the Indians standing round the hole, it was really exciting to hear them talk of the owner. As there was difficulty in procuring rope, I had a sapling cut and let down the hole, by means of which I descended with a lantern. The news of my intention had spread among the Indians, and all left off work and hurried to the spot. The hole was about four feet deep, and, just as my head sunk below the surface, I was startled by an extraordinary scratching and scampering. A huge iguana ran along the wall, and escaped through the orifice by which I had entered.

54. The Palace at Labná viewed from a high tree (Thompson, circa 1890)

The chamber was entirely different in shape from those I had seen before. The latter were circular, and had dome-shaped ceilings. This had parallel walls and the triangular-arched ceiling; in fact, exactly like the apartments above ground. It was eleven feet long, seven wide, and ten high to the centre of the arch. The walls and ceiling were plastered, and the floor was cement, all hard. A centipede was the only tenant after the evasion of the iguana.

While I was making these measurements, the Indians kept up a low conversation around the hole. A mystery hung around it, transmitted to them by their fathers, and connected with an indefinable sense of apprehension. This mystery might have been solved at any time in five minutes, but none of them had ever thought of doing it. The old man begged me to come out, saying that if I died they would have to answer for it. They had all sense enough to take their hands

55. Yucatec Maya and diamond rattlesnake in front of the Palace, Labná (probably Thompson, circa 1890)

out of the fire without being told, but probably to this day they believe that in that hole is the owner of the building. When I came out they looked at me with admiration. They told me that there were other places of the same kind, but they would not show them to me, lest some accident should happen. As my attempt drew them all from work, and I could not promise myself any satisfactory result, I refrained from insisting.

This chamber was formed in the roof of the lower building. That building contained two corridors, and we had always supposed that the great interval between the arches of the parallel corridors was a solid mass of masonry. The discovery of this chamber brought to light a new feature in the construction of these buildings. Whether the other roofs, or any of them, contained chambers, it is impossible to say. Not suspecting anything of the kind, we had made no search for them. They may exist, but with the holes covered up and hidden by the growth and decay of vegetation. Heretofore I had inclined to the opinion that the subterraneous chambers I had met with were intended for cisterns or reservoirs of water. The position of this in the roof of a building seemed adverse to such an idea, as, in case of a breach, the water might find its way into the apartment below.

At the foot of the terrace was a tree, hiding part of the building. Though holding trees in some degree of reverence, around these ruined cities it was a great satisfaction to hear them fall. This one was a noble ramon, which I had ordered to be cut down, and being engaged in another direction, I returned, and found that the Indians had not done so. They said it was so hard that it would break their axes. These little axes seemed hardly capable of making any impression upon the trunk, and I gave them directions, perhaps still more barbarous, to cut away the branches and leave the trunk. They hesitated, and one of them said, in a deprecating tone, that this tree served as food for horses and cattle, and their mistress had always charged them not to cut down such. The poor fellow seemed perplexed between the standing orders of the rancho and the special instructions to do what I required.

The ramon tree was growing out of the mouth of a cave which the Indians said was an ancient well. I should perhaps not have observed it, but for the discussion about cutting down the tree. I had no great disposition for another subterraneous scramble, but descended the cavity for the purpose of taking a bird's-eye view of the mouth. On one side was a great ledge of stone projecting as a roof, and under this was a passage in the rock, choked up by masses of fallen stone. It was impossible to continue if I had been so disposed, but there was every reason to believe that formerly there had been some wild passage through the rocks as at Xcoch and Chack, which led to a subterraneous deposite of water, and that this had been one of the sources from which the ancient inhabitants procured their supply.

From the number of Indians at our command, and their alacrity in working, we had been enabled to accomplish much in a very short time. In three days they finished all that I required of them. When I dismissed them, I gave a half dollar extra to be divided among seventeen.

The evening closed [in Sabachshé] with a general gathering of the Indians under the arbour in front of the casa real. We had provided for their entertainment a sheep and a turkey, to which Bernaldo had devoted the day. At sundown all was ready. We insisted upon seating the old alcalde on a chair. Bernaldo served out meat and tortillas, and the alcalde presided over the agua ardiente, which, as it was purchased of himself, and to prove that it was not bad, he tasted before serving the rest. Supper over, we began our conversation, which consisted entirely of questions on our part and answers on theirs, a manner of discourse even in civilized life difficult to be kept up long. There was no unwillingness to give information, but there was a want of communicativeness which made all intercourse with them unprofitable and unsatisfactory. In fact, however, they had nothing to communicate. They had no stories or traditions; they knew nothing of the origin of the ruined buildings. These were standing when they were born; had existed in the time of their fathers; and the old men said that they had fallen much within their own memory. In one point, however, they differed from the Indians of Uxmal and Zayi. They had no superstitious feelings with regard to the ruins, were not afraid to go to them at night, or to sleep in them. When we told them of the music that was heard sounding among the old buildings of Zayi, they said that if it were heard among these, they would all go and dance to it.

Our next point of destination was the rancho of Kewick, three leagues distant. Mr. Catherwood set out with the servants and luggage, Dr. Cabot and myself following in about an hour. The Indians told us there was no difficulty in finding the road, and we set out alone. The face of the country was rolling, and more open than any we had seen. We passed through two Indian ranchos, and a league beyond came to a dividing point. Both were footpaths. In about an hour the direction we selected changed so much that we turned back, and, after a toilsome ride, reached again the dividing point, and turned into the other path. This led us into a wild savanna surrounded by hills. Very soon we found tracks leading off in different directions, among which we became perfectly bewildered. In the midst of our perplexities we came upon an Indian leading a wild colt, who, without asking any questions, or waiting for any from us, waved us back, and led us across the plain into another path, following which some distance, he again struck across, and put us into still another.

The whole region was so wild we hardly believed that such a path could lead to a village or rancho; but, withal, there was one interesting circumstance. In our desolate and wandering path we had seen five high mounds, holding aloft the ruins of ancient buildings. Doubtless there were more buried in the woods. At three o'clock we entered a dense forest, and came suddenly upon the casa real of Kewick, standing alone, almost buried among trees. It stood on the platform of an ancient terrace, strewed with the relics of a ruined edifice. The steps of the terrace had fallen and been newly laid, but the walls were entire, with all the stones in place. Conspicuous in view was Mr. Catherwood with our servants and luggage, and, as we rode up, it seemed a strange confusion of things past and present. Mr. Catherwood dispelled the floating visions by his first greeting, an assurance that the casa real was full of fleas.

This proprietor was a full-blooded Indian, the first of this ancient but degraded race whom we had seen in the position of landowner and master. He was about forty-five years old, highly respectable in appearance and manners. He had inherited the land from his fathers, did not know how long it had been transmitted, but believed that it had always been in his family. The Indians on the rancho were his servants, and we had not seen in any village or on any hacienda men of better appearance, or under more excellent discipline. This produced on my mind a strong impression that, indolent, ignorant, and debased as the race is under the dominion of strangers, the Indian even now is not incapable of fulfilling the obligations of a higher station than his destiny has placed him. It is not true that he is fit only to labour with his hands; he is capable of directing the labour of others. As this Indian master sat on the terrace, with his dependants crouching round him, I could imagine him the descendant of a long line of caciques who once reigned in the city, the ruins of which were his inheritance. Involuntarily we treated him with a respect we had never shown to an Indian before. Our respect may have proceeded from the discovery that our new acquaintance was a man of property, possessed not merely of acres, and Indians, and unproductive real estate, but also of that great desideratum in these trying times, ready money. We had given Albino a dollar to purchase eggs with, who objected to it as too large a coin to be available on the rancho, but on his return informed us, with an expression of surprise, that the master had changed it the moment it was offered to him.

Our hasty dinner over, we asked for Indians to guide us to the ruins, and were somewhat startled by the objections they all made on account of the garrapatas. Frequently we came in contact with a bush covered with these insects, from which thousands swarmed upon us, like moving grains of sand, and scattered till the body itself seemed crawling. Our horses suffered more than ourselves, and it became a habit, whenever we dismounted, to rasp their sides with a rough stick. During the dry season the little pests are killed off by the heat of the sun, and devoured by birds, but for which I verily believe they would make the country uninhabitable. All along we had been told that the dry season was at hand. But we began to despair of any dry season, and had no hopes of getting rid of them. Nevertheless, we were somewhat startled at the warning conveyed by the reluctance of the Indians. When we insisted upon going, they gave us another alarming intimation by cutting twigs, with which, from the moment of starting, they whipped the bushes on each side, and swept the path before them.

Beyond the woods we came out into a comparatively open field, in which we saw on all sides through the trees the Xlap-pahk, or old walls, now grown so familiar, a collection of vast remains and of many buildings. The façades were not so much ornamented as some we had seen, but the stones were more massive, and the style of architecture was simple, severe, and grand. Nearly every house had fallen, and one long ornamented front lay on the ground cracked and doubled up as if shaken off by the vibrations of an earthquake, and still struggling to retain its upright position, the whole presenting a most picturesque and imposing scene of ruins. Night came upon us while gazing at a mysterious painting, and we returned to the casa real to sleep.

Early the next morning we were again in the apartment [with] the painting at which we were gazing the evening before. The end wall had fallen inward; the others remained. The ceiling, as in all the other buildings, was formed by two sides rising to meet each other, and covered within a foot of the point of junction by a flat layer of stones. In all the other arches, without a single exception, the layer was perfectly plain: but this had a single stone distinguished by a painting, which covered the whole surface presented to view. The painting itself was curious. The colours were bright, red and green predominating; the lines clear and distinct. The whole was more perfect than any painting we had seen. But its position surprised us more than the painting itself. It was in the most out-of-the-way spot in the whole edifice, and but for the Indians we might not have noticed it at all. Why this layer of stones was so adorned, or why this particular stone was distinguished above all others in the same layer, we were unable to discover, but we considered that it was not done capriciously nor without cause. We had long been of opinion that every stone in those ancient buildings, and every design and ornament that decorated them, had some certain though now inscrutable meaning.

This painting exhibits a rude human figure, surrounded by hieroglyphics, which doubtless contain the whole of its story. From its position in the wall, it was impossible to draw it without getting it out and lowering it to the ground, which I was anxious to accomplish, not only for the sake of the drawing, but for the purpose of carrying it away. The only way of getting at it was by digging down through the roof. The Indians had no crowbar, but loosening the mortar with their machetes, and prying apart the stones by means of hard wood saplings with the points sharpened, they excavated down to the layer on the top of the arch. The stone lapped over about a foot on each side, and was so heavy that it was impossible to hoist it out of the hole. Our only way, therefore, was to lower it down into the apartment.

The proprietor made no objections to my carrying it away, but it was too heavy for a mule-load, and the Indians would not undertake to carry it on their shoulders. The only way of removing it was to have it cut down to a portable size. When we left, the proprietor accompanied me to the village to procure a stonecutter for that purpose, but there was none. Unable to do anything with the stone, I engaged the proprietor to place it in an apartment sheltered from rain. If I do not mistake the character of my Indian friend and inheritor of a ruined city, it now lies subject to my order. I hereby authorize the next American traveller to bring it away at his own expense, and deposite it in the National Museum at Washington.

The same scarcity of water which we had found all over this region, except at Sabachshé, exists here also. The aguada was a small, muddy pond, with trees growing on the sides and into the water, which, in any other country, would be considered an unfit watering-place for beasts. The proprietor and all the Indians told us that in the dry season the remains of stone embankments were still visible, made, as they supposed, by the ancient inhabitants. The bank was

knee deep with mud. A few poles were laid out on supporters driven into the mud, and along these the Indians walked to dip up water. At the time our horses were brought down to drink; but they had to be watered out of the calabashes of the Indians.

At two o'clock we returned to the casa real. We had "done up" another ruined city, and were ready to set out again. But we had one serious impediment in the way. I have mentioned that on our arrival at this place we gave Albino a dollar, but I omitted to say that it was our last. On setting out on this journey, we had reduced our personal luggage to hammocks and petaquillas, oblong straw baskets without fastenings, unsafe to carry money in. Silver, the only available coin, was too heavy to carry about the person. At Sabachshé we discovered that our expenses had overrun our estimates, and sent Albino back to Nohcacab with the keys of our money trunk, and directions to follow us in all haste. The time calculated for his overtaking us had passed. We should have thought nothing of a little delay but for our pressing necessities. Some accident might have happened to him, or the temptation might have been too strong.

Our affairs were approaching a crisis, and the barbarism of the people of the country in matters of finance was hurrying it on. If we

56. Catherwood sketch of a small drawing found on the ceiling of a ruined structure at Kiuic

wanted a fowl, food for horses, or an Indian to work, the money must be ready at the moment. Throughout our journey it was the same; every order for the purchase of an article was null unless the money accompanied it. Brought up under the wings of credit, this system was always odious to us. We could attempt nothing on a liberal and enlightened scale, were always obliged to calculate our means, and could incur no expense unless we had the money to defray it on the spot. This, of course, trammelled enterprise, and now, on a mere miscalculation, we were brought suddenly to a stand still. On counting the scattering medios of private stock, we found that we had enough to pay for transporting our luggage to the village of Xul, but if we tarried over the night and Albino did not come, both ourselves and our horses must go without rations in the morning, and then we should have no means of getting away our luggage. It was really perplexing to know what to do; but it was very certain that if we remained at the rancho, as soon as a medio was not forthcoming the moment it was wanted we were undone. Our chance would be better at the village, and we determined to break up and go on.

At three o'clock we set out, and at half past five we made a dashing entry into the village of Xul, with horses, and servants, and carriers, and just one solitary medio left. On the opposite side of the plaza was one of those buildings which had so often sheltered us in time of trouble, but now I hesitated to approach the convent. The fame of the cura of Xul had reached our ears. Report said that he was rich, and a moneymaking man, and odd. Among his other possessions, he was lord of a ruined city which we proposed to visit, particularly interesting to us from the circumstance that, according to the accounts, it was then inhabited by Indians. We wished to procure from him facilities for exploring this city to advantage, and doubted whether it would be any recommendation to his favour as a rich man to begin our acquaintance by borrowing money.

But, although rich, he was a padre. Without dismounting, I rode over to the convent. The padre came out to meet me, and told me that he had been expecting us every day. I dismounted, and he took my horse by the bridle, led him across the corridor, through the sala, and out to the yard. He asked why my companions did not come over, and, at a signal, in a few minutes their horses followed mine through the sala.

Don José Gulielmo Roderigues, the cura of Xul, was a Guachapino, or native of Old Spain. Like all the old Spaniards in the country, he was somewhat proud. He was educated a Franciscan friar. But thirty years before, on account of the revolutions and the persecution of his order, he fled from Spain, and took refuge in Yucatan. On the destruction of the Franciscan Convent in Merida he secularized, and entered the regular church; had been cura of Ticul and Nohcacab; and about ten years before had been appointed to the district of Xul. His curacy was one of those called beneficiaries; i.e., in consideration of building the church, keeping it in repair, and performing the duties and services of a priest, the capitation tax paid by the Indians, and the fees allowed for baptism, marriages, masses, salves, and funeral services, after deducting one seventh for the Church, belonged to himself personally. At the time of his appointment, the village was a mere Indian rancho. The land comprehended in his district was, in general, good for maize, but, like all the rest of that region, it was destitute of water. His first object had been to remedy this deficiency, to which end he had dug a well two hundred feet deep, at an expense of fifteen hundred dollars. Besides this, he had large and substantial cisterns, equal to any we had seen in the country, for the reception of rain-water. By furnishing this necessary of life in abundance, he had drawn around him a population of seven thousand.

To us there was something more interesting than this creation of a village and a population in the wilderness. Here, again, was the same strange mingling of old things with new. The village stands on the site of an aboriginal city. In the corner of the plaza now occupied by the cura's house, the yard of which contains the well and cisterns, once stood a pyramidal mound with a building upon it. The cura had himself pulled down this mound, and levelled it so that nothing was left to indicate even the place where it stood. With the materials he had built the house and cisterns, and portions of the ancient edifice now formed the walls of the new. With singular good taste, showing his practical turn of mind, and a vein of antiquarian feeling, he had fixed in conspicuous places many of the old carved stones. Along the corridor of the convent was a long seat of time-polished stones taken from the ruins of an ancient building, and in every quarter might be seen these memorials of the past, connecting links between the living and the dead, and serving to keep alive the memory of the fact that on this spot once stood an ancient Indian city.

At that moment we stood upon a giddy height. To ask the loan of a few dollars might lower us materially. The evening was wearing away when, to our great satisfaction, we heard the clattering of horses' hoofs. Albino made his appearance. The production of a bag of dollars fixed us in our high position, and we were able to order Indians for the next day. We finished the evening with a warm bath in a hand basin, under the personal direction of the cura, which relieved somewhat the burning of garrapata bites, and then retired to our hammocks.

Early the next morning we set out for the rancho of Nohcacab, three leagues distant. We had not gone far when Mr. C. complained of a slight headache. Wishing to ride moderately, Dr. Cabot and myself went on, leaving him to follow with the luggage. At nine o'clock we reached the rancho. The first huts were enclosed by a well-built stone wall, along which appeared, in various places, sculptured fragments from the ruins. Beyond was another wall, the entrance to which was by a gateway formed of two sculptured monuments of curious design and excellent workmanship, raising high our expectations in regard to the ruins on this rancho, and sustaining the accounts we had heard of them.

The proprietor was waiting to receive us. Having taken possession of an empty hut, and disposed of our horses, we accompanied him to look over the rancho. What he regarded as most worth showing was his tobacco crop, lying in some empty huts to dry, which he contemplated with great satisfaction, and the well, which he looked at with as much sorrow. It was three hundred and fifty-four feet deep, and even at this great depth it was dry.

While thus engaged, our baggage carriers arrived with intelligence that Mr. Catherwood was taken ill, and they had left him lying in the road. I immediately applied to the proprietor for a coché and Indians, and he undertook to get them ready. In the mean time I saddled my horse and hastened back to Mr. Catherwood, whom I found lying on the ground under the shade of the tree by the fountain, wrapped up in all the coverings he could muster, even to the

57. Modern view of carved stone figures, Labná

saddlecloths of the horses. While he was in this state, two men came along, bestriding the same horse, and bringing sheets and ponchas to make a covering for the coché. Then came a straggling line of Indians, each with a long pole, and withes to lash them together.

The path was narrow, lined on each side with thorn bushes, the spikes of which stuck in the naked flesh of the Indians as they carried the coché. They were obliged to stop frequently and disentangle themselves. On reaching the rancho I found Doctor Cabot down with a fever. A cold shivering crept over me, and in a few minutes we were all three in our hammocks. Our host had been employed in preparing breakfast upon a large scale, and seemed mortified that there was no one to do it justice. I had it brought to the side of my hammock. My effort made him happy, and I began to think my prostration was merely the reaction from over-excitement. By degrees what I began to please our host I continued for my own satisfaction. My equanimity was perfectly restored, and, breakfast over, I set out to look at the ruins.

Passing through one of the huts, we soon came to a steep hill covered with trees, up which the proprietor had cut a road two or three yards wide, leading to a building standing upon a terrace on the brow of the hill. The interior was entire, but without any distinguishing features. We came to three other buildings standing on the same range, without any important variations in the details. I was thoroughly disappointed. There were no subjects for the pencil and nothing to carry away. The proprietor seemed mortified that he had not better ruins to show us, but I gave him to understand that it was not his fault. Nevertheless, it was really vexatious, with such a troop of Indians at command, that there was nothing for us to do. The Indians sympathized in the mortification of their master, and, to indemnify me, told me of two other ruined cities, one of which was but two leagues from the village of Xul.

I returned and made my report, and Mr. Catherwood immediately proposed a return to the village. It was late in the evening when we arrived, but the cura received us as kindly as before. During the evening I made inquiries for the place of which the Indians had told me. It was but two leagues distant, but of all who happened to drop in, not one was aware of its existence. The cura, however, sent for a young man who had a rancho in that direction, and who promised to accompany me.

At six o'clock the next morning we started, neither Mr. Catherwood nor Doctor Cabot being able to accompany me. At the distance of about two leagues we reached an Indian rancho, where we learned from an old woman that we had passed the path leading to the ruins. Retracing our steps, and crossing the camino real, we entered the woods on the other side, and cut a path up the side of a hill, on the top of which were the ruins of a building. The outer wall had fallen, leaving exposed to view the inner half of the arch. This arch was plastered and covered with painted figures in profile, much mutilated, but in one place a row of legs remained, which seemed to have belonged to a procession, and at the first glance brought to my mind the funeral processions on the walls of the tombs at Thebes. In the triangular wall forming the end of the room were three compartments, in which were figures, some having their heads adorned with plumes, others with a sort of steeple cap, and carrying on their heads something like a basket. Two were standing on their hands with their heels in the air. These figures were about a foot high, and painted red. The drawing was good, the attitudes were spirited and life-like. Even in their mutilated state, they were by far the most interesting paintings we had seen in the country.

There was one other building, and these two, my guide said, were all, but probably others lie buried in the woods.

In a few minutes we mounted to return to the village. Ruins were increasing upon us, to explore which thoroughly would be the work of years. We had but months, and were again arrested by illness. For some days, at least, Mr. Catherwood would not be able to resume work. I was really distressed by the magnitude of what was before us, but, for the present, we could do nothing, and I determined at once to change the scene. The festival of Ticul was at hand, and that night it was to open with *el báyle de las Mestizas,* or the Mestiza ball. Ticul lay in our return route, nine leagues from the village of Xul, but I determined to reach it that evening. My companion did not sympathize in my humour; his vaquero saddle hurt him, and he could not ride faster than a walk. I took his hard-trotting horse and uneasy saddle, and gave him mine. Pushing on, at eleven o'clock we reached Xul, where I had my horse unsaddled and washed, ordered him a good mess of corn, and two boiled eggs for myself. In the mean time, Mr. Catherwood had a recurrence of fever and ague, and my horse was led away. But the attack proved slight, and I had him brought out again. At two o'clock I resumed my journey, with a sheet, a hammock, and Albino. The heat was scorching. Albino would have grumbled at setting out at this hour, but he, too, was ripe for the fiesta of Ticul.

In an hour we saw in the woods on our right large mounds, indicating that here, too, had once stood an ancient city. I rode in to look at them, but the buildings which had crowned them were all fallen and ruined, and I only gained an addition to the stock of garrapatas already on hand. We had not heard of these ruins at the village, and, on inquiring afterward, I could find no name for them.

At the distance of three leagues we commenced ascending the sierra, and for two hours the road lay over an immense ledge of solid rock. My horse's hoofs clattered and rang at every step, and, though strong and sure-footed, he stumbled and slid in a way that was painful and dangerous to both horse and rider. It was impossible to go faster than a walk, and, afraid that night would overtake us, in which case, as there was no moon, we might lose our way, I dismounted and hurried on, leading my horse.

It was nearly dark when we reached the top of the last range. On the very brink stood the church of La Hermita, below the village of Oxcutzcab, and beyond a boundless wooded plain, dotted in three places with villages. There were ruined mounds in the neighbourhood, which I intended to look at in passing, but we had still four leagues to make, and pushed on. We roused the barking dogs of two villages, and at nine o'clock rode into the plaza of Ticul. It was crowded with Indians, blazing with lights, and occupied by a great circular scaffold for a bull-ring, and a long, enclosed arbour. Strains of music gave notice that the *báyle de las Mestizas* had already begun.

Our trunks had been ordered over from Nohcacab, and, making a hurried toilet, I hastened to the ball-room. The crowd outside opened a way, Don Philippe Peon beckoned to me as I entered, and in a moment more I was seated in one of the best places. After a month in Indian ranchos, that day toiling among ruins, almost driven to distraction by garrapatas, clambering over a frightful sierra, and making a journey worse than any sixty miles in our country, all at once I settled down at a fancy ball, amid music, lights, and pretty women, in the full enjoyment of an armchair and a cigar.

CHAPTER ELEVEN

Bolonchén and Dzibilnocac

esides the great business of balls, bull-fights, Daguerreotyping, and superintending the morals of the padres [during] the fiesta of Ticul, I had some light reading in a manuscript entitled "Ancient Chronology of Yucatan; or, a simple Exposition of the Method used by the Indians to compute Time." This essay was presented to me by the author, Don Pio Perez. I had been advised that this gentleman was the best Maya scholar in Yucatan, and that he was distinguished in the same degree for the investigation and study of all matters tending to elucidate the history of the ancient Indians. His attention was turned in this direction by the circumstance of holding an office in which old documents in the Maya language were constantly passing under his eyes.

From the analysis made by Don Pio, I am enabled to state the interesting fact that the calendar of Yucatan, though differing in some particulars, was substantially the same with that of the Mexicans. It had a similar solar year of three hundred and sixty-five days, divided in the same manner, first, into eighteen months of twenty days each, with five supplementary days; and, secondly, into twenty-eight weeks of thirteen days each, with an additional day.

It had the same method of distinguishing the days of the year by a combination of those two series, and the same cycle of fifty-two years, in which the years, as in Mexico, are distinguished by a combination of the same series of thirteen, with another of four names or hieroglyphics. Don Pio acknowledges that in Yucatan there is no certain evidence of the intercalation (similar to our leap year, or to the Mexican secular addition of thirteen days) necessary to correct the error resulting from counting the year as equal to three hundred and sixty-five days only.

Besides the cycle of fifty-two years common to the Yucatecans and Mexicans, and, as Don Pio Perez asserts, to the Indians of Chiapas, Oaxaca, and Soconusco, those of Yucatan had another age of two hundred and sixty, or of three hundred and twelve years, equal to five or six cycles of fifty-two years, each of which ages consisted of thirteen periods (called Ajau or Ajau Katun) of twenty years each, according to many authorities, but, in Don Pio's opinion, of twenty-four years.

The fact that though the inhabitants of Yucatan and Mexico speak different languages, their calendar is substantially the same, I regard as extremely interesting and important, for this is not like a similarity of habits, which may grow out of natural instincts or identity of position. A calendar is a work of science, founded upon calculations, arbitrary signs, and symbols, and the similarity shows that both nations acknowledged the same starting points, attached the same meaning to the same phenomena and objects, which meaning was sometimes arbitrary, and not such as would suggest itself to the untutored. It shows common sources of knowledge and processes of reasoning, similarity of worship and religious institutions. In short, it is a link in a chain of evidence tending to show a common origin in the aboriginal inhabitants of Yucatan and Mexico. For this discovery we are indebted to Don Pio Perez.

On setting out our direction was again south, and again our road was over the sepulchres of cities. At the distance of two miles we saw "old walls" on an eminence; a little farther three ruined buildings; and beyond these we came to the ruins of Sacbey. These consist of three buildings, irregularly disposed. One faces the south, and has three small doorways. Another is about the size of the former, and has three apartments, with two columns in the centre doorway. The third is so ruined that its plan could not be made out. Near as they were to the village, the padrecito had never seen them. They stand about a hundred feet from the path, but so completely buried among

58. *Page 174:* Figure on the east façade of the "Atlantean Building" (Palace of the Figures), Xculoc (Stephens' Schoolhoke) (date unknown)

the trees, that, though I had visited them before under the guidance of an Indian, I passed now without observing them.

A short distance beyond is one of the most interesting monuments of antiquity in Yucatan. It is a broken platform or roadway of stone, about eight feet wide and eight or ten inches high, crossing the road, and running off into the woods on both sides. I have before referred to it as called by the Indians Sacbey, which means, in the Maya language, a paved way of pure white stone. The Indians say it traversed the country from Kabah to Uxmal; and that on it couriers travelled, bearing letters to and from the lords of those cities, written on leaves or the bark of trees. It was the only instance in which we had found among the Indians anything like a tradition. While we were standing upon the road, an old Indian came up from the other direction, bending under a load, who, in crossing it, stopped, and, striking his stick against the stones, uttered the words Sacbey, and Kabah, and Uxmal. At the same time our carriers came up, the old sexton at their head, who, depositing his burden upon the ancient road, repeated Sacbey, and then favoured us with an oration, in which we could only distinguish Kabah and Uxmal.

At the distance of two leagues we reached Xampon, where stand the remains of an edifice which, when entire, must have been grand and imposing, and now, but for the world of ruins around, might excite a stranger's wonder. It stood alone, and an Indian had planted a milpa around it. From this "old walls" were again visible, which the

59. Modern view of restored sacbé, Labná

60. West façade of North
Building, Chunhuhub
(Teobert Maler, circa 1900)

Indians called Kalupok. Beyond we saw at a distance two other
places, called Hiokowitz and Kuepak, ruined and difficult of access,
and we did not attempt to reach them. It added to the effect of the ruins scattered in this region, that they were not on a camino real, but
on a little-frequented milpa path, in some places so overgrown that
we found it difficult to force a passage. The heat was intense. We exhausted our waccals of water, and as there was no stream or foun-

tain, our only chance of a supply was from a deposite of rain-water in the hollow of some friendly rock.

At two o'clock we reached a small clearing, in which stood an arbour of leaves, and under it a rude cross, facing the road. Beyond was an overgrown path, which had been opened to enable me to visit the ruins of Zekilna. This place had been the object of one of my bootless visits from Nohcacab. The account I had heard was of an apart-

ment containing an altar for burning copal, with traces of its use as left by the ancient inhabitants. When I had arrived where it was necessary to turn off, it was some time before the Indian could discover any signs of a path. Perceiving the discomfort and hardship that must attend an exploration in so desolate a place, I did most earnestly hope that the path would lead to nothing that might require a second visit.

Leading my horse as the Indian cleared the way, we came to a broken, stony ascent, climbing up which I discovered that we were upon the top of an ancient terrace. Running off lengthwise from this terrace was a small building, which the Indian pointed out as containing the altar and copal. Passing the first door, he went on to the second, put his head in cautiously, and, without entering, drew back. I found an apartment differing in nothing from the most ordinary we had seen in the country. For some time I could not get the Indian to enter. When he did, standing in the doorway, and looking around cautiously, he waved his finger horizontally, according to the manner of the Indians, to indicate that there was nothing. Fortunately, I learned

61. "Third Castillo" (a structure that Stephens missed), Chunhuhub (Maler, circa 1900)

that the road we had left led to the ruins of Chunhuhu. It shows the difficulty I had in ascertaining the juxtaposition of places, that though this was one of the places which I intended to visit, until this man mentioned it I had not been able to learn that it lay in the same neighbourhood.

The next morning at daylight we sent Albino with the Indians to begin clearing around the ruins, and after breakfast we followed. The path lay through a savanna covered with long grass, and at the distance of a mile we reached two buildings.

The first stands on a substantial terrace, but lower than most of the others. The end on the left has fallen, carrying with it one doorway, so that now only four appear. The doorway was the largest and most imposing we had seen in the country, but, unfortunately, the ornaments over it were broken and fallen. In the centre apartment the back corridor is raised, and the ascent to it is by three steps. All the doorways were plain except the centre one. It is in a dilapidated condition, but still presents bold and striking ornaments. Even on this scale, however, the details of the sitting figures above the cornice do not appear.

On a lower terrace is another building. It had a freshness about it that suggested the idea of something more modern than the others. The whole was covered with a coat of plaster but little broken, and it confirmed the opinion we had entertained before, that the fronts of all the buildings had been thus covered.

While we were engaged in making a clearing, two young men came down from the top of the building, with long guns, the locks covered with deer-skin, and all the accoutrements of cacadores, or hunters. They were tall, fine-looking fellows, fearless and frank in appearance and manner. Dr. Cabot's gun was the first object that attracted their attention, after which they laid down their guns, and, as if for the mere sport of swinging their machetes, were soon foremost in making the clearing.

We were so pleased with their appearance that we proposed to one of them to accompany us in our search after ruins. The elder was quite taken with the idea of rambling, but soon said, with a rather disconsolate tone, that he had a wife and children. His hermanito, or younger brother, named Dimas, had no such ties, and he continued with us until we left the country. These men we had never heard of till they came upon us with their guns. Their manly bearing as hunters inspired confidence, and the only suspicious circumstance was that they were willing to take us without references. But we found afterward that they had both known us at Nohcacab.

From the terrace of the first building we saw at a distance a high hill, almost a mountain, on the top of which rose a wooded elevation surrounding an ancient building. There was something extraordinary in its position, but the young men told us it was entirely ruined, and, although it was then but eleven o'clock, if we attempted to go to it, we could not return till after dark. They told us, also, of others at the distance of half a league, more extensive, and some of which, they said, were, in finish and preservation, equal to these.

At one o'clock, under the guidance of Dimas, we set out to look for them. It was desperately hot. We passed several huts, and at one of them asked for some water; but it was so full of insects that we could barely taste it. Dimas led us to the hut of his mother, and gave us some from a vessel in which the insects had settled to the bottom.

We ascended the spur of a high hill, and coming down into a thickly-wooded valley, after the longest half league we ever walked, we saw through the trees a large stone structure. On reaching it, we came to a large mound faced on all sides with stone. Crossing over the top, we looked down upon an overgrown area, having on each side a range of ruined buildings, with their white façades peering through the trees. Beyond, seemingly inaccessible, was the high hill with the ruins on the top, which we had seen from the terrace of the first building. Hills rose around us on every side. The stillness of the grave rested upon the ruins, and the notes of a little flycatcher were the only sounds we heard.

The ruins in sight were much more extensive than those we had first visited, but in a more ruinous condition. We descended the mound to the area in front, and, bearing down the bushes, we reached an edifice. It has two apartments, and conspicuous in the façade are representations of three uncouth human figures, in curious dresses, with their hands held up by the side of the head, supporting the cornice [see Fig. 58]. These ruins, Dimas told us, were called Schoolhoke. Like the others, they stand on what is called the savanna of Chunhuhu. The ruined building on the top of the hill, visible from both places, seems towering as a link to connect them together. Supposing the two piles of ruins to have formed part of the same city, there is reason to believe that it once covered as much ground and contained as many inhabitants as any yet presented.

We returned to the rancho worn down with fatigue, just in time to escape a violent rain. This brought within, as an accompaniment to the fleas of the night before, our carriers and servants. We had eleven hammocks in close juxtaposition, and through the night a concert of nasal trombones, with Indian variations. The rain continued all the next day, and as no work could be done, Mr. Catherwood took advantage of the opportunity to have another attack of fever. We were glad of [the rain] on another account, for we had kept a man constantly employed in the woods searching for water. Our horses had exhausted all the rocky cavities around, and we could not have held out another day.

The next morning, Mr. Catherwood went to make a drawing of the last building, and Doctor Cabot and myself to visit another ruined city, all to meet at Bolonchen in the evening. We were warned that the path we proposed taking was not passable on horseback. For the first league our arms and legs were continually scratched and torn by briers. Our Indian guide moved easily on foot, just clearing the branches on each side and overhead. We had one alternative, which was to dismount and lead our horses. Unused to having favours shown them, they pulled back, so that the labour of dragging them on added greatly to the fatigue of walking.

At one o'clock we came to a rancho of Indians, where we bought some tortillas and procured a guide. Leaving the camino real, we turned again into a milpa path, and in about an hour came in sight of another ruined city, known by the name of Ytsimpte. From the plain on which we approached we saw on the brow of a hill, a range of buildings laid bare to view, the trees having just been felled. As we drew near we saw Indians engaged in continuing the clearing. On arriving at the foot of the buildings, Albino found that the clearing was made by order of the alcalde of Bolonchen, in expectation of our visit and for our benefit!

These ruins lie in the village of Bolonchen, and the first apartment we entered showed the effects of this vicinity. All the smooth stones of the inner wall had been picked out and carried away for building purposes. The edifice had one apartment, and a grand staircase rose in the centre to the top. This staircase was in a ruinous condition, but the outer stones of the lower steps remained, richly ornamented with sculpture. Probably the whole casing on each side had once possessed the same rich decoration.

Beyond this was another large building, square and peculiar in its plan. At the extreme end the whole façade lay unbroken on the ground, held together by the great mass of mortar and stones, and presenting the entire line of pillars with which it had been decorated. In the doorway of an inner apartment was an ornamented pillar, and on the walls was the print of the mysterious red hand. Turn which way we would, ruin was before us. At right angles with the first building was a line of ruined walls, following which I passed the headless trunk of a sculptured body lying on the ground. The legs, too, were gone. At the end was an arch, which seemed, at a distance, to stand entire and alone, like that named the arch of triumph at Kabah. But it proved to be only the open and broken arch of a ruined building. From the extent of these remains, the masses of sculptured stones, and the execution of the carving, this must have been one of the first class of the aboriginal cities.

A short ride brought us to the suburbs of the village of Bolonchen, and we entered a long street. It was late in the afternoon. Indian children were playing in the road, and Indians, returned from their work, were swinging in hammocks within the huts. As we advanced, we saw a vecino sitting in the doorway thrumming a guitar. It was, perhaps, a scene of indolence, but it was one of quiet and contentment, of comfort and even thrift. All looked at us with curiosity, but without distrust. Every face bore a welcome, and, as we rode through, all gave us a friendly greeting. At the head of the street the plaza opened upon us on a slight elevation, with groups of Indian women in the centre drawing water from the well, and relieved against a background of green hills rising above the tops of the houses, which, under the reflection of the setting sun, gave a beauty and picturesqueness of aspect that no other village in the country had exhibited.

Bolonchen derives its name from two Maya words: *Bolon,* which signifies nine, and *chen,* wells. From time immemorial, nine wells formed at this place, and these wells are now in the plaza of the village. These wells were circular openings cut through a stratum of rock. The water was at that time ten or twelve feet from the surface, in all at the same level. The source of this water is a mystery to the inhabitants, but there are some facts which seem to make the solution simple. The wells are mere perforations through an irregular stratum of rock, all communicate, and in the dry season a man may descend in one and come out by another at the extreme end of the plaza. It is manifest, therefore, that the water does not proceed from springs. Besides, the wells are all full during the rainy season. When this is over the water begins to disappear, and in the heat of the dry season it fails altogether. It would appear that under the surface there is a great rocky cavern, into which the floods of the rainy season find a way by crevices or other openings, and, having little or no escape, are retained, and furnish a supply so long as they are augmented by the rains.

The custody and preservation of these wells form a principal part of the business of the village authorities. But with all their care,

62. Catherwood drawing
of the cave at Bolonchén

the supply lasts but seven or eight months in the year. This year, on
account of the long continuance of the rainy season, it had lasted
longer than usual, and was still abundant. The time was approaching,
however, when these wells would fail, and the inhabitants be driven
to an extraordinary cueva. There was one great difficulty in the way
of our visiting the cueva. Since the commencement of the rainy season it had not been used; and every year there was a work of several
days to be done in repairing the ladders. As this, however, was our
only opportunity, we determined to make the attempt.

At the distance of half a league from the village, we disencumbered ourselves of superfluous apparel, and, each with a torch in
hand, entered a wild cavern. The descent, by ladder, was precipitous.

Here all light from the mouth of the cavern was lost, but we soon reached the brink of a great perpendicular descent, to the very bottom of which a strong body of light was thrown from a hole in the surface. As we stood on the brink of this precipice, under the shelving of an immense mass of rock, seeming darker from the stream of light thrown down the hole, gigantic stalactites and huge blocks of stone assumed all manner of fantastic shapes, and seemed like monstrous animals or deities of a subterranean world.

From the brink on which we stood, an enormous ladder, of the rudest possible construction, led to the bottom of the hole. It was eighty feet long, and about twelve feet wide, made of the rough trunks of saplings lashed together lengthwise, and supported all the way down by horizontal trunks braced against the face of the rock. The ladder was double, having two sets or flights of rounds, divided by a middle partition, and the whole fabric was lashed together by withes. It was very steep, seemed precarious and insecure, and confirmed the worst accounts we had heard of the descent into this remarkable well.

Our Indians began the descent, but the foremost had scarcely got his head below the surface before one of the rounds slipped, and he only saved himself by clinging to another. The ladder having been made when the withes were green, these were now dry, cracked, and some of them broken. We attempted a descent with some little misgivings, but, by keeping each hand and foot on a different round, with an occasional crash and slide, we all reached the foot of the ladder.

On one side of the cavern is an opening in the rock. Entering, we soon came to an abrupt descent, down which was another long and trying ladder. The cave was damp, and the rock and the ladder were wet and slippery. It was evident that the labour of exploring this cave was to be greatly increased by the state of the ladders, and there might be some danger. But, even after all that we had seen of caves, there was something so wild and grand in this that we could not bring ourselves to give up the attempt. It was impossible to carry a torch, and we were obliged to feel our way in the dark, or with only such light as could reach us from the torches above and below. At the foot of this ladder was a large cavernous chamber, from which irregular passages led off in different directions to deposites of water. Doctor Cabot and myself took one of the passages indicated by the Indians.

Moving on by a slight ascent over the rocks, we came to the foot of a third ladder, two or three steps beyond another, both which we had to go up, and six paces farther a fifth, descending. A little be-

yond we descended another ladder, and yet a little farther on we
came to one—the seventh—the length and general appearance of
which induced us to pause and consider. This long ladder was laid on
a narrow, sloping face of rock, protected on one side by a perpendicular wall, but at the other open and precipitous. Holding by the side
of the ladder next the rock, we descended, crashing and carrying
down the loose rounds, so that when we got to the bottom we had
cut off all communication with Albino. He could not descend, and,
what was quite as inconvenient, we could not get back. It was now
too late to reflect. We told Albino to throw down our torches, and go
back for Indians and rope to haul us out.

   In the mean time we moved on by a broken, winding passage,
and came to a ladder, at the foot of which we entered a low and sti-
fling passage. Crawling along this on our hands and feet, we came to
a rocky basin full of water. Before reaching it one of our torches had
gone out, and the other was then expiring. From the best calculation
I can make, we were then fourteen hundred feet from the mouth of
the cave, and at a perpendicular depth of four hundred and fifty feet.
We were black with smoke, grimed with dirt, and dripping with perspiration. Water was the most pleasant spectacle that could greet our
eyes; but it did not satisfy us to drink it only. Our expiring torch
warned us to forbear. In the dark we might never be able to find our
way back to upper earth. Trusting that if we did not reappear in the
course of the week Mr. Catherwood would come to the rescue, we
whipped off our scanty covering, and stepped into the pool. It was
just large enough to prevent us from interfering with each other, and
we achieved a bath which, perhaps, no white man ever before took at
that depth under ground.

   The Indians call this basin Chacka, which means red water. This
we did not know at the time, and we did not discover it, for to economize our torch we avoided flaring it. Hurrying out, we made a rapid
toilet, and, groping our way back, with our torch just bidding us farewell, we reached the foot of the broken ladder. Albino returned with
Indians and ropes. We hauled ourselves up, and got back to the open
chamber from which the passages diverged. Here the Indians pointed
out another, which we followed till it became lower than any we had
yet explored; and we came to another basin of water. This is called
Puouelha, meaning that it ebbs and flows like the sea. The Indians
say that it recedes with the south wind, and increases with the northwest. They add that when they go to it silently they find water; but
when they talk or make a noise the water disappears. Perhaps it is
not so capricious with white men, for we found water, and did not ap-

proach it with sealed lips. The Indians say, besides, that forty women once fainted in this passage, and that now they do not allow the women to go to it alone.

In returning we turned off twice by branching passages, and reached two other basins of water. When we got back to the foot of the great staircase, exhausted and almost worn out, we had the satisfaction of learning that there were seven in all, and we had missed three. The third is called Sallab, which means a spring; the fourth Akahba, on account of its darkness; the fifth Chocohá, from the circumstance of its being always warm; the sixth Ooiha, from being of a milky colour; and the seventh Chimaisha, because it has insects called ais.

It was a matter of some regret that we were not able to mark such peculiarities as might exist in these waters, particularly that we were not provided with barometer and thermometer to ascertain the relative heights and temperatures. But the sources of the water and the geological formation of the country were matters of secondary interest to us. The great point was that when the wells in the plaza fail, the village turns to this cave, and four or five months in the year derives from this source its only supply. It was the sole watering place of one of the most thriving villages in Yucatan, containing a population of seven thousand souls. Perhaps even this was surpassed in wonder by the fact that though the fame of the Cueva of Bolonchen extends throughout Yucatan, from the best information we could procure, not a white man in the village had ever explored it.

Early the next morning we resumed our journey. On leaving the village we were soon again in the wilderness. Keeping as near as possible what we understood to be the direction, [we] came out upon a muddy aguada, covered with weeds, and beyond this a sugar rancho, the first we had seen in Yucatan, indicating that we were entering a different section of country. We had escaped the region of eternal stones, and the soil was rich and loamy. A league beyond this we reached the rancho of Santa Rosa.

The next morning we started for the ruins of Labphak. It was luxurious to ride on a road free from stones. In an hour we entered a forest of fine trees, and a league beyond found a party of Indians, who pointed us to a narrow path just opened, wilder than anything we had yet travelled. After following this some distance, the Indians stopped, and made signs to us to dismount. In a few minutes we saw peering through the trees the white front of a lofty building. It had three stories, the uppermost consisting of a bare dead wall, [a] casa cerrada. The building was overgrown with gigantic trees. We moved on from door to door, and wandered through its desolate chambers. For the first time in the country we found interior staircases, one of which was entire, every step in its place. The stones were worn, and we almost expected to see the foot-prints of the former occupants. With hurried interest we moved on till we reached the top. This commanded an extensive view over a great wooded plain. The sky was overcast, and portended the coming of another Norte. The wind swept over the ruined building, so that in places we were obliged to cling to the branches of the trees to save ourselves from falling. An eagle stayed his flight through the air and hovered over our heads. At a great height Doctor Cabot recognised it as one of a rare species, the first which he had seen in the country, and stood with his gun ready, hoping to carry it home with him as a memorial of the place. But the proud bird soared away.

The roof and a portion of the façade [of] the lowest range have fallen, and almost buried the centre doorways. Each staircase consists of two flights, with a platform at the head of the first, which forms the foot of the second. They lead out upon the roof, under the projection which stands like a watchtower in the wall of the second range, and from this range two interior staircases lead out in the same way to the platform of the third.

In the second and third ranges there are no openings of any kind except those at the head of the staircases. At first sight of this plain, solid wall we thought we had really at last found a casa cerrada. But working our way round the platform of the terrace, we found ranges of doorways opening into apartments. This was merely a back wall without doors or windows. And we made another much more interesting and important discovery. The elevation which we came upon first, facing west, noble and majestic as it was, was actually the rear of the building. The front, facing east, presented the tottering remains of the grandest structure that now rears its ruined head in the forests of Yucatan.

In front was a grand courtyard, with ranges of ruined buildings, forming a hollow square. In the centre a gigantic staircase rose from the courtyard to the platform of the third story. On the platform of the second terrace, at each end, stood a high square building like a tower, with the remains of rich ornaments in stucco. On the platform of the third, at the head of the grand staircase, on each side stood two oblong buildings, their façades adorned with colossal figures and ornaments in stucco; seemingly intended as a portal to the structure on the top. In ascending the grand staircase, cacique, priest, or stranger had before him this gorgeously ornamented portal, and

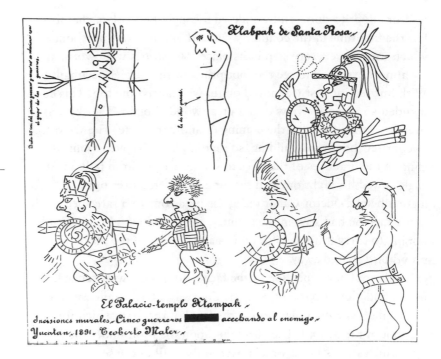

63. Maler drawing of
graffiti at the Palace,
Xtampak (Stephens'
Labphak)

passed through it to enter the centre apartment of the upper story.

This apartment is perfectly plain. But in this lofty chamber were strange memorials, tokens of recent occupation, indicating, amid the desolation and solitude around, that within a few years this ruined edifice, from which the owners had perhaps fled in terror, or been driven by the sword, had been the refuge and abode of man. In the holes of the archway were poles for the support of hammocks, and at each end were swinging shelves made of twigs and rods. When the cholera swept like a scourge over this isolated country, the inhabitants of the villages and ranchos fled for safety to the mountains and the wilderness. This desolate building was repeopled, this lofty chamber was the abode of some scared and stricken family. Here, amid hardships and privations, they waited till the angel of death passed by.

The lower range consists of narrow apartments on all four of the sides. The grand staircase forms the foundation for the support of the two upper ranges. It has no communication with any of the apartments. Whether the interior really is solid or contains apartments remains a question for future explorers.

In two places are carved tablets set in the wall, as at Palenque, and, except at Palenque, this was the only place in all our wanderings in which we found bas-reliefs. We were now moving in the direction of Palenque, though, of course, at a great distance from it. The face of the country was less stony, and the discovery of these bas-reliefs, and the increase and profusion of stuccoed ornaments, induced the impression that, in getting beyond the great limestone surface, the builders of these cities had adapted their style to the materials at hand, until, at Palenque, instead of putting up great façades of rudely-carved stone, they decorated the exterior with ornaments in stucco, and, having fewer carved ornaments, bestowed upon them more care and skill. Though resembling those at Palenque in general character, the bas-reliefs are greatly inferior in design and execution. Standing in the outer wall, they are much defaced and worn. Both were composed of separate stones; but the subjects on the different pieces appeared to want adaptation to each other, and almost suggested that they were fragments of other tablets, put together without much regard to design of any kind.

My hammock was swung in the front apartment. Directly over my head was the dim outline of a faded red painting like that first seen at Kewick. On the walls were the prints of the mysterious red hand, and around were the tokens of recent occupation. What tales of fear and wonder these old walls, could they speak, might disclose. We had a large fire built in one corner of the apartment, but we heard no moschetoes, and there were no fleas. During the night we all woke up at the same moment, only to congratulate each other and enjoy the consciousness of feeling ourselves free from these little nuisances.

Except a small ruined structure which we passed on the way to this building, as yet we had seen only this one with the ranges around the courtyard. It was clear that it did not stand alone. But we were so completely buried in the woods that it was utterly impossible to know which way to turn in search of others. In making our clearing we had stumbled upon two circular holes, like those found at Uxmal, which the Indians called chultunes, or cisterns, and which they said existed in all parts; and Doctor Cabot, in pursuit of a bird, had found a range of buildings at but a short distance, disconnected from each other, and having their façades ornamented with stucco.

Going out to the path from which we had turned off to reach this edifice, and proceeding a short distance, we saw through the trees the corner of a large building, which proved to be a great parallelogram, enclosing a hollow square. In the centre of the front range a grand but ruined staircase ascended from the ground to the top of the building, and, crossing the flat roof, we found a corresponding staircase leading down into the courtyard. The richest ornaments were on the side facing the courtyard, being of stucco, and on each side of the staircase were some of new and curious design. Unfortunately, they were all in a ruinous condition. The whole courtyard was overgrown, so that the buildings facing it were but indistinctly visible, and in some places not at all.

There is no place which we visited that we were so reluctant to leave unfinished. It remains a rich and almost unbroken field for the future explorer. To excite his imagination and to show that the love of the marvellous is not confined to any one country, I add that, upon the strength of a letter of mine, giving an account of the discovery of this place, and mentioning the vestiges of six buildings, we found, on our return to Merida, that these six had gone on accumulating, and had not been fairly brought to a stop till they had reached six hundred!

The reader may not consider the country through which we have been travelling as over-burdened with population, but in the district of Nohcacab, the people did so consider it. Oppressed by the large landed proprietors, many of the enterprising yeomanry of this district determined to seek a new home in the wilderness. Bidding farewell to friends and relatives, after a journey of two days and a half they reached the fertile plains of Zibilnocac, from time immemorial an Indian rancho. Here the soil belonged to the government. Every man could take up what land he pleased, full scope was offered to enterprise, and an opportunity for development not afforded by the over-peopled region of Nohcacab. Long before reaching it we had heard of this new village of Iturbide. In five years, from twenty-five inhabitants it had grown into a population of fifteen hundred.

Toward dark, we reached Iturbide, standing on the outposts of civilization, the Chicago of Yucatan. The plaza is on the ground formerly occupied by an old milperia, or cornfield. Five years before it was probably enclosed by a bush fence; now, at one corner rises a thatched house, with an arbour before it, and a table under the arbour, at which, perhaps, at this moment the principal inhabitants are playing monte. On the other corner stood a casa de paja (thatched house) from which the thatching had been blown away, and in which were the undisposed-of remains of an ox for sale. Along the sides were whitewashed huts, and on one corner a large, neat house; then a small edifice with a cross in the roof, marking it as a church; and, finally, an open casa publica, very aptly so called, as it had no doors.

Such are the edifices which have sprung up in the new village. Attached to each house was a muddy yard, where large black pigs were wallowing in the mire, the special objects of their owner's care, soon to become large black hogs, and to bring ten or twelve dollars a piece in the Campeachy market. But it was not for these we had come to Iturbide.

Within the plaza were memorials of older and better times, indications of a more ingenious people than the civilized whites by whom it is now occupied. At one end was a mound of ruins, which had once supported an ancient building; and in the centre was an ancient well. There could be no question about the antiquity of this well. The people all said that it was a work of the antiguos, and paid respect to it and valued it highly, for it had saved them the labour and expense of digging a new one for themselves. It was about a yard and a quarter wide at the mouth, and eight yards in depth, circular, and constructed of stones laid without plaster or cement of any kind. The

64. West façade of "tower building," Dzibilnocac (date unknown)

stones were all firmly in their places, and had a polish which, with creases made by ropes in the platform at the top, indicated the great length of time that water had been drawn from it.

Besides these memorials, from a street communicating with the plaza we saw a range of great mounds, the ruins of the ancient city of Zibilnocac. On the way to the ruins we passed another ancient well, of the same construction with that in the plaza, but filled up with rubbish, and useless. The Indians called it Stu-kum, the word meaning a calabash with the seeds dried up. A short walk brought us into an open country. The field was in many places clear of trees, and covered only with plantations of tobacco, and studding it all over were lofty ranges and mounds, enshrouded in woods, through which white masses of stone were glimmering, and rising in such quick succession, and so many at once, that Mr. Catherwood said, almost despondingly, that the labours of Uxmal were to begin again.

Among them was one long edifice, having at each end what seemed a tower. Our numerous escort took no interest in the ruins, could give us no information about them, nor even knew the paths that led to them. The building before us was more ruined than it seemed from a distance, but in some respects it differed from all the others we had seen. It required much clearing. When this was signified to our attendants, we found that among them all there was not a single machete. Finally, one man came along with his machete, and then others, until five were at work. They were occupied the greater part of the day, but to the last there were some trees, obstructing the view of particular parts, which I could not get cut down.

The next morning an Indian held an umbrella over Mr. Catherwood's head to protect him from the sun, and, while drawing, several times he was obliged by weakness to lie down and rest. I was disheartened by the spectacle and felt very much disposed to break up the expedition and go home, but Mr. Catherwood persisted.

This building differed in form from any we had seen, and had square structures rising in the centre and at each end. These were called towers. The façades of the towers were all ornamented with sculptured stone. Several of the apartments had tobacco leaves spread out in them to dry. In the centre, one apartment was encumbered with rubbish, cutting off the light from the door, but we saw on one of the stones the dim outline of a painting like that at Kewick. In the adjoining apartment were the remains of paintings like those near the village of Xul, reminding me of processions in Egyptian tombs. The colour of the flesh was red, as was always the case with the Egyptians in representing their own people. Unfortunately, they were too much mutilated to be drawn, and seemed surviving the general wreck only to show that these aboriginal builders had possessed more skill in the least enduring branch of the graphic art.

The first accounts we heard of these ruins date back to the time of my first visit to Nohpat. Among the Indians there was one who, while we were lunching, mentioned these ruins in exaggerated terms, particularly a row of painted soldiers. On pushing my inquiries, he said these figures carried muskets, and was so pertinacious on this point that I concluded he was either talking entirely at random, or of the remains of old Spanish structures. I noted the place in my memorandum book. Having had it for a long time upon our minds, none proved more unlike what we expected to find. We looked for remains distinguished for their beauty and high state of preservation. Instead we found an immense field, grand, imposing, and interesting from its vastness, but all so ruined that, with the exception of this one building, little of the detail could be discovered.

Back of this building was a tobacco patch, the only thriving thing we saw at Iturbide; and on the border another ancient well, now, as in ages past, furnishing water, and from which the Indian attending the tobacco patch gave us to drink. Beyond were towering mounds and vestiges, indicating the existence of a greater city than any we had yet encountered. In wandering among them Dr. Cabot and myself counted thirty-three, all of which had once held buildings aloft. The field was so open that they were all comparatively easy of access, but the mounds themselves were overgrown. I clambered up them till the work became tiresome and unprofitable. They were all, as the Indians said, puras piedras, pure stones; no buildings were left; all had fallen. Though happy it was our fortune to wander among these crumbling memorials of a once powerful and mysterious people, we almost mourned that our lot had not been cast a century sooner, when, as we believed, all these edifices were entire.

CHAPTER TWELVE

Maní

ollowing a broad wagon road made for the passage of the horse and cart, we came to a large aguada. Ever since our arrival in the country, we had been told that these aguadas were artificial, and, like the ruined cities we were visiting, the works of the ancient inhabitants. At first we had considered these accounts unreliable. But we were now in a region where the people were entirely dependant upon the aguadas. All considered them the works of the antiguos; and we obtained at length what we had long sought for, precise information which would not admit question or doubt.

In 1835, Señor Trego, a gentleman engaged in making sugar, turned his attention to this aguada. He took advantage of the dry season to make an examination. On clearing out the mud, he found an artificial bottom of large flat stones many layers deep. These were laid upon each other, and the interstices were filled in with clay of a different character than any in the neighborhood. Near the centre, he discovered four ancient wells. And he found upward of four hundred pits, holes into which the water filtered, and which, with the wells, were intended to furnish a supply when the aguada should be dry.

It so happened that the next year was one of unusual scarcity of water. That year, Señor Trego said, more than a thousand horses and mules came to this aguada with barrels on their backs, and carried away water. Families established themselves along the banks; small shops were opened. The aguada supplied them all. When this failed, the wells and the pits held out till the rainy season came on.

Usually, at this season, the aguada was dry, and the people were drawing from the wells and pits. This year, happily for them, but unluckily for us, water was still abundant. Still it was a thing of high interest to see this ancient reservoir recovered and restored to its original uses, and, as we rode along the bank, to have indicated to us the particular means and art used to render it available. Hundreds are perhaps now buried in the woods, which once furnished this element of life to the teeming population of Yucatan.

Leaving the aguada, our road lay over a level and wooded plain, then wet and muddy from the recent rains. In the afternoon we passed the campo santo of Macoba, and very soon, ascending a hill, we saw through the trees the "old walls" of the ancient inhabitants. It was one of the wildest places we had seen, and we were somewhat excited on approaching it, for we had heard that the old city was repeopled, and that Indians were again living in the buildings. It was almost evening. Smoke was issuing from the ruins, and, as seen through the trees, the very tops seemed alive with people. But as we approached we almost turned away with sorrow. It was like the wretched Arabs of the Nile swarming around the ruined temples of Thebes, a mournful contrast of present misery and past magnificence. The doors were stopped with leaves and branches; the sculptured ornaments on the façades were blackened by smoke rolling from the doorways. All around were the confusion and filthiness of Indian housekeeping.

Our appearance in this wilderness had created astonishment among the Indians. All day, whenever we drew near to the buildings, the women and children ran inside, and now, when they found us entering their habitations, they all ran out of doors. The old major domo, unused to such a commotion, followed us close, anxiously, but respectfully, without uttering a word. When we closed the book and told him we had finished, he raised both hands, and, with a relieved expression, exclaimed, "Gracias a Dios, la obra es acabada!" "Thank God, the work is done!"

We were again preparing to move, but, on the eve of setting out, we learned that Bernaldo wanted to vary the monotony of travelling

65. *Page 196:* Catherwood drawing of an aguada near Macobá

by getting married. He had met at the well an Indian girl of thirteen, he himself being sixteen. While assisting her to draw water, some tender passages had taken place between them, and he had disclosed to Albino his passion and his wishes. But he was trammelled by that impediment which all over the world keeps asunder those who are born for each other, viz., want of fortune. The girl made no objections on this score, nor did her father. On the contrary, the latter, being a prudent man, who looked to the future well-establishing of his daughter, considered Bernaldo, though not in the actual possession of fortune, a young man of good expectations, by reason of the wages that would be due to him from us. The great difficulty was to get ready money to pay the padre. Bernaldo was afraid to ask for it, and the matter was not communicated to us until at the moment of setting out. It was entirely against hacienda law to marry off the estate. Don Simon would not like it; and, in the hurry and confusion of setting out, we had no time to deliberate. We therefore sent him on before us.

Our road lay through the same great forest in which the ruins stood. At the distance of a league we descended from the high ground, and reached a small aguada. The road for some distance was hilly until we came out upon a great savanna covered with a growth of bushes, which rose above our heads, excluding every breath of air, without shielding us from the sun. At one o'clock we reached the suburbs of the rancho of Puut. The settlement was a long line of straggling huts. Mr. Catherwood stopped at one of them for a cup of water. Water, in the Maya language, is expressed by the word *ha*, but, being that morning rather out of practice, Mr. Catherwood had asked for *ka*, which means fire, and the woman brought him a lighted brand. He motioned that away, but still continued asking for *ka*, fire. The woman went in, sat down, and made him a straw cigar, which she brought out to him. Sitting in the broiling sun, and perishing with thirst, he dropped his Maya, and by signs made her understand what he wanted, when she brought him water.

Albino had not come up with us, and passing through one Indian rancho, we came to another, in which were many paths, and we were at a loss which to take. The men were all away, and we were obliged to chase the women into their very huts to ask directions. At the last hut we cornered two, who were weaving cotton, and came upon them with our great effort in the Maya language, "Tush y am bé—" "Is this the way to—." We had acquired great facility in asking this question, but if the answer went beyond "yes" or "no," or an indication with the hand, as was the case on this occasion, it was entirely beyond our attainments. The woman gave us a very long, and probably a very civil answer, but we could not understand a word of it. Finding it impossible to bring them to monosyllables, we asked for a draught of water and rode on.

At two o'clock we reached the foot of a stony sierra. From the top we saw the village of Becanchen, where, on arriving, we rode through the plaza, and up to a large house, the front of which was adorned with a large red painting of a major domo on horseback, leading a bull into the ring. We inquired for the casa real, and were directed to a miserable thatched house, where a gentleman stepped out and recognized Mr. Catherwood's horse, which had belonged to Don Simon Peon. Through the horse he recognised me, having seen me with Don Simon at the fair at Jalacho, on the strength of which he immediately offered his house for a posada, or inn.

We were still on the great burial-ground of ruined cities. In the corridor of the house were sculptured stones, which our host told us were taken from the ancient buildings in the neighbourhood. They had also furnished materials for the foundation of every house on the plaza; and besides these there were other memorials. In the plaza were eight wells, then furnishing an abundant supply of water, and bearing that stamp of the hand of the ancient builders. Below the plaza was water gushing from the rocks, filling a clear basin beneath, and running off till it was lost in the woods. It was the first time in our whole journey that we had seen anything like a running stream, and after the parched regions through which we had passed, of almost inaccessible caves, muddy aguadas, and little pools in the hollows of rocks, it was a refreshing and delightful spectacle.

The name of this village is derived from this stream of water, being compounded of the Maya words *Becan,* running, and *chen,* a well. Twenty years ago a solitary Indian came into it, and made a clearing for his milpa. In doing so he struck upon the running stream, followed it until he found the water gushing from the rock, and the whole surface now occupied by the plaza pierced with ancient wells. The Indians gathered round the wells, and a village grew up, which now contains six thousand inhabitants.

Having little or no intercourse with the capital, this village was the first which Doctor Cabot's fame had not reached, and our host took me aside to ask me in confidence whether Doctor Cabot was a real medico. He wanted the medico to visit a young Indian whose hand had been mangled by a sugar-mill. Doctor Cabot made some inquiries, the answers to which led to the conclusion that it would be necessary to cut off the hand. Unluckily, he had left his amputating instruments behind. He had a hand-saw for miscellaneous uses, which would serve in part, and Mr. Catherwood had a large spring-knife of admirable temper, which Doctor Cabot said would do, but the former flatly objected to its conversion into a surgical instrument. It had been purchased at Rome twenty years before, and in all his journeyings had been his travelling companion. After such an operation he would never be able to use it again. Strong arguments were urged on both sides, and it became tolerably manifest that, unless amputation was necessary to save the boy from dying, the doctor would not get the knife.

Reaching the house, we saw the Indian sitting in the sala, the hand torn off to within about an inch of the wrist, and the stump swollen into a great ball six inches in diameter, perfectly black, and literally alive with vermin. At the first glance I retreated into the yard, and thence into the kitchen, when a woman engaged in cooking ran out, leaving her vessels boiling over the fire. I superintended her cooking, and dried my damp clothes, determined to avoid having anything to do with the operation. Fortunately for me and Mr. Catherwood's knife, Doctor Cabot considered that it was not advisable to amputate. It was ten days since the accident happened, and the wound seemed to be healing.

At this place we determined to separate; Mr. Catherwood to go on direct to Peto, a day and a half's journey distant, to recruit, while Doctor Cabot and I made a circuitous movement to the village of Mani. While speaking of our intention, a by-stander told us of ruins on his hacienda of Zaccacal, eight leagues distant by a milpa road.

Early the next morning Doctor Cabot and I set out with Albino and a single Indian. At half past nine we reached a large aguada, the banks of which were so muddy that it was impossible to get down to it to drink. A league beyond we reached another, surrounded by fine shade trees, with a few ducks floating quietly upon its surface. As we rode up Dr. Cabot shot a trogan, one of the rare birds of that country, adorning by its brilliant plumage the branches of an overhanging tree. It was very hot. Suffering from thirst, we passed some Indians under the shade of a large seybo tree eating tortillas and chili, to whom we rode up, confident of procuring water. They either had none, or, as Albino supposed, hid it away as we approached. At one o'clock we came to another aguada, but the bank was so muddy that it was impossible to get to the water without miring our horses or ourselves, and we were obliged to turn away without relief from our distressing thirst. Beyond this, to our great satisfaction we reached the hacienda of Zaccacal.

Toward evening, escorted by the major domo and a vaquero, I set out for the ruins. The vaquero led the way on horseback, and we followed, dismounting at the top of a stone terrace. On this terrace was a circular hole like those at Uxmal, but much larger. Looking down into it till my eyes became accustomed to the darkness, I saw a large chamber with three recesses in different parts of the wall, which the major domo said were doors opening to passages that went under ground to an extent entirely unknown. I descended, and found the chamber of an oblong form. The doors, as the major domo called them, were merely recesses about two feet deep. Touching one of them with my feet, I told him that the end of his passage was there, but he said it was closed up, and persisted in asserting that it led to an indefinite extent. It was difficult to say what these recesses were intended for. They threw a mystery around the character of these subterranean chambers, and unsettled the idea of their being all intended for wells.

Beyond this, on a higher terrace, were two buildings, one of which was in a good state of preservation, and the exterior was ornamented all around with pillars set in the wall, somewhat different from those in the façades of other buildings, and more fanciful. The interior consisted of but a single apartment. The ceiling was high, and in the layer of flat stones along the centre of the arch was a single stone, like that seen for the first time at Kewick, ornamented with painting.

This building stood in front of another more overgrown and ruined, which had been an imposing and important edifice. The plan was complicated, and the exterior of one part was rounded, but the rounded part was a solid mass, and within the wall was straight. In the back wall was a recess, once occupied, perhaps, by a statue. Altogether, there was much about this edifice that was new and curious; and there were other cerros, or mounds, of undistinguishable ruins.

We had accomplished a journey which we were assured was impracticable. Now we were coming upon the finest portion of the state, famed for its rich sugar plantations. We met heavy, lumbering vehicles drawn by oxen and horses, carrying sugar from the haciendas. Very soon we reached Tekax, one of the four places in Yucatan bearing the name of a city, and I must confess that I felt some degree of excitement. Throughout Yucatan our journey had been so quiet, so free from danger or interruption of any kind, that, after my Central American experience, it seemed unnatural. Yucatan was in a state of open rebellion against Mexico; we had heard of negotiations, but there had been no tumult, confusion, or bloodshed. Tekax alone had broken the general stillness, and while the rest of the country was perfectly quiet, this interior city had got up a small revolution.

According to reports, this revolution was got up by three individuals who belonged to the party in favour of declaring independence of Mexico. The elections had gone against their party, and alcaldes in favour of a reannexation to Mexico were installed in office. In the mean time commissioners arrived from Santa Ana to negotiate with the government of Yucatan, urging it not to make any open declaration, but to continue quietly in its state of independence de facto until the internal difficulties of Mexico were settled, when its complaints would be attended to and its grievances redressed. Afraid of the influence which these commissioners might exercise, the three patriots of Tekax resolved to strike for liberty, went round among the ranchos of the sierra, and collected a band of more than half-naked Indians, who, armed with machetes, a few old muskets, and those primitive weapons with which David slew Goliath, descended upon Tekax, and, to the great alarm of the women and children, took possession of the plaza, set up the figure of Santa Ana, pelted him with stones, put some bullets into him, burned him to ashes, and shouted "Viva la independencia." Few of them had ever heard of Santa Ana, but this was no reason why they should not pelt him with stones and burn him in effigy. They knew nothing of the relations between Yucatan and Mexico, and by the cry of independencia they meant a release from tribute to the government and debts to masters. With but little practice in revolutions, they threw out the formidable threat that they would march three hundred men against the capital, and compel a declaration of independence.

Intelligence of these movements soon reached Merida, and fearful menaces of war were bandied from one city to the other. Each waited for the other to make the first demonstration. At length the capital sent forth its army, which reached Ticul while Doctor Cabot was still there. It was then within one day's march of the seat of rebellion, but halted to rest, and to let the moral effect of its approach go on before. In three days the regular army resumed its march, with cannon in front, colours flying, drums beating, and the women of Ticul laughing, sure that there would be no bloodshed. The same day it reached Tekax, and the next morning, instead of falling upon each other like so many wild beasts, the officers and the three patriot leaders were seen walking arm in arm together in the plaza. The former promised good offices to their new friends, two reales apiece to the Indians, and the revolution was crushed.

Such were the accounts we had received, always coupled with sweeping denunciations of the population of Tekax as revolutionary and radical, and the rabble of Yucatan. Having somewhat of a leaning to revolutions in the abstract, I was happy to find that, with such a bad reputation, its appearance was finer, and more promising than that of any town I had seen, and I could not but think it would be well for Yucatan if many of her dead-and-alive villages had more such rabble.

It was unprecedented for strangers to pass through this place. European saddles, holsters, and arms were strange, and, including Albino, we made up the cabalistic number of three which got up the late revolution. Knowing the curiosity we excited, without dismounting or exchanging a word with an inhabitant, we passed through the plaza and continued on our journey.

Our road lay for some distance along the sierra. It was broad, open, and the sun beat fiercely upon us. At half past ten we reached Akil, and rode up to the casa real. In the steps and foundation were sculptured stones from ruined mounds in the immediate neighbourhood. The road along the yard of the church ran through a mound, leaving part on each side, and the excavated mass forming on one side the wall of the convent yard. The rest of the wall, the church, and the convent were built with stones from the ancient buildings.

At half past five we reached Mani, again finding over the door and along the sides of the casa real sculptured stones, some of them of new and curious designs. In one compartment was a seated figure, with what might seem a crown and sceptre, and the figures of the sun and moon on either side of his head, curious and interesting in themselves, independent of the admonition that we were again on the site of an aboriginal city. Day after day we rode into places unknown beyond the boundaries of Yucatan, with no history attached to them. Mani, however, rises above the rest, and, compared with the profound obscurity in which other places are enveloped, its history is plainly written.

When the haughty caciques of Maya rebelled against the supreme lord, and destroyed the city of Mayapan, the reigning monarch was left with only the territory of Mani. Here, reduced in power to the level of the other caciques, the race of the ancient lords of Maya ruled undisturbed until the time of the Spanish invasion. The shadow of the throne rested over it; and long after the conquest it bore the proud name of la Corona real de Mani.

I had heard of this place on my first visit to Uxmal, of relics and heirlooms in the hands of the cacique, and of ruins, which we were advised were not worth visiting. The morning did not open with much promise. On first emerging we found about the door of the casa real a crowd of loungers. Some of them were intoxicated, and there were many impudent boys watching every movement and turning aside to laugh when they could do so unobserved.

We set out to look at the ruins, and the crowd followed at our heels. At the end of a street leading to the well we saw a long building, pierced in the middle by the street. We saw at a glance that it was not the work of the antiguos, but had been erected by the Spaniards since the conquest, and yet we were conducted to it as one of the same class with those we had found all over the country. Its true history is perhaps as much unknown as that of the more ancient buildings. In its tottering front were interspersed sculptured stones taken from the aboriginal edifices, and thus, in its own decay, it publishes the sad story that it had risen upon the ruins of another race.

At the rear of the casa real were the remains of large mounds. In the wall round the square of the church was a large circular upright stone. Our guide told us that in the suburbs there were other mounds; but, without leaving the streets, we saw enough to satisfy us that Mani stood on the site of an ancient town of the same general character with all the others.

Returning to the casa real, Albino inquired of the ancient relics, and the Indians brought a copy of Cogolludo, wrapped with great care. While we were looking at it they brought out and unrolled on the floor an old painting on cotton cloth. The design was a coat of arms bordered with the heads of [a group of] murdered ambassadors, [sent by] of the cacique of Mani to solicit other chiefs to render obedience to the Spaniards. In the centre is a tree growing out of a box, representing the sapote tree at Zotuta, under which the murder was committed, and which, the Indians say, is still standing. The painting had evidently been executed by an Indian, and probably very near the time of the occurrence which it was intended to commemorate. It is an object of great reverence among the Indians of Mani. In fact, throughout our whole journeyings, either in Central America or Yucatan, it was the first and only instance in which we met with any me-

morial in the hands of the Indians, tending to keep alive the memory
of any event in their history. But this must not be imputed to them as
a reproach. History shows clearly enough that this now abject and degraded race did cling with desperate and fatal tenacity to the memory
of those ancestors whom they know not now. The records of their
conquerors show the ruthless and savage policy pursued by the Spaniards to root this memory from their minds. Here, in this very town,
we have a dark and memorable instance.

In 1571, twenty-nine years after the foundation of Merida, some
Indians of Mani relapsed and became idolaters, practising in secret
their ancient rites. Intelligence of their backsliding reached the ears of
the provincial in Merida, who came to Mani in person, and forthwith established himself as inquisitor. Some who had died obstinately
in the secret practice of idolatrous rites had been buried in sacred
ground. He ordered their bodies to be dug up, and their bones
thrown into the fields. In order to strike terror into the minds of the
Indians, and root out the memory of their ancient rites, on a day appointed for that purpose, attended by the principal of the Spanish nobility, and in the presence of a great multitude of Indians, he made
them bring together all their books and ancient characters, and
publicly burned them, thus destroying at once the history of their
antiquities.

The sight of this painting made me more earnest in pushing my
inquiries for other memorials, but this was all; the Indians had no
more to show. I then inquired of the alcalde for ancient archives. He
knew nothing about them, but said we could examine for ourselves.
We procured the keys, and returned to the casa real. When we un-
locked the door we had thirty or forty persons to enter with us.

Among the books and archives of the municipality was one large
volume which had an ancient and venerable appearance, being bound
in parchment, tattered, and worm-eaten, and having a flap to close
like that of a pocket-book. Unhappily, it was written in the Maya language, and perfectly unintelligible. The dates, however, showed that
these venerable pages were a record of events which had taken place
within a very few years after the entry of the Spaniards into the country. As I pored over them, I was strongly impressed with the belief
that they contained matter which might throw some light upon the
subject of my investigations.

Being Sunday, a crowd of curious and lazy lookers-on surrounded the table, but they could not distract my attention. Though
all could speak the Maya, none could read it. Nevertheless, I contin-

ued to turn over the pages. On the 157th page, in a document which bore the date of 1557, I saw the word *Vxmal*. Here I stopped, and called upon the by-standers. The schoolmaster was the only one who could even attempt to give me any assistance, but he was not familiar with the Maya as a written tongue, and said that this, having been written nearly three hundred years before, differed somewhat from that of the present day, and was more difficult to comprehend. Other places were referred to in the document, the names of which were familiar to me, and I observed that the words immediately preceding Vxmal were different from those preceding the other names. The presumption was that Uxmal was referred to in some different sense.

In turning to the end of the document I found a loose sheet of foolscap paper; and upon it was a curious map, also dated in 1557, of which Mani was the centre. Vxmal was laid down upon it, and indicated by a peculiar sign, different from that of all the other places named. On the back of the map was endorsed a long instrument of the same date, in which the word *Vxmal* again occurred, and which, beyond doubt, contained matter relating to other places named in the map. With the assistance of the schoolmaster I compared this with the one written in the book, and ascertained that the latter was a recorded copy of the other.

A few pages beyond was another document, bearing date in 1556, and in this, again, the word Vxmal appeared. The alcalde sent for an Indian clerk of the municipality. But he was not in the village, and an old Indian was brought who had formerly served in that capacity. After staring stupidly at the pages, he said he had grown so old that he had forgotten how to read. My only course was to have copies made, which the schoolmaster set about immediately, and late in the afternoon he placed them in my hands. In the evening, by the permission of the alcalde, I took the book to my quarters, and looked over every page, running my finger along every line, in search of the word Uxmal. But I did not meet with it in any other place, and probably the documents referred to are the most ancient, if not the only ones in existence of ancient date, in which that name is mentioned.

The copies I carried with me to my friend Don Pio Perez, who discovered some errors. At his instance, my good friend the cura Carillo went over to Mani, and made exact copies of the map and documents. He also made diligent search through the Maya archives for other papers mentioning Uxmal, or referring to it in any way, but found none.

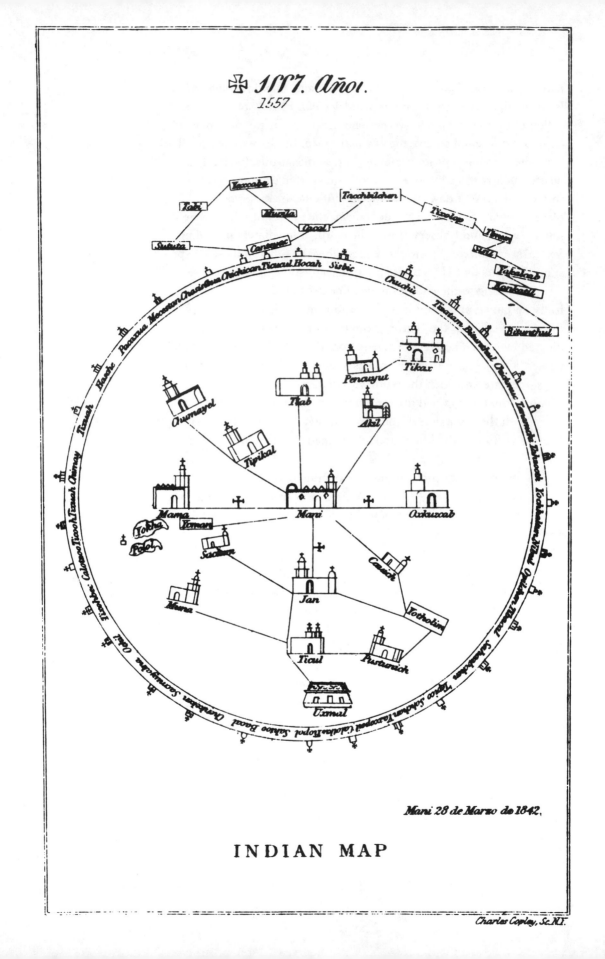

INDIAN MAP

Now what was Uxmal? I am safe in supposing that it was not a mere hacienda, for at that early period of the conquest haciendas had not begun to be established. The title papers of Don Simon Peon show that the first grant of it was made for the purposes of a hacienda one hundred and forty-five years afterward, at which time the land was waste and belonged to the crown, and had small settlements of Indians upon it, who were publicly and notoriously worshipping the devil in the ancient buildings. It was not, then, a hacienda. Was it a Spanish town? There is no indication, record, or tradition that a Spanish town was ever established at Uxmal. The general belief is that there never was any. Don Simon is sure of it, and in that confidence I fully participate. But as the strongest proof on this point, I call in this ancient map. It is a fact perhaps more clearly established than any other in the history of the conquest, that in every Indian village in which the Spaniards made a settlement, with that strong religious enthusiasm which formed so remarkable a feature in their daring and unscrupulous character, their first act was the erection of a church. Now it will be remarked that nearly all the places laid down on the map are indicated by the sign of a church. Most of them now exist, all have aboriginal names, and the inference is that they were at that time existing aboriginal towns, in which the Spaniards had erected churches. Several of these places we had visited. We had seen churches reared upon the ruins of ancient buildings, and in their immediate vicinity vestiges and extensive ruins of the same general character with those at Uxmal.

But Uxmal is not indicated by the sign of a church. This I consider evidence that no church was erected there, and that while the Spaniards were establishing settlements in other Indian towns, for some unknown reason, perhaps on account of its unhealthiness, at Uxmal they made none. But it will be seen farther, that Uxmal not only is not indicated by the sign of a church, but is indicated by one entirely different, of a peculiar and striking character. In my opinion, this sign was intended to represent what would most clearly distinguish a large place without a church from those in which churches had been erected. The conclusion is irresistible that at the time when the Judge Don Felipe Manriques arrived *at* Uxmal, it was an existing inhabited aboriginal town. In each reference to his arrival at Uxmal, it is mentioned that he was accompanied by his interpreter. He would not need an interpreter if the place was desolate, or if it was a hacienda, or a Spanish town. He could need an interpreter only when the place was occupied by the aborigines, whose language he did not un-

66. *Opposite:* Catherwood drawing of a 1557 map of the region that Stephens discovered in Maní

derstand, and such, I cannot help believing, was actually the case. I can easily believe, too, that its depopulation and desolation within the hundred and forty years preceding the royal grant for the purposes of a hacienda, were the inevitable consequence of the policy pursued by the Spaniards in their subjugation of the country.

Monday, March 7. Before daylight we left Mani. We stopped that night at Tixmeach. The next morning at half past nine we reached Peto, where we found Mr. Catherwood and our luggage on the hands of our friend Don Pio Perez. At Peto we [also] found letters and packets of newspapers from home, forwarded to us from Merida, and, except attending to them, our time was devoted almost exclusively to long and interesting conversations with Don Pio on matters connected with the antiquities of the country. I cannot sufficiently express my obligations to this gentleman for the warm interest he took in facilitating our pursuits. Besides preparing a series of verbal forms and other illustrations of the grammar of the Maya language, he gave me a vocabulary in manuscript, containing more than four thousand Maya words, and an almanac, prepared by himself, according to the Indian system of computation, for the year from the 16th of July, 1841, to the 15th of July, 1842.

Besides these, he furnished me with the copy of one other document, which, if genuine and authentic, throws more light upon aboriginal history than any other known to be in existence. It is a fragment of a Maya manuscript, written from memory by an Indian, at some time not designated, and entitled "Principal epochs of the ancient history of Yucatan." It purports to give the series of "katunes," or epochs, from the time of the departure of the Toltecs from the country of Tulapan until their arrival at this, as it is called, island of Chacno-uitan, occupying, according to Don Pio's computation of katunes, the lapse of time corresponding with that between the years 144 and 217 of the Christian era.

It assigns dates to the discovery of Bacalar and then of Chichen Itza, both within the three epochs corresponding with the time between A.D. 360 and A.D. 432; the colonization of Champoton, and its destruction; the times of wandering through the uninhabited forests, and establishing themselves a second time at Chichen Itza, within epochs corresponding with the lapse between A.D. 888 and A.D. 936. [It assigns] the epoch of the colonization of Uxmal, corresponding with the years between A.D. 936 and A.D. 1176; the epochs of wars between the governors of Chichen Itza and Mayapan; the destruction of the latter city by the Uitzes of the Sierras; and the arrival of the Spaniards, adding that "Holy men from the East came with them." The manuscript terminates with the epoch of the first baptism and the arrival of the first bishop.

How far it is to be regarded as authentic I am not able to say, but [it is] the only known manuscript in existence that purports to be written by an Indian in his native language, giving an account of the events in the ancient history of this country. It may conflict in some particulars with opinions expressed by me, but I consider the discovery of the truth as far more important than the confirmation of any theory of my own. I may add that, in general, it bears out and sustains the views presented in these pages.

CHAPTER THIRTEEN

Chichén Itzá

ver since we left home we had had our eyes upon Chichen. We had become eager to reach it, and the increasing bulk of these volumes warns me that I must not now linger on the road. The first night we stopped at the village of Taihxiu, the second at Yaxcaba, and at noon of the third day we reached Pisté, about two miles distant from Chichen. We had heard some unpropitious accounts concerning the hospitality of the proprietor of the hacienda, and thought it safer not to alarm him by going upon him with appetites sharpened by a hard day's ride, but first to lay the village under a moderate contribution.

At four o'clock we left Pisté, and very soon we saw rising high above the plain the Castillo of Chichen. In half an hour we were among the ruins of this ancient city, with all the great buildings in full view, casting prodigious shadows over the plain, and presenting a spectacle which, even after all that we had seen, once more excited in us emotions of wonder. The camino real ran through the midst of them, and the field was so open that, without dismounting, we rode close in to some of the principal edifices. Night was approaching, and, fairly dragging ourselves away, we rode on, and in a few minutes reached the hacienda. Vaqueros were shouting, and a large drove of cattle was pouring in at the gate. We were about following, but a crowd of men and women on the steps of the hacienda shouted to us not to come in, and a man ran toward us, throwing up both hands, and shut the gate directly in our faces. This ominous demonstration did not mean anything churlish; on the contrary, all was done out of kindness. We had been expected for three months. The major domo conducted us to a house directly opposite the gate of the hacienda. The next morning, under the guidance of an Indian of the hacienda, we prepared for a preliminary survey.

The ruins of Chichen are nine leagues from Valladolid, the camino real to which passes directly through the field. The great buildings tower on both sides of the road in full sight of all passers-by, and from the fact that the road is much travelled, the ruins of Chichen are perhaps more generally known to the people of the country than any other in Yucatan.

Immediately on our arrival at Chichen we heard of a countryman, Mr. John Burke. In 1838 Mr. Burke came from Valladolid to

67. *Page 212:* North elevation of La Iglesia, Chichén Itzá (1934)

68. Reconstruction of Chichén Itzá, from the north

the village of Cawa, six leagues distant from Chichen. One of the young men told him of old buildings on this hacienda, from one of which Valladolid was visible. Mr. Burke rode over, and on the fourth of July stood on the top of the Castillo, spyglass in hand, looking out for Valladolid. Two years afterward, they were visited by the Baron Frederichstahl, and by him first brought to the notice of the public, both in Europe and this country. This visit was made in the prosecution of a route recommended to him by me after my return from my former interrupted journey of exploration among the ruins of Yucatan.

The whole circumference occupied by the buildings is about two miles, the diameter two thirds of a mile, though ruined buildings appear beyond these limits. We went first to the principal buildings on the opposite side of the camino real. The path led through the cattle-yard of the hacienda, from which we passed out at one end by a range of bars into the field of ruins. The buildings were large, and some were in good preservation. In general, the façades were not so elaborately ornamented as some we had seen, seemed of an older date, and the sculpture was ruder, but the interior apartments contained decorations and devices that were new to us, and powerfully interesting. All the principal buildings were within a comparatively small compass. In fact, they were in such proximity that by one o'clock we had visited every building, examined every apartment, and arranged the whole plan and order of work.

The name of Chichen is another instance showing the importance attached in that dry country to the possession of water. It is compounded of the two Maya words *chi,* mouth, and *chen,* well. Among the ruins are two great senotes, which, beyond doubt, furnished water to the inhabitants of the ancient city. Since the establishment of a hacienda and the construction of a well, these had fallen into disuse. Doctor Cabot had undertaken to open a path in one of them down to the water, for the purpose of bathing, which, in that hot climate, was as refreshing as food. We came upon him just as he had finished, and, besides his Indian workmen, he had the company of a large party of Mestizo boys from the village of Pisté, who were already taking advantage of his labours, and were then swimming, diving, and perched all about in the hollows of the rocks.

On our journey from Peto, we had entered a region where the sources of the supply of water again formed a new and distinctive feature in the face of the country. These, too, are called senotes, but they differ from those before presented, being immense circular holes with broken, rocky, perpendicular sides from fifty to one hundred feet

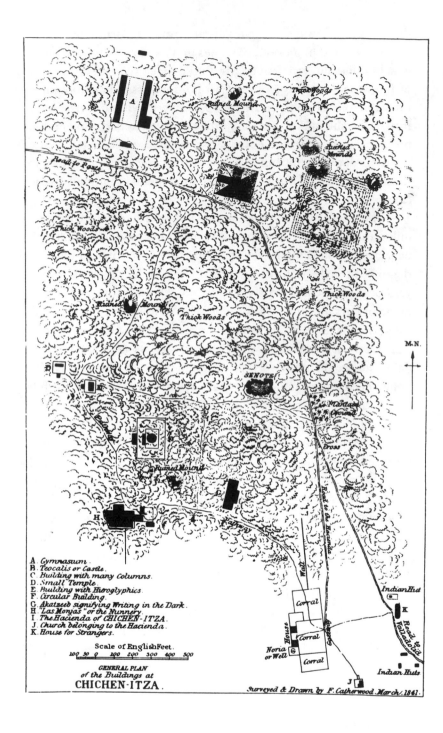

69. Catherwood map of
Chichén Itzá

deep, and having at the bottom a great body of water, of an unknown depth, always about the same level, supposed to be supplied
by subterranean rivers.

This senote was oblong, about three hundred and fifty feet in
length. The sides were perpendicular, except in one place, which was
broken so as to form a steep, winding descent to the water. The path
is to a certain extent artificial, as we saw in one place the vestiges of
a stone wall along the brink. Every day, when the sun was vertical
and scarcely endurable on the surface of the earth, we bathed in this
deep senote.

There was another circumstance which, though painful in itself,
added materially to the spirit with which we commenced our labours
at Chichen. Under the anticipation of a failure of the next crop, corn
had risen from two reales to a dollar the load. The distress occa-
sioned in this country by the failure of the corn crop cannot well be
imagined. In 1836 this calamity occurred. Along the coast a supply
was furnished from the United States, but it would not bear the expense of transportation into the interior. In this region corn rose to
four dollars a load, which put the staff of life completely beyond the
reach of the Indians. Famine ensued, and the poor Indians died of
starvation. At the time of our arrival, the servants of the hacienda
had consumed their small stock, and, with no hope from their milpas, with the permission of the master were about moving away to regions where the pressure would be less severe. Our arrival arrested
this movement. The poor Indians crowded round the door of our hut,
begging employment, and scrambling for the reales which Albino distributed among them. But all the relief we could afford them was of
short duration, and it may not be amiss to mention that Yucatan is
now groaning under famine superadded to the horrors of war.

Following the path from our door through the cattle-yard of the hacienda, the reader will reach [a] building [that] faces the east. It does
not stand on an artificial terrace, but the earth seems to have been excavated for some distance before it, so as to give it elevation of position. The exterior is without ornament of any kind. A grand staircase, now entirely in ruins, rises in the centre to the roof of the
building. On each side of the staircase are two doorways; at each end
is a single doorway, and the front facing the west has seven. The
whole number of apartments is eighteen. The west front opens upon
a large hollow surface, whether natural or artificial it is not easy to
say. In the centre of this is one of those features before referred to, a
solid mass of masonry, standing out from the wall, high as the roof,

and corresponding, in position and dimensions, with the ruined staircase on the eastern front. This projection is not necessary for the support of the building; it is not an ornament, but a deformity. Whether it be really a solid mass, or contain interior chambers, remains to be ascertained by the future explorer.

At the south end the doorway opens into a chamber, round which hangs a greater and more impenetrable mystery. The lintel of this doorway is of stone, and on the soffite, or under part, is sculptured. This tablet, and the position in which it exists, have given the name to the building, which the Indians call Akatzeeb, signifying the writing in the dark; for, as no light enters except from the single doorway, the chamber was so dark that the drawing could with difficulty be copied. It was the first time in Yucatan that we had found hieroglyphics sculptured on stone, which, beyond all question, bore the same type with those at Copan and Palenque. The sitting figure seems performing some act of incantation, or some religious or idolatrous rite, which the "writing in the dark" undoubtedly explains, if one could but read it.

Leaving this building, and following the path indicated in the map, we reach a modern stone fence, dividing the cattle-field of the hacienda, on the other side of which appears through the trees, between two other buildings, the end façade of a long, majestic pile, called the Monjas, or Nuns. Over the doorway are twenty small cartouches of hieroglyphics in four rows, five in a row. Over these stand out in a line six bold projecting curved ornaments, like that presented from the House of the Governor at Uxmal, resembling an elephant's trunk, and the upper centre space over the doorway is an irregular circular niche, in which portions of a seated figure, with a head-dress of feathers, still remain. The rest of the ornaments are of that distinctive stamp, characteristic of the ancient American cities.

The front of the same building is composed of two structures entirely different from each other, one of which forms a sort of wing to the principal edifice. This has two doorways opening into chambers, behind each of which is another, now filled up several feet with mortar and stones, and appearing to have been originally filled up solid to the ceiling, making again casas cerradas. The great structure to which the wing adjoins is apparently a solid mass of masonry, erected only to hold up the two ranges of buildings upon it. A grand staircase fifty-six feet wide, the largest we saw in the country, rises to the top. On one side of the staircase a huge breach has been made by the proprietor, for the purpose of getting out building stone, which discloses

70. *Opposite:* Main façade of Las Monjas, Chichén Itzá (Charnay, 1860)

only solid masonry. On the top of the structure stands a range of buildings, with a platform extending all round.

From the back of this platform the grand staircase rises again. The third range is, unfortunately, in a ruinous condition. It is to be observed that in this, as in all the other cases, these ancient architects never placed an upper building on the roof of a lower one, but always back, so as to rest on a structure solid from the ground, the roof of the lower range being merely a platform in front of the upper one.

This building seems to have been constructed only with reference to the second range of apartments, upon which the art and skill of the builders have been lavishly expended. The broad platform around it, though overgrown with grass several feet high, formed a noble promenade, commanding a magnificent view of the whole surrounding country.

219   *Las Monjas*

On the side of the staircase are five doorways, of which the three centre ones are what are usually called false doors, appearing to be merely recesses in the wall. The compartments between the doorways contained combinations of ornaments of unusual taste and elegance, both in arrangement and design. The two extreme doorways open into chambers, in each of which are three long recesses in the back wall, extending from the floor to the ceiling, all of which, from the remains still visible, were once ornamented with paintings. At each end of the building was another chamber, with three niches, and on the other side, facing the south, the three centre doorways, corresponding with the false doors on the north side, opened into an apartment having nine long niches in the back wall. All the walls from the floor to the peak of the arch had been covered with painted designs, now wantonly defaced, but the remains of which present colours in some places still bright and vivid. Among these remains detached portions of human figures continually recur, well drawn, the heads adorned with plumes of feathers, and the hands bearing shields and spears.

Descending again to the ground, at the end of the wing stands what is called the Eglesia, or Church, its comparatively great height adding very much to the effect of its appearance. It has three cornices, and the spaces between are richly ornamented. The sculpture is rude but grand. The principal ornament is over the doorway, and on each side are two human figures in a sitting posture, but, unfortunately, much mutilated. The portion of the façade above the second cornice is merely an ornamented wall, like those before mentioned at Zayi and Labná [see Figs. 67 and 71].

This building is in a good state of preservation. The interior consists of a single apartment, once covered with plaster, and along the top of the wall under the arch are seen the traces of a line of medallions or cartouches in plaster, which once contained hieroglyphics. The Indians have no superstitious feelings about these ruins, except in regard to this building; they say that on Good Friday of every year music is heard sounding. But this illusion was destined to be broken. In this chamber we opened our Daguerreotype apparatus, and on Good Friday were at work all day, but heard no music.

Passing on northward from the Monjas, we reach the edifice conspicuous among the ruins of Chichen, and unlike any other we had seen, except one at Mayapan much ruined. It is circular in form, and is known by the name of the Caracol, or winding staircase, on account of its interior arrangements. It stands on the upper of two terraces. A grand staircase containing twenty steps rises to the platform of this terrace. On each side of this staircase, forming a sort of balus-

221 *La Iglesia*

71. Catherwood drawing
of La Iglesia, Chichén Itzá

trade, were the entwined bodies of two gigantic serpents, three feet wide, portions of which are still in place. Among the ruins of the staircase we saw a gigantic head, which had terminated at one side the foot of the steps.

The platform of the second terrace is reached by another staircase. In the centre of the steps, and against the wall of the terrace, are the remains of a pedestal, on which probably once stood an idol. On the platform stands the building. It has four small doorways facing the cardinal points. A great portion of the upper part and one of the sides have fallen. Above the cornice the roof sloped so as almost to form an apex. When entire, even among the great buildings around, this structure must have presented a striking appearance. The doorways give entrance to a circular corridor. The inner wall has also four doorways, smaller than the others, and standing at intermediate points of the compass, facing northeast, northwest, southwest, and southeast. These doors give entrance to a second circular corridor, four feet wide; and in the centre is a circular mass, apparently of solid stone. In one place was a small square opening choked up with stones, which I endeavoured to clear out; but the stones falling into the narrow corridor made it dangerous to continue. The roof was so tottering that I could not discover to what this opening led. It was about large enough to admit the figure of a man in a standing position, to look out from the top. The walls of both corridors were plastered and ornamented with paintings, and both were covered with the triangular arch. The plan of the building was new, but, instead of unfolding secrets, it drew closer the curtain that already shrouded, with almost impenetrable folds, these mysterious structures.

72. Catherwood drawing of the Caracol, Chichén Itzá

Northwest from the Caracol stands [a] building called by the Indians Chichanchob, meaning Red House. The terrace is still in good preservation, and as we approached it on our first visit, a cow was coming quietly down the steps.

The building is still strong and substantial. Above the cornice it was richly ornamented, but the ornaments are now much decayed. It has three doorways, which open into a corridor running the whole width of the building. Along the top of the back wall was a stone tablet, with a row of hieroglyphics extending all along the wall. Many of them were defaced, and, from their height, in an awkward position to copy; but we had a scaffold erected, and obtained copies of the whole. The building has a back corridor, consisting of three chambers, all of which retain the marks of painting. From the convenience of its arrangements, with the platform of the terrace for a promenade, and the view of a fine open country in front, we should have been tempted to take up our abode in it.

All these buildings are within three hundred yards of the staircase of the Monjas; from any intermediate point all are in full sight. The field is open, and intersected by cattle-paths. The buildings, staircases, and terraces were overgrown, but Indians being at hand in sufficient force, they were easily cleared, and the whole was finished with a despatch that had never before attended our progress.

These are the only buildings on the west side of the camino real which are still standing. Great vestiges exist of mounds with remains of buildings upon them, and colossal stones and fragments of sculpture at their feet, which it would be impossible to present in detail.

Passing among these vestiges, we come out upon the camino

223   *Caracol and Red House*

73. Reconstruction of the Red House and the Caracol, Chichén Itzá

real, and, crossing it, again enter an open field, containing the extraordinary edifice which, on first reaching the field of ruins, we rode in on horseback to examine. It consists of two immense parallel walls. One hundred feet from the northern extremity, facing the open space between the walls, stands on an elevation a building containing a single chamber, with the front fallen, and, rising among the rubbish, the remains of two columns, elaborately ornamented with sculpture; the whole interior wall being exposed to view, covered from the floor to the peak of the arch with sculptured figures in bas-relief, much worn and faded. At the other end, setting back, is another building, also ruined, but exhibiting the remains of two columns richly ornamented with sculptured figures in bas-relief.

In the centre of the great stone walls, exactly opposite each other, and at the height of twenty feet from the ground, are two massive stone rings, four feet in diameter. On the rim and border were two sculptured entwined serpents. These walls, at the first glance, we considered identical in their uses and purposes with the parallel structures supporting the rings at Uxmal, of which I have already expressed the opinion that they were intended for the celebration of some public games. I have in all cases adopted the names of buildings which I found assigned to them on the spot, where any existed, and where there were none I have not attempted to give any. At Chichen all the principal buildings have names. This is called an Eglesia, or Church, of the antiguos, which was begun, but not finished, and the great open walls present not a bad idea of one of their gigantic churches before the roof is put on. But as we have already one Eglesia, and there is historical authority which shows clearly the object and uses of this extraordinary structure, I shall call it the Gymnasium or Tennis-court.

In the account of the diversions of Montezuma, by Herrera, we have the following:

"The King took much Delight in seeing Sport at Ball, which the Spaniards have since prohibited, because of the Mischief that often hapned at it; and was by them call'd *Tlachtli,* being like our Tennis. The Ball was made of the Gum of a Tree that grows in hot Countries, which, having Holes made in it, distils great white Drops, that soon harden, and, being work'd and moulded together, turn as black as Pitch. The Balls made thereof, tho' hard and heavy to the Hand, did bound and fly as well as our Foot-balls, there being no need to blow them; nor did they use Chaces, but vy'd to drive the adverse Party that is to hit the Wall, the others were to make good, or strike it over.

They struck it with any Part of their Body, as it hapned, or they could
most conveniently; and sometimes he lost that touched it with any
other Part but his Hip, which was look'd upon among them as the
greatest Dexterity; and to this Effect, that the Ball might rebound the
better, they fastened a Piece of stiff Leather on their Hips. They
might strike it every time it rebounded, which it would do several
Times one after another, in so much that it look'd as if it had been
alive. They play'd in Parties, so many on a Side, for a Load of
Mantles, or what the Gamesters could afford, at so many Scores.
They also play'd for Gold, and Feather-work, and sometimes play'd
themselves away, as has been said before. The Place where they play'd
was a ground Room, long, narrow, and high, but wider above than
below, and higher on the Sides than at the Ends, and they kept it very
well plaster'd and smooth, both the Walls and the Floor. *On the side
Walls they fix'd certain Stones, like those of a Mill, with a Hole quite
through the Middle,* just as big as the Ball, and he that could strike it
through there won the Game; and in Token of its being an extraordinary Success, which rarely hapned, he had a Right to the Cloaks of
all the Lookers-on, by antient Custom, and Law amongst Gamesters;
and it was very pleasant to see, that as soon as ever the Ball was in
the Hole, the Standers-by took to their Heels, running away with all
their Might to save their Cloaks, laughing and rejoicing, others

74. Ball court, Chichén
Itzá (date unknown)

scouring after them to secure their Cloaks for the Winner, who was oblig'd to offer some Sacrifice to the Idol of the Tennis-court, and the Stone through whose Hole the Ball had pass'd. Every Tennis-court was a Temple, having two Idols, the one of Gaming, and the other of the Ball. On a lucky Day, at Midnight, they perform'd certain Ceremonies and Enchantments on the two lower Walls and on the Midst of the Floor, singing certain Songs, or Ballads; after which a Priest of the great Temple went with some of their Religious Men to bless it; he uttered some Words, threw the Ball about the Tennis-court four Times, and then it was consecrated, and might be play'd in, but not before. The Owner of the Tennis-court, who was always a Lord, never play'd without making some Offering and performing certain Ceremonies to the Idol of Gaming, which shows how superstitious they were, since they had such Regard to their Idols, even in their Diversions. Montezuma carry'd the Spaniards to this Sport, and was well pleas'd to see them play at it, as also at Cards and Dice."

The general features are so identical as to leave no doubt that this structure was erected for precisely the same object as the Tennis-court in the city of Mexico. The temples are at hand in which sacrifices were offered, and we discover in this something more important than the mere determining of the character of a building. In the similarity of diversions we see a resemblance in manners and institutions, and trace an affinity between the people who erected the ruined cities of Yucatan and those who inhabited Mexico at the time of the conquest. In the account of Herrera, moreover, we see incidentally the drawing of a funeral pall over the institutions of the natives. We learn that the sport which "Montezuma took much delight in seeing," and which was a favourite diversion of the people, "the Spaniards have since prohibited."

At the southern extremity of the eastern wall stands [a] building consisting of two ranges, one even with the ground, and the other above it, being in a good state of preservation, and having conspicuous a procession of tigers or lynxes. From its lofty position, with trees growing around it and on the roof, the effect is beautifully picturesque. It has, besides, a far higher interest, and on some considerations may perhaps be regarded as the most important structure that we met with in our whole exploration of ruins.

The lower building, standing on the ground, is in a ruinous condition: the front has fallen, and shows only the remains of two columns covered with sculptured figures. The fall of the front has laid

227 *Temple of the Jaguar*

bare the entire wall of the chamber, covered from one end to the other with elaborately-sculptured figures in bas relief.

Exposed for ages to a long succession of winds and rains, the characters were faded and worn. Under the glare of a tropical sun the lines were confused and indistinct, and the reflection of the heat was so intense that it was impossible to work before it except for an hour or two in the afternoon, when the building was in the shade. The head-dress of the figures is, as usual, a plume of feathers, and in the upper row each figure carries a bundle of spears or a quiver of arrows. All these figures were painted. The Indians call this chamber Stohl, and say that it represents a dance of the antiguos; and these bas-reliefs, too, have a distinct and independent value. In the large work of Nebel, entitled "Voyage Pittoresque et Archéologique dans le Mexique," is a drawing of the stone of sacrifice in the Museum of Mexico, now for the first time published. It contains a procession of figures in bas-relief, which, though differing in detail, are of the same general character with those sculptured on the wall of this building. The stone was dug up in the plaza of Mexico, near the spot on which stood, in the time of Montezuma, the great teocalis of that city. The

75. Front upper chamber showing base of serpent columns, Temple of the Jaguar, Chichén Itzá (date unknown)

76. Sculptured wall in the
Temple of the Jaguar,
Chichén Itzá (date
unknown)

resemblance forms another connecting link with the very people who
occupied the city of Mexico at the time of the conquest. And the
proofs go on accumulating. In the upper building, though broken
and disfigured, is perhaps the greatest gem of aboriginal art which on
the whole Continent of America now survives.

The means of access to this building are gone. We reached it by
clambering over fallen stones. The door opens upon the platform of
the wall, overlooking the Tennis-court. The front corridor was supported by massive pillars, portions of which still remain, covered
with elaborate sculptured ornaments. The lintel of the inner doorway
is a beam of sapote richly carved. The jambs are partly buried, and
above the rubbish appear sculptured figures with rich head-dresses,
which anywhere else we should have considered it necessary to bring
to light and copy.

But between these jambs we enter an inner chamber, the walls
and ceiling of which are covered, from the floor to the peak of the
arch, with designs in painting, representing, in vivid colours, human
figures, battles, houses, trees, and scenes of domestic life, and conspicuous on one of the walls is a large canoe. The first feeling of gratified
surprise was followed by heavy disappointment, for the whole was
mutilated and disfigured. In some places the plaster was broken off;
in every part deep and malignant scratches appeared in the walls, and

while individual figures were entire, the connexion of the subjects could not be made out. For a long time we had been tantalized with fragments of painting, giving us the strong impression that in this more perishable art these aboriginal builders had made higher attainments than in that of sculpture, and we now had proofs that our impression did them justice. The colours are green, yellow, red, blue, and a reddish brown, the last being invariably the colour given to human flesh. These paintings exhibit a freedom of touch which could only be the result of discipline and training under masters. But they have a higher interest than any that attaches to them as mere specimens of art; for among them are seen designs and figures which call forcibly to mind the well-known picture writings of the Mexicans. If these analogies are sustained, this building attached to the walls of the Tennis-court stands an unimpeachable witness that the people who inhabited Mexico at the time of the conquest belonged to the same great race which furnished the builders of the ruined cities in Yucatan.

But to continue. Southeast from this rises the Castillo, the first building which we saw, and from every point of view the grandest

77. Catherwood drawing of a portion of the same wall

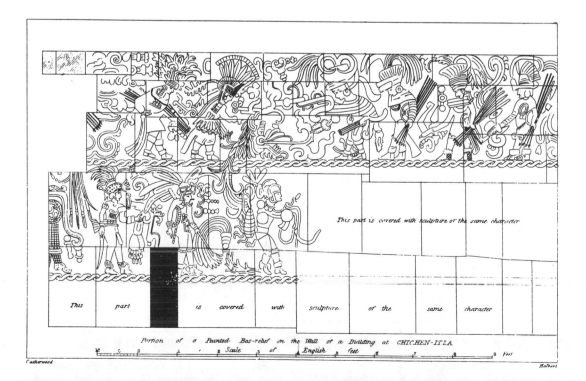

This part is covered with sculpture of the same character

This   part   is   covered   with   sculpture   of the   same   character

Portion   of   a   Painted   Bas-relief   in   the   Wall   of   a   Building   at   CHICHEN-ITZA

Scale   of   English   feet

Catherwood   Halbert and most conspicuous object that towers above the plain [see Figs. 1 and 2]. Every Sunday the ruins are resorted to as a promenade by the villagers of Pisté, and nothing can surpass the picturesque appearance of this lofty building while women, dressed in white, with red shawls, are moving on the platform, and passing in and out at the doors. The mound does not face the cardinal points exactly, though probably so intended. In all the buildings, from some cause not easily accounted for, while one varies ten degrees one way, that immediately adjoining varies twelve or thirteen degrees in another. On the west side is a staircase thirty-seven feet wide; on the north, the staircase is forty-four feet wide. On the ground at the foot of the staircase, forming a bold, striking, and well conceived commencement to this lofty range, are two colossal serpents' heads, ten feet in length, with mouths wide open and tongues protruding. No doubt they were emblematic of some religious belief, and in the minds of an imaginative people, passing between them to ascend the steps, must have excited feelings of solemn awe.

Single doorways on the top of the mound face the east, south, and west, having massive lintels of sapote wood covered with elaborate carvings, and the jambs are ornamented with sculptured figures. The sculpture is much worn, but the head-dress, ornamented with a plume of feathers, and portions of the rich attire, still remain. The face is well preserved, and has a dignified appearance. It has, too, earrings, and the nose bored, which, according to the historical accounts, was so prevalent a custom in Yucatan, that long after the conquest the Spaniards passed laws for its prohibition.

78. Castillo, Chichén Itzá
(Charnay, 1860)

The doorway facing the north gives access to a corridor. In the back wall of this corridor is a single doorway, having sculptured jambs, over which is a richly-carved sapote beam, and giving entrance to an apartment. In this apartment are two square pillars, having sculptured figures on all their sides, and supporting massive sapote beams covered with the most elaborate carving of curious and intricate designs, but so defaced and timeworn that, in the obscurity of the room, it was extremely difficult to make them out. We passed a whole day within this lofty chamber, from time to time stepping out upon the platform to look down upon the ruined buildings of the ancient city, and an immense field stretching on all sides beyond.

From this lofty height we saw for the first time groups of small columns, which, on examination, proved to be remarkable and unintelligible remains. They stood in rows of three, four, and five abreast, many rows continuing in the same direction, when they changed and pursued another. They were very low, many of them only three feet high, while the highest were not more than six feet, and consisted of several separate pieces, like millstones. Many of them had fallen, and in some places they lie prostrate in rows, all in the same direction, as if thrown down intentionally. I had a large number of Indians at work clearing them, and endeavouring to trace their direction to the end. In some places they extended to the bases of large mounds, on

79. Serpent's head at the base of the Castillo, Chichén Itzá (date unknown)

which were ruins of buildings and colossal fragments of sculpture, while in others they branched off and terminated abruptly. I counted three hundred and eighty, and there were many more; but so many were broken, and they lay so irregularly, that I gave up counting them. They were entirely too low to have supported a roof under which persons could walk. The idea at times suggested itself that they had upheld a raised walk of cement, but there were no remains visible.

I have now closed my brief description of the ruins of Chichen, having presented, with as little detail as possible, all the principal buildings of this ancient city. Ruined mounds exist, and detached portions of sculpture strew the ground, exhibiting curious devices, which often arrested us in wandering among them, but which I shall not attempt to give. They were the ruins of which we had formed the largest expectations, and these expectations were more than realized. And they had additional interest in our eyes from the fact that the broad light of day beams upon their history. The first settlement of the Spaniards in the interior was made at this very spot.

80. Modern view of the colonnade at the Temple of the Warriors from the Castillo, Chichén Itzá

Strange as it may appear, no detailed account of these extraordinary buildings, so different from any to which the Spaniards were accustomed, exists. The only existing notice of the journey [of] Don Francisco Montejo to Chichen from the coast says, that from a place called Aké, the Spanish soldiers set out, directing their course for Chichen Itza, where they determined to stop and settle, as it appeared a proper place, on account of the strength of the great buildings that were there, for defence against attacks by the Indians. We do not even learn whether these buildings were inhabited or desolate. Herrera says that the Indians in this region were so numerous, that in making the distribution which the adelantado was allowed by the terms of the royal grant, the least number which fell to the lot of a Spaniard was two thousand.

Having regard, however, to the circumstances of the occupation and abandonment of Chichen by the Spaniards, their silence is perhaps not extraordinary. At this place the adelantado made a fatal mistake, and, lured by the glitter of gold in another province, divided his forces, and sent one of his best captains, with fifty men, in search of it. From this time calamities and dangers pressed upon him. Altercations began with the Indians; provisions were withheld, the Spaniards were obliged to seek them with the sword, and all that they ate was procured at the price of blood. At length the Indians determined upon their utter destruction. Immense multitudes surrounded the camp of the Spaniards, hemming them in on all sides. The Spaniards, seeing themselves reduced to the necessity of perishing by hunger, determined to die bravely in the field, and went out to give battle. The most sanguinary fight they had ever been engaged in then took place. The Spaniards fought for their lives, and the Indians to remain masters of their own soil. Masses of the latter were killed, but great slaughter was made among the Spaniards, and, to save the lives of those who remained, the adelantado retreated to the fortifications. One hundred and fifty of the conquerors were dead. Nearly all the rest were wounded, and if the Indians had attacked them in their retreat they would have perished to a man.

Unable to hold out any longer, they took advantage of a night when the Indians were off their guard. As soon as all was still they tied a dog to the clapper of a bell-rope, putting some food before him, but out of his reach, and with great silence marched out from the camp. The dog, when he saw them going, pulled the cord in order to go with them, and afterward to get at the food. The Indians, supposing that the Spaniards were sounding the alarm, remained quiet, waiting the result, but a little before daylight, perceiving that the bell did not cease ringing, they drew near the fortification, and found it deserted. In the mean time the Spaniards escaped toward the coast. In the meager and disconnected accounts of their dangers and escape, it is, perhaps, not surprising that we have none whatever of the buildings, arts, and sciences of the fierce inhabitants of Chichen.

I shall close with one general remark. These cities were not all built at one time, but are the remains of different epochs. Chichen, though in a better state of preservation than most of the others, has a greater appearance of antiquity. Some of the buildings are no doubt older than others, and long intervals may have elapsed between the times of their construction.

The Maya manuscript places the first discovery of Chichen within the epochs corresponding with the time between A.D. 360 and A.D. 432. From the words used, it may be understood that the discovery was then made of an actual existing city, but it is a fair construction of these words to suppose that nothing more is meant than a discovery of what the words Chi-chen import, viz., the mouths of wells, having reference to the two great senotes, the discovery of wells be-

81. Modern view of the sacred cenote and the remains of a small building, Chichén Itzá

ing, among all primitive people, and particularly in the dry region of Yucatan, an event worthy to be noted in their history.

One of these senotes I have already mentioned; the other I did not visit till the afternoon preceding our departure from Chichen. Setting out from the Castillo, we ascended a wooded elevation, which seemed an artificial causeway leading to the senote. The senote was the largest and wildest we had seen. In the midst of a thick forest, an immense circular hole, with cragged, perpendicular sides, trees growing out of them and overhanging the brink. A hawk was sailing around it, looking down into the water, but without once flapping its wings. The water was of a greenish hue. A mysterious influence seemed to pervade it, in unison with the historical account that the well of Chichen was a place of pilgrimage, and that human victims were thrown into it in sacrifice. In one place, on the very brink, were the remains of a stone structure, probably connected with ancient superstitious rites; perhaps the place from which the victims were thrown into the dark well beneath.

CHAPTER FOURTEEN

Valladolid to Cozumel

t was still in the gray of the morning when we caught our last view of the great buildings, and set out for Valladolid. From Valladolid it was our purpose to prosecute our exploration through a region less known than any we had yet visited. From accounts we supposed that in two places on the coast called Tancar and Tuloom, what were taken for old Spanish forts were aboriginal buildings. Our business at Valladolid was to make arrangements for reaching them, and at the same time for coasting round Cape Catoche, and visiting the Island of Cozumel. We had been told that at Valladolid we should be able to procure all necessary information about the ruins on the coast.

The city of Valladolid had some notoriety, as being the place at which the first blow was struck in the revolution now in progress against the dominion of Mexico. There, for the first time, the Indians were brought out in arms. Utterly ignorant of the political relation between Mexico and Yucatan, they came in from their ranchos and milpas under a promise that their capitation tax should be remitted. After the success of the first outbreak the government endeavoured to avoid the fulfillment of this promise, but was compelled to compromise by remitting the tax upon women, and the Indians still look forward to emancipation from the whole. What the consequences may be of finding themselves, after ages of servitude, once more in the possession of arms, and in increasing knowledge of their physical strength, is a question of momentous import to the people of that country, the solution of which no man can foretell.

And Valladolid had been the theatre of stranger scenes in ancient times. According to historical accounts, it was once haunted by a demonio of the worst kind, called a demonio parlero, a talking devil, who held discourse with all that wished at night, speaking like a parrot, answering all questions put to him, touching a guitar, playing the castanets, dancing and laughing, but without suffering himself to be seen.

Afterward he took to throwing stones in garrets, and eggs at the women and girls, and, says [one] pious doctor, "an aunt of mine, vexed with him, said, 'Go away from this house, devil,' and gave him a blow in the face which left the nose redder than cochineal." He became so troublesome that the cura went to one of the houses which he frequented to exorcise him, but in the mean time El Demonio went to the cura's house and played him a trick. After this he began slandering people, and got the whole town at swords' points to such an extent that it reached the ears of the bishop at Merida, who forbade speaking to him under pain of heavy spiritual punishments. At first the demonio fell to weeping and complaining, then made more noise than ever, and finally took to burning houses. The vecinos sought Divine assistance, and the cura, after a severe tussle, drove him out of the town.

It is almost impossible to conceive what difficulty we had in learning anything definite concerning the road we ought to take. There were but two persons in the town who could give us any information, and what they gave was most unsatisfactory. We determined on going to the village of Chemax, from which, we were advised, there was a direct road to Tancah, where a boat was on the stocks, and probably then finished, which we could procure for a voyage down the coast.

The road was broad, and had been lately opened for carretas and calesas. On the way we met a large straggling party of Indians, returning from a hunting expedition in the forests along the seacoast. Naked, armed with long guns, and with deer and wild boars slung on their backs, their aspect was the most truculent of any people we had seen. They seemed ready at any moment for battle.

82. *Page 236:* Caracol, Castillo, and Temple of the Warriors from Las Monjas, Chichén Itzá (circa 1934)

It was some time after dark when we reached the village. The outline of the church was visible through the darkness, and beside it was the convent, with a light streaming from the door. The cura was sitting at a table surrounded by the officials of the village, who started at the clatter of our horses. When we appeared in the doorway, if a firebrand had been thrown among them they could not have been more astounded. The village was the last between Valladolid and Tancah, and the surprise caused by our appearance did not subside when we told them that we were on our way to the latter. They all told us that it was impossible. Tancah was a mere rancho, seventy miles distant, and the whole intermediate country was a dense forest.

Turning back formed no part of our deliberations. The only question was whether we should undertake the journey on foot. Our alternative was to go to the port of Yalahao, which is almost at right angles from Tancah, and thence take a canoa. This would subject us to the necessity of two voyages along the coast, going and returning, and would require, perhaps, a fortnight to reach Tancah, which we had expected to arrive at in three days. But there were villages and ranchos on the road, and the chance of a canoa was so much greater that, under the circumstances, we were glad of such an alternative.

The village of Chemax contains nearly ten thousand inhabitants, and was in existence at the time of the conquest. The curacy of Chemax comprehended within its jurisdiction all between it and the sea. The cura Garcia had drawn up a report of the condition and character of the region under his charge, and its objects of curiosity and interest, from which I copied the following notice in regard to ruins known by the name of Coba.

"In the eastern part of this village, at eight leagues' distance, near one of the three lagunas, is a building that the indigenes call Monjas. It consists of various ranges of two stories, all covered with arches, closed with masonry of rude stone. Its interior pavement is preserved, and on the walls of one are some painted figures in different attitudes, showing, without doubt, according to the supposition of the natives, that these are the remains of that detestable worship so commonly found. From this edifice there is a paved road running to the southeast to a limit that has not been discovered with certainty, but some aver that it goes in the direction of Chichen Itza."

The cura himself had never visited these ruins. They were all buried in forest; there was no rancho or other habitation near. As our time was necessarily to be much prolonged by the change we were obliged to make, we concluded that it would not be advisable to go and see them.

But the cura had much more interesting information. On his own hacienda of Kantunile, sixteen leagues nearer the coast, were several mounds, in one of which, while excavating for stone to be used in building, the Indians had discovered a sepulchre containing three skeletons, which, according to the cura, were those of a man, a woman, and a child, but all, unfortunately, so much decayed that in attempting to remove them they fell to pieces.

At the head of the skeletons were two large vases of terra cotta, with covers. In one of these was a large collection of Indian ornaments, beads, stones, and two carved shells. The carving on the shells is in bas-relief, and very perfect. It is of the same type with the figure on the Ticul vase, and those sculptured on the wall at Chichen. The other vase was filled nearly to the top with arrow-heads, not of flint, but of obsidian. As there are no volcanoes in Yucatan from which obsidian can be procured, the discovery of these proves intercourse with the volcanic regions of Mexico. Besides these, and more interesting than all, on the top of these arrow-heads lay a *penknife with a horn handle*. All these the cura had in his possession, carefully preserved in a bag, which he emptied on a table for our examination.

The penknife attracted our particular attention. The horn handle was much decayed, and the iron or steel was worn and rusted, This penknife was never made in the country. How came it in an Indian sepulchre? I answer, when the fabrics of Europe and this country came together, the white man and the red had met. The figures carved on the shells, those little perishable memorials, accidentally disinterred, identify the crumbling bones in that sepulchre with the builders of Chichen. Those bones were laid in their grave after a penknife had found its way into the country. Speculation and ingenuity may assign other causes, but, in my opinion, at the time of the conquest Indians were actually living in and occupying those very cities on whose great ruins we now gaze with wonder. A penknife—one of the petty presents distributed by the Spaniards—reached the hands of a cacique, who died in his native town, and was buried with the rites and ceremonies transmitted by his fathers. At the time of the conquest a penknife was doubtless considered precious, worthy of being buried with the heirlooms of its owner, and of accompanying him to the world of spirits. I was extremely anxious to procure these memorials. The cura said, with Spanish courtesy, that they were mine. But he evidently attached great value to them, and, much as I desired it, I could not, with any propriety, take them.

I am obliged to hurry over our journey to the coast. The road was lonely and rugged, mostly a complete crust of stone, broken and

83. *Opposite:* Modern view of the Temple of the Paintings, Cobá

sharp pointed, which almost wore out our horses. It was desperately hot. We had no view except the narrow path before us, and we stumbled along, wondering that such a stony surface could support such a teeming vegetation.

In the afternoon of the third day we were approaching the port. When within about a league of it, we came out upon a low, swampy plain, with a grove of cocoanut trees before us, indicating, and, at the same time, hiding, the port of Yalahao. The road lay over a causeway, then wet and slippery, with numerous holes, and sometimes completely overflowed. On each side was a sort of creek, and in the plain were large pools of water.

The village was a long, straggling street of huts, elevated a few feet above the washing of the waves. In passing along it, for the first time in the country we came to a bridge crossing a brook, with a fine stream of running water in sight on the left. Our horses seemed as much astonished as ourselves, and we had great difficulty in getting them over the bridge. On the shore was another spring bubbling within reach of the waves.

We rode to a house belonging to our friend the cura. It stood so near the sea that the waves had undermined part of the long piazza in

84. Catherwood drawing of the port of Yalahao

front; but the interior was in good condition, and a woman tenant in possession. Wherever we went we seemed to be the terror of the sex, and before we had fairly made a beginning, she abandoned the house and left us in quiet possession. Toward evening we sat in the doorway and looked out upon the sea. The waves were rolling almost to our door, and Doctor Cabot found a new field opened to him in flocks of large seafowl strutting along the shore and screaming over our heads.

It is not many years since the coast of Cuba and the adjacent continent were infested by bands of desperadoes. Tales of piracies and murders which make the blood run cold are fresh in the remembrance of many. The sailor still repeats or listens to them with shuddering interest, and in those times, this port was notorious as a rendezvous for these robbers of the sea.

We found one great deficiency at this place: there was no ramon for the horses. At night we turned them loose in the village; but the barren plain furnished them no grazing, and they returned to the house. Early in the morning we despatched Dimas to a ramon tree two leagues distant, that being the nearest point at which any could be procured; and in the mean time I set about searching for a canoa, and succeeded in engaging one, but not of the best class, and the patron and sailors could not be ready in less than two or three days.

This over, we had nothing farther to do in Yalahao. I rambled for a little while in the Castillo, a low fortress, with twelve embrazures, built for the suppression of piracy, but the garrison of which, from all accounts, connected themselves somewhat closely with the pirates. It was now garrisoned by a little Mestizo tailor, who had run away from Sisal with his wife to avoid being taken for a soldier. The meekest possible tenants of a fort, they paid no rent, and seemed perfectly happy.

We completed laying in our stock of provisions, to wit, chocolate, sweetened bread, beef and pork in strings, two turtles, three bushels of corn, and implements for making tortillas. To avoid the long journey back through the interior, we determined to send Dimas with our horses to the port of Silan. On our return, we should continue down the coast and meet him there. At nine o'clock we were taken off in a small dug-out, and put on board our canoa. We had no leave-takings. The only persons who took any interest in our movements were Dimas, who wanted to go with us, the woman whom we had dispossessed of the house, and the agent of the canoa, who had no desire to see us again.

Our canoa was known in the port of Yalahao by the name of El Sol, or the Sun. It was thirty-five feet long and six feet wide at the top, but curving toward the bottom. It carried two large sails, with the peaks held up by heavy poles secured at the masts; had a space of eight or ten feet clear in the stern. All the rest was filled with luggage, provisions, and water-casks. We had not been on board till the moment of embarcation, and prospects seemed rather unpromising for a month's cruise. There was no wind; the sails were flapping against the mast. The sun beat down upon us, and we had no mat or awning of any kind, although the agent had promised one. Our captain was a middle-aged Mestizo fisherman, hired for the occasion. Our voyage was one to which we had always looked forward with interest. The precise object was to discover vestiges or remains of the great buildings of lime and stone which, according to the historical accounts, surprised and astonished the Spaniards.

At eleven o'clock the breeze set in. At twelve the patron asked if he should run ashore for us to dine, and at half past one the breeze was so strong against us that we were obliged to come to anchor under the lee of Point Moscheto. This was an island about two leagues distant from Yalahao, with a projecting point, which we had to double. We could have walked round it in an hour, but in El Sol, it seemed to stand out like Cape Horn. Our bark had no keel, and could do nothing against the wind. We went ashore on a barren, sandy beach, bathed, shot, and picked up shells. Toward evening the wind fell, and we crawled round the point, when we came to anchor again. It was now dark, and El Sol could not travel at night. The patron made all secure; we had a big stone for anchor, and rode in water knee deep.

The next morning, with the rising of her great namesake, El Sol was under way. At one o'clock another bold point intercepted us. It was a great object to get round it, for the wind would then be fair. El Sol made a vigorous effort, but by this time the breeze had become strong, and we were fain to come to anchor. Toward evening the breeze again died away, we slowly got round the point, and at half past eight came to anchor, having made six leagues on our voyage.

Our captain told us that this desolate point was Cape Catoche, the memorable spot on the Continent of America at which the Spaniards first landed, and approaching which, says Bernal Dias, we saw at the distance of two leagues a large town, which, from its size, it exceeding any town in Cuba, we named Grand Cairo. The Spaniards set out for it, and passing by some thick woods, were attacked by Indians in ambuscade. Near the place of this ambuscade, he adds, were three buildings of lime and stone, wherein were idols of clay, with diabolical countenances, &c. Navigators and geographers, however, have assigned different localities to this memorable point, and its true position is, perhaps, uncertain.

At daylight we were again under way, and soon were opposite the entrance to a passage known to the fishermen as the Boca de Iglesia, from the ruins of a church visible at a great distance. This church was one of the objects I intended to visit, but our captain told us that we could not approach nearer than a league. A long muddy flat intervened. He said, too, that the church was certainly Spanish, and stood among the ruins of a Spanish town destroyed by the bucaniers, or, in his words, by the English pirates. The wind was ahead. Anxious to lose no advantage, we made sail for the island of Contoy. It was dark when we came to anchor, and we were already distressed for water. Our casks were impregnated with the flavour of agua ardiente, and the water was sickening. Through the darkness we saw the outline of a desolate rancho. Our men went ashore, and, moving round it with torches, made a fine piratical appearance; but they found no water.

Before daylight we were roused by the screaming of seabirds. In the gray of the morning, the island seemed covered with a moving canopy, and the air was noisy with their clamour. At eleven o'clock we reached the island of Mugeres, notorious in that region as the resort of Lafitte the pirate. On the farther point of the island we had a distant view of one of those stone buildings which were our inducement to this voyage along the coast.

While looking at it from the prow of the canoa, with the patron by my side, he broke from me, seized a harpoon, and pointing with it to indicate the direction to the helmsman, we came silently upon a large turtle, apparently asleep, which must have been somewhat surprised on waking up with three or four inches of cold steel in his back. There are three kinds of turtles which inhabit these seas; the Cahuamo, the eggs of which serve for food, and which is useful besides only for its oil; the Tortuga, of which the meat as well as the eggs is eaten, which also produces oil, and of which the shell is worth two reales the pound; and the Karé, of which the shell is worth ten dollars a pound. It was one of this kind that had crossed our path. I immediately negotiated with the patron for the purchase of the shell. The outer scales of the back, eight in number, are all that is valuable. Their weight he estimated at four pounds, and the price in Campeachy he said was ten dollars a pound, but he was an honest fellow, and let me have it at two pounds and a half, for eight dollars a pound. I had the satisfaction of learning afterward that I had not paid more than twice as much as it was worth.

In the afternoon we steered for the mainland, passing the island of Kancune, a barren strip of land, with sand hills and stone buildings visible upon it. The whole of this coast is lined with reefs of rocks, having narrow passages which enable a canoe to enter and find shelter; but it is dangerous to attempt the passage at night. The patron came to anchor at about four o'clock under the lee of the point of Nesuc.

At daylight the next morning we were again under way, and, with a strong and favourable wind, steered from the coast for the island of Cozumel. Very soon, we felt the discomfort and even insecurity of our little vessel. The waves broke over us, wetting our luggage and ourselves. At about four o'clock in the afternoon we were upon the coast of Cozumel, and here we made a discovery that our patron was not familiar with the coast of this island. It was bound with reefs; there were only certain places where it was practicable to run in, and he was afraid to make the attempt. Sailing along till he saw a passage among the reefs, he laid the old canoe into it, and then threw out the big stone, but at some distance from the shore. On the outer reef was the wreck of a brig. Her naked ribs were above the water, and the fate of her mariners no one knew.

The next morning, after some hours spent in groping about, we encountered a strong current of perhaps four miles an hour. At length we furled sails and betook ourselves to poles. After two hours' hard work, we reached the little Bay of San Miguel, on which stood [an abandoned] rancho established by the pirate Molas. The clearing around it was the only one on the island. This bay had a sandy beach extending some distance to a rocky point, but even here the water was discoloured by sunken reefs. In the case of a norther it was an unsafe anchorage ground; El Sol would be driven upon the rocks. The captain wished to leave us on the shore, and go in search of a better harbour. But we objected, and directed him to run her up close. Standing on the bow, and leaping with our setting poles, we landed upon the desolate island of Cozumel.

Above the line of the shore was a fine table of land, on which were several huts thatched with palm leaves. One was large and commodious, divided into apartments, and contained rude benches and tables, as if prepared for our immediate occupation. Back of the house was an enclosure for a garden, overgrown, but with any quantity of tomatoes, ripe, wasting, and begging to be put into a turtle soup then in preparation on board the canoe.

The situation commanded a view of the sea. Barely distinguishable, in the distance was the coast of Yucatan. On the bank were large forest trees which had been spared in the clearing, and orange

and cocoanut trees planted by Molas. The place had a sort of piratical aspect. In the hut were doors and green blinds from the cabin of
some unlucky vessel, and reeving blocks, tar buckets, halliards, drink-
ing gourds, fragments of rope, fishing nets, and two old hatches were
scattered on the ground. The first object we discovered was a well of
pure and abundant water, which we fell upon at the moment of landing. This well had a higher interest. We saw in it, at first glance, the
work of the same builders with whose labours on the mainland we
were now so familiar, being, like the subterranean chambers at Uxmal, dome shaped, but larger both at the mouth and in the interior.
This well was shaded by a large cocoanut tree. We hauled up under it
one of the hatches, and, sitting around it on blocks, had served up
the turtle which had been accomplishing its destiny on board the canoa. With our guns resting against the trees, long beards, and canoa
costume, we were, perhaps, as piratical-seeming a trio as ever scuttled
a ship at sea.

When I resolved to visit Cozumel I was not aware that it was uninhabited. Knowing it to be but thirty miles long, I supposed that a
thorough exploration could be made. But even before landing we saw
that this would be impossible. The whole island was overgrown with
trees. Except along the shore or within the clearing around the hut, it
was impossible to move in any direction without cutting a path. If we
should cut by the compass through the heart of the island, we might
pass within a few feet of a building without perceiving it. Fortunately, however, on the borders of the clearing there were vestiges of
ancient population. One of them, two hundred feet from the sea,
even now visible above the tops of the trees, stands on a terrace, and
has steps on all four of its sides. The low building had four doors facing the cardinal points. The exterior is of plain stone, but was stuccoed and painted, traces of which are still visible. The doorways open
into a narrow corridor, which encompasses a small room, having a
doorway opening to the centre. South-southeast from this stands another building raised upon a terrace, consisting of a single apartment,
having two doorways and a back wall seven feet thick. The height is
ten feet, the arch is triangular, and on the walls are the remains of
paintings.

Doubtless, many more buildings lie buried in the woods; but to
us these were pregnant with instruction. The building standing close
to the sea answers the description of "towers" seen by Grijalva and
his companions as they sailed along the coast. The *ascent is by steps,
the base is very massive,* the *building is small at the top,* it is *about
the height of two men placed one above the other.* It is an interesting

fact, moreover, that not only our patron and sailors called this building a "tower," but in a late article published in the proceedings of the Royal Geographical Society at London, this building, with others of the same general character, is indicated by the name of a "tower."

There is strong reason to believe that the Spaniards landed for the first time on the shore of which this building stands, that the building presented is the very tower in which the Spaniards saw the performance of idolatrous rites. Perhaps it is the same temple from which Bernal Dias and his companions rolled the idols down the steps. And more than this, these buildings were identically the same with those on the mainland. If we had seen hundreds, we could not have been more firmly convinced that they were all erected and occupied by the same people. They afford abundant and conclusive proof that the ruined cities on the continent, the building of which has been ascribed to races lost, perished, and unknown, were inhabited by the very same Indians who occupied the country at the time of the conquest.

At the rear of the last building, buried in the woods, is another memorial, perhaps equal in interest to any now existing on the island of Cozumel. It is the ruins of a Spanish church. The front wall has almost wholly fallen, but the side walls are standing to the height of about twenty feet. The plastering remains, and along the base is a line of painted ornaments. The interior is encumbered with the ruins of the fallen roof, overgrown with bushes; a tree is growing out of the great altar. The history of this church is as obscure as that of the ruined temples whose worship it supplanted. When it was built or why it was abandoned, and, indeed, its very existence, are utterly unknown to the inhabitants of New Spain.

But I have a particular reason for presenting this ruined church. It is a notion pervading all the old Spanish writers, that at some early day Christianity had been preached to the Indians. Connected with this is the belief that the cross was found by the first conquerors in the province of Yucatan as a symbol of Christian worship. Prophecies are recorded supposed to show a traditionary knowledge of its former existence, and foretelling that from the rising of the sun should come a bearded people and white, who should carry aloft the sign of the cross, which their gods could not reach, and from which they should fly away. The same vague idea exists to this day. In general, when the padres pay any attention to the antiquities of the country, they are always quick in discovering some real or imaginary resemblance to the cross. A strong support of this belief is advanced in the "Cozumel Cross" at Merida, found on the island of Cozumel, and

249   *"Cozumel Cross"*

85. *Opposite:* Ruins on Cozumel Island (date unknown)

supposed to have been an object of reverence among the Indians before their conversion to Christianity.

Until the destruction of the Franciscan convent it stood on a pedestal in the patio, and, we were told, from the time when it was placed there, no lightning had ever struck the building, as had often happened before. It is now in the Church of the Mejorada. In looking for it at that place, Mr. Catherwood and myself were invited into the cell of an octogenarian monk who told us that he had himself dug it up from among the ruins, and had it set up where it is now seen. It is of stone, has a venerable appearance of antiquity, and has extended on it in half relief an image of the Saviour, made of plaster, with the hands and feet nailed. At the first glance we were satisfied that, whatever might be the truth in regard to its early history, it was, at least, wrought into its present shape under the direction of the monks. And though, at that time, we did not expect ever to know anything more about it, the ruins of this church cleared up in our minds all possible mystery connected with its existence.

In front of the building is a cemented platform, broken and uprooted by trees, but still preserving its form. On this stand two square pillars, which, we supposed, had once supported crosses. We were immediately impressed with the belief that one of these missing symbols was that now known as the "Cozumel Cross." It had probably been carried away by some pious monk at or about the time when the church became a ruin and the island depopulated. Though crosses may have been found in Yucatan, the connecting of the "Cozumel Cross" with the ruined church on the island completely invalidates the strongest proof offered that the cross was ever recognised by the Indians as a symbol of worship.

Toward evening we took a bath. While in the water black clouds gathered suddenly, thunder rolled, lightning flashed, and sea-birds flew screaming over our heads. Rain following quickly, we snatched up our clothing and ran for the hut. Looking back for a moment, we saw our canoa under way, with scarcely a yard of mainsail, like a great bird flying over the water. As she turned the point of the island and disappeared our fears were roused. From experience we judged it impossible for her to live through a storm so sudden and violent. The patron was not familiar with the coast, there was but one place in which he could find shelter, a narrow passage, difficult to enter even by daylight, and night was almost upon him. Mr. Catherwood had timed the precise moment when he turned the point, and we knew that the canoa would not be able to reach the cove before dark, but would have to ride through the storm, and, perhaps, be driven to sea.

It was fearful to think of the danger of the poor patron and sailors. Mingled with these fears was some little uneasiness on our own account. All our luggage and provisions were on board. If she never returned we should be five Robinson Crusoes, all alone on a desert island. As the storm raged our apprehensions ran high, and we had got so far as to calculate our chances of reaching the mainland by a raft, finding some relief in the occupation of moving our hammocks to avoid the rain as it beat through the thatched roof.

CHAPTER FIFTEEN

Tulum

On the third day, at twelve o'clock, the canoa hove in sight, working her way round the point, and in a short time was at her old anchorage ground. From the simple and unaffected account of the patron, night had overtaken him, and he supposed that he had run by the cove, when a flash of lightning disclosed the narrow passage. He turned the old canoa short into the very middle of it. In passing through he struck upon a sunken rock, lost one man overboard, caught him by the light of another flash, and in a moment was in still water.

We filled our water casks, in an hour were on board, and left, solitary as we found it, the once populous island of Cozumel. A hawk mourning over its mate, which we carried away, was the only living thing that looked upon our departure.

The opposite coast of Yucatan was dimly visible. The wind was high, the sea rough, and a strong current was sweeping us down toward the point of Cape Catoche. About an hour before dark we got across the current, and stood up along the coast, passing three low, square buildings, but the sea was so rough that we could not land to examine them. The account of the expedition of Grijalva says, "After leaving the island of Cozumel we saw three large villages, separated two miles from each other. They contained a great number of stone houses, with high towers, and covered with straw." This *must* have been the very part of the coast where these villages were seen. The whole is now covered with forest, but it is not unreasonable to suppose that the stone buildings visible on the shore are tokens of the buried towns in the interior. We ran on till after dark, and came to anchor under a projecting point, behind a reef of rocks.

At daylight we were again under way. We passed three more square buildings; but as the coast was rocky we could not land without endangering the safety of our precious canoa. Far off, on a high cliff, stood the Castillo of Tuloom, the extreme point at which we were aiming. At twelve o'clock we turned a point, and came upon a long, sandy beach, forming a bay, at the head of which was a small collection of huts, composing the rancho of Tancar. The entrance was difficult, being hemmed in by sunken reefs and rocks. Two women were standing in the doorway of one of the huts.

Our first inquiries were upon the subject of ruins. A short path through the woods leads to a milpa, in which are numerous remains of ancient buildings standing on terraces, but all small and dilapidated. These buildings once stood erect in full view from the sea, but now the stranger sails along the coast unconscious that among the trees lie shrouded the ruins of an aboriginal town.

In the afternoon we set out for the ruins of Tuloom. Our road lay for a mile and a half along the shore. The beach was sandy, and in some places so yielding that we sank above the ankles, and found it a relief to take off our shoes and stockings, and wade in the edge of the water. At the end of the beach was a high rocky promontory, standing out into the sea. This we ascended. In half an hour we came unexpectedly upon a low building, apparently an altar. Beyond the cliff became more rugged and barren. Amid all its barrenness, from the crevices of the rocks sprang a thick growth of scrubby wild palm, covering the whole surface of the cliff. Toiling through this, we reached another low building, from the top of which we saw El Castillo, but with a great chasm between. Afraid of being overtaken by darkness on this wild range, we turned back. Night was upon us when we again reached the shore. The sandy beach was now a welcome relief. At a late hour we again reached the hut, having come to a rapid conclusion that a frequent repetition of this walk would be neither pleasant nor profitable, and that, in order to get through our

86. *Page 252:* Castillo and Temple 5 viewed from the north, Tulum (circa 1930)

work, it would be necessary again to take up our abode among the ruins.

The next morning we set out for that purpose, escorted by a fine lad of about twenty. Ascending the cliff, and passing beyond the two buildings we had seen the day before, we descended from the rear of the last to the head of the chasm. Ascending again at the other end of the ravine, we entered a gloomy forest, and, passing a building on the left, with "old walls" visible in different places indistinctly through the trees, reached the grand staircase of the Castillo. The steps, the platform of the building, and the whole area in front were overgrown with trees, large and principally ramon, which, with their deep green foliage and the mysterious buildings around, presented an image of a grove sacred to Druidical worship.

We were amid the wildest scenery we had yet found in Yucatan. Besides the deep and exciting interest of the ruins themselves, we had around us what we wanted at all the other places, the magnificence of nature. Clearing away the platform in front, we looked over an immense forest; walking around the moulding of the wall, we looked out upon the boundless ocean, and deep in the clear water at the foot

255   *Castillo at Tulum*

87. Catherwood drawing of the Castillo, Tulum

of the cliff we saw gliding quietly by a great fish eight or ten feet long.

The front of the Castillo is still in good preservation. In the doorway are two columns, making three entrances, with square recesses above them, all of which once contained ornaments. In the centre one fragments of a statue still remain. The interior is divided into two corridors; the one in front had at each end a stone bench. Again on the walls we found the mysterious prints of the red hand. A single doorway leads to the back corridor, which has a stone bench extending along the foot of the wall. On each side of the doorway are stone rings, intended for the support of the door, and in the back wall are oblong openings, which admit breezes from the sea. Both apartments have the triangular-arched ceiling, and both had a convenience and pleasantness of arrangement that suited us well as tenants.

The sea wall of the Castillo rises on the brink of a high, broken, precipitous cliff, commanding a magnificent ocean view. The wall is solid, and has no doorways or entrances of any kind. At evening, when the work of the day was ended and our men returned to the hut, we sat down on the moulding of the wall, and regretted that the doorways of our lofty habitation had not opened upon the sea. Night, however, wrought a great change in our feelings. An easterly storm came on, and the rain beat heavily against the sea wall. We were obliged to stop up the oblong openings, and congratulated ourselves upon the wisdom of the ancient builders.

Within the area in front of the Castillo were several small ruined

88. Castillo viewed from Temple 5, Tulum (circa 1930)

buildings, which seemed intended for altars. Opposite the foot of the steps was a square terrace, with steps on all four sides. The platform was overgrown with trees, under the shade of which Mr. Catherwood set up his camera to make his drawing; the picturesque effect being greatly heightened by his keeping one hand in his pocket, to save it from the moschetoes, and his tying his pantaloons around his legs to keep ants and other insects from running up.

Adjoining the lower room of the south wing were extensive remains, one of which contained a chamber forty feet wide and nineteen deep, with four columns that had probably supported a flat roof. In another, lying on the ground, were the fragments of two tablets, of the same character with those at Labphak.

Forty feet from the Castillo stands a small isolated building. Over the doorway is the same curious figure we saw at Sayi, with the head down and the legs and arms spread out; and along the cornice were other curious and peculiar ornaments. The doorway is very low. Throughout the country at times we had heard the building of these cities ascribed to corcubados, or hunchbacks. The unusual lowness of all the doorways, with the strangeness and desolation of all around, almost gave colour to the most fanciful belief.

The day ended without our making any advances beyond this immediate neighbourhood, but the next was made memorable by the unexpected discovery that this forest-buried city was encompassed by a wall, which had resisted all the elements of destruction at work upon it, and was still erect and in good preservation. Since the beginning of our exploration we had heard of city walls, but all vestiges of them elsewhere had been uncertain, and our attempts to trace them unsatisfactory. We set out without much expectation of any decided result, and, all at once found ourselves confronted by a massive stone structure running at right angles to the sea. Following its direction, we soon came to a gateway and watch-tower. We passed through the gateway, and followed the wall outside, keeping as close to it as the trees and bushes would permit, down to the sea. We immediately set about a thorough exploration, and without once breaking off, measured it from one end to the other.

This wall forms a parallelogram abutting on the sea. We began our survey on the cliff at the southeast angle, where the abutment is much fallen. We attempted to measure along the base, but the close growth of trees and underbrush made it difficult to carry the line, and we mounted to the top. Even then it was no easy matter. Trees growing beside the wall threw their branches across it, thorns, bushes, and vines of every description grew out of it, and at every step we were

89. Stucco figure of
"diving god" over the inner
door of Temple 25, Tulum
(circa 1930)

obliged to cut down the Agave Americana, which pierced us with its
long, sharp points. The sun beat upon us, moschetoes, flies, and
other insects pestered us, but, under all annoyances, the day employed on the summit of this wall was one of the most interesting we
passed among ruins.

The wall is composed of rough, flat stones, laid upon each other
without mortar or cement of any kind. The south side has two gate-
ways. At the distance of six hundred and fifty feet the wall turns at

90. West gateway on the
south side of the wall
surrounding Tulum (circa
1930)

right angles, and runs parallel to the sea. At the angle, elevated so as
to give a commanding view, is [a] watch-tower. The interior is plain,
and against the back wall is a small altar, at which the guard might
offer up prayers for the preservation of the city. But no guard sits in
the watch-tower now; trees are growing around it. Within the walls
the city is desolate and overgrown, and without is an unbroken forest. The battlements, on which the proud Indian strode with his bow
and arrow, and plumes of feathers, are surmounted by immense
thorn bushes and overrun by poisonous vines. The city no longer
keeps watch; the fiat of destruction has gone out against it. In solitude it rests, the abode of silence and desolation.

The west line, parallel with the sea, has a single gateway; at the angle is another watch-tower, and the wall then runs straight to the sea. The whole circuit is twenty-eight hundred feet. On the north side of the wall, near the east gateway, is a building divided into two principal and two smaller rooms, the ceilings of which had entirely fallen. At one corner is a senote, with the remains of steps leading down to it, and containing brackish water. Near this was a hollow rock, which furnished us with our supply.

Toward the southeast corner of the wall, on the brow of the cliff, stands a building [that] discloses an entirely new principle of construction. The ceiling has four beams of wood laid on the top of the wall, with smaller beams laid across the larger so closely as to touch. On these crossbeams is a thick mass of mortar and large pebbles, which was laid on moist, and now forms a solid crust, being the same materials which we had seen in ruins on the floors of other rooms. Against the back wall was an altar, with a rude triangular stone upon it, which seemed to bear marks of not very distant use. On each side of the doorway were large sea-shells fixed in the wall for the support of the doors.

It was our belief that the walls enclosed only the principal, perhaps the sacred buildings, and that ruins existed to a great distance beyond; but we did not consider it worth while to attempt any exploration. In fact, our occupation of this walled city was too much dis-

91. "Watchtower" (Structure 55) at the northwest corner of wall surrounding Tulum (circa 1930)

turbed to allow us to think of remaining long. A legion of fierce usurpers, already in possession, were determined to drive us out, and after hard work by day, we had no rest at night. We held our ground against the moschetoes of Tuloom for two nights, but on the third, one after the other, we crawled out of our hammocks to the platform before the door. The moon was shining magnificently, lighting up the darkness of the forest, and drawing a long silvery line upon the sea. For a time we felt ourselves exalted above the necessity of sleep, but by degrees drowsiness overcame us, and at last we were all stretched at full length on the ground. The onslaught was again terrible. We returned to our hammocks, but found no peace, and emerging again, kindled a large fire, and sat down to smoke till daylight.

The next morning we finished what remained to be done, and, after an early dinner, prepared to leave the ruins. While the men were arranging their loads I gave Doctor Cabot a direction to a point in the wall, where, in measuring around it, Mr. Catherwood and I had started two ocellated turkeys. He set out to cut his way in a straight line with his hunting knife, and very soon, while sitting on the steps of the Castillo, I heard him calling to me that he had come upon another building which we had not seen. Having occasion to economize shoe leather for the walk back over the cliff, I at first hesitated about going to it, but he insisted. He was so near that we communicated without any particular effort of voice, but I could see nothing of him or of the building. Following his path, I found him standing before it. Working our way around it we discovered two others near by, almost invisible, so dense was the foliage of the trees. Our plans were all deranged, for we could not go away without drawings of these buildings. We returned to the steps of the Castillo, and summoned all hands to council. The men had their back-loads ready, Bernaldo reported two tortillas as the stock of provisions on hand, and the idea of another night in the Castillo struck us with dismay. We had been so long accustomed to sleep that it had become part of our nature. A night's rest was indispensable, and we determined to break up and return the next day.

By the time Mr. Catherwood arrived on the ground the next morning the clearing of the first building was made. This building faces the west, and consists of two stories. The exterior had been richly decorated, and above the cornice were fragments of rich ornaments in stucco. The lower story has four columns, making five doorways opening into a narrow corridor, which runs round and encloses on three sides a chamber in the centre. The walls of the corridor on both sides were covered with paintings, but green and mildewed from the rankness of vegetation in which the building is smothered. A small doorway in front opens into the chamber; of this, too, the walls were covered with paintings, decayed and effaced. Against the back wall was an altar for burning copal.

The building on the top stands directly over the lower chamber, and corresponds with it in dimensions, this being the only instance we met with in which one room was placed directly over another. There was no staircase or other visible means of communication between the lower and upper stories. At the rear of this building were others attached to it, or connected with it, but uprooted and thrown down by trees. Among the ruins were two stone tablets with rounded surfaces, six feet six inches high, having upon them worn and indistinct traces of sculpture.

At [a] short distance is the [other] building, with a staircase in the centre, two pillars in the doorway, and, over the centre, the head of a mutilated figure. The interior is divided into two principal and parallel apartments. At the north extremity of the inner one is a smaller apartment, containing an enclosed altar for burning copal. The roof had fallen, and trees were growing out of the floor.

Near this is another building, larger than the last, constructed on the same plan, but more ruined. These buildings were all within about two hundred feet of the steps of the Castillo. We were in the very act of leaving before we discovered them, and but for the accidental attempt of Doctor Cabot to cut through in search of birds, or if he had happened to cut a few yards to the right hand or the left, we should have gone away ignorant of their existence.

It will be borne in mind that when this city was inhabited and clear of trees, the buildings were all visible from the sea. The Spaniards are known to have sailed along this coast. The narrative of the expedition of Grijalva, taken up at the point at which we left it, after crossing from Cozumel, continues: "We ran along day and night, and the next day toward sunset we saw a bourg, or village, so large that Seville would not have appeared larger or better. We saw there a very high tower. There was upon the bank a crowd of Indians, who carried two standards, which they raised and lowered as signs to us to come and join them. The same day we arrived at a bay, near which was a tower, the highest we had seen. We remarked a very considerable village; the country was watered by many rivers. We discovered a bay *where a fleet would have been able to enter.*"

This account is certainly not so accurate as a coast survey would be at this day, but it is more minute than most accounts of the early voyages of the Spaniards, and, in my opinion, it is all sufficient to identify this now desolate city. After crossing over from Cozumel,

twenty-four hours sailing would bring them to this part of the coast; and the next circumstance mentioned, viz., the discovery of a bay where a fleet would have been able to enter, is still stronger, for at the distance of about eight leagues below Tuloom is the Bay of Ascension, always spoken of by the Spanish writers as a harbour in which the whole Spanish navy might lie at anchor. It is the only bay along the coast from Cape Catoche into which large vessels can enter, and constrains me to the belief that the desolate place now known as Tuloom was that "bourg, or village, so large that Seville would not appear larger or better," and that the Castillo, from which we were driven by the moschetoes, was that "highest tower which the Spaniards had seen."

Farther, it is my firm belief that this city continued to be occupied by its aboriginal inhabitants long after the conquest, for Grijalva turned back from the Bay of Ascension, again passed without landing, and after the disastrous expedition of Don Francisco Montejo, the Spaniards made no attempt upon this part of the coast, so that the aborigines must have remained for a long time in this place unmolested. And the strong impression of a comparatively very recent occu-

92. East façade of Temple 20 and Stela 2, Tulum (circa 1930)

pation is derived from the appearance of the buildings themselves, which, though not less ruined, owing to the ranker growth of trees, had in some instances an appearance of freshness and good keeping that, amid the desolation and solitude around, was almost startling.

Outside of the walls are several small buildings, no doubt intended for adoratorios, or altars. One stands on a terrace, having a circular platform, on the brow of the cliff, overlooking the sea. The doorway faces the north. The interior consists of a single chamber, and against the back wall is an altar in such a state of preservation as to be fit for its original uses. Near the foot of the steps, overgrown by the scrubby wild palm which covers the whole cliff, is a small altar, with ornaments in stucco, one of which seems intended to represent a pineapple. These wanted entirely the massive character of the buildings, and are so slight that they could almost be pushed over with the foot. They stand in the open air, exposed to strong easterly winds, and almost to the spray of the sea. It was impossible to believe that the altar had been abandoned three hundred years. Within that time some guardian eye had watched over it, some pious hand had repaired it, and long since the arrival of the Spaniards the Indian had performed before it his idolatrous rites.

We found this one of the most interesting places we had seen in our whole exploration of ruins. I shall close with one remark. The whole triangular region from Valladolid to the Bay of Ascension on one side, and the port of Yalahao on the other, is not traversed by a single road. It is a region entirely unknown; no white man ever enters it. Ruined cities no doubt exist. [We were] told of a large building many leagues in the interior, known to an old Indian, covered with paintings in bright and vivid colours. With difficulty we contrived to see this Indian, but he was extremely uncommunicative; said it was many years since he saw the building; that he had come upon it in the dry season while hunting, and should not be able to find it again. It is my belief that within this region cities like those we have seen in ruins were kept up and occupied for a long time, perhaps one or two centuries, after the conquest, and that, down to a comparatively late period, Indians were living in them, the same as before the discovery of America. In fact, I conceive it to be not impossible that within this secluded region may exist at this day, unknown to white men, a living aboriginal city, occupied by relics of the ancient race, who still worship in the temples of their fathers.

Our journey in this direction is now ended, and our course is homeward. We were detained one day at Tancar by a storm, and on Tuesday morning the patron came to us in a hurry with a summons on board; the wind had veered so that he could get out of the harbour. The wind was still high, and the sea so rough, and kept the little canoa in such commotion, that in half an hour nearly all our party were sea-sick. We had a strong wind and fair, and late in the afternoon put in at Nesuc, where we had stopped before, distinguished by its solitary palm tree.

Early in the morning we were again under way, and coasted to the point of Kancune, where we landed in front of a rancho then occupied by a party of fishermen. A short walk brought us to the point, on which stood two dilapidated buildings, one entirely fallen, and the other having dimensions like the smallest of those seen at Tuloom. It was so intensely hot, and we were so annoyed by millions of sand-flies, that we did not think it worth while to stay, but returned to the hut, embarked, and, crossing over, in two hours reached the island of Mugeres. Near the shore were immense flocks of sea-birds, sitting on the piles of a turtle enclosure. Over our heads was a cloud of white ibises, and, somewhat to the surprise of the fishermen, our coming to anchor was signalized by a discharge of heavy bird artillery, and a splashing into the water to pick up the dead and wounded. In wading ashore we stuck in a mud-bank, and had time to contemplate the picturesque beauty of the scene before us. It was a small sandy beach, with a rocky coast on each side, and trees growing down to the water, broken only by a small clearing opposite the beach, in which were two palm leaf huts, and an arbour covered with palm leaves. Under the arbour hung three small hammocks, and a hardy, sun-dried fisherman sat repairing a net, with two Indian boys engaged in weaving a new one. The old fisherman, without desisting from his work, invited us to the hammocks, and, to satisfy our invariable first want on this coast, sent a boy for water, which, though not good, was better than that on board.

The island was famed among the fishermen as the rendezvous of Lafitte the pirate, and the patron told us that our host had been his prisoner two years. This man was about fifty-five, tall and thin, and his face was so darkened by the sun that it was hard to say whether he was white or of mixed blood. We remarked that he was not fond of talking of his captivity. He said he did not know how long he was a prisoner nor where he was taken. As the business of piracy was rather complicated in these parts, we conceived a suspicion that he had not been a prisoner entirely against his will. His fellow-fishermen had no narrow feelings on the subject, and perhaps gave a preference to piracy as a larger business, and one that brought more ounces, than catching turtles. They seemed, however, to have an idea that los Ingleses entertained different views, and the prisoner, el pobre, as our patron called him, said those things were all over, and it was best not to disturb them. He could not, however, help dropping a few words in behalf of Lafitte, or Monsieur Lafitta; he did not know whether it was true what people said of him, but he never hurt the poor fishermen. Led on by degrees he told us that Lafitte died in his arms, and that his widow, a señora del Norte from Mobile, was then living in great distress at Silan, the port at which we intended to disembark.

The island of Mugeres is between four and five miles long, half a mile wide, and four miles distant from the mainland. The ruins were at the north end. For a short distance we kept along the shore, and then struck into a path cut straight across the island. About half way across we came to a santa cruz, or holy cross, set up by the fishermen, at which place we heard distinctly the sound of the breakers on the opposite shore. To the right a faint track was perceptible, which soon disappeared altogether. But our guides knew the direction, and, cutting a way with the machete, we came out upon a high, rocky, perpendicular cliff, which commanded an immense expanse of ocean, and against which the waves, roused by the storm of the night before, were dashing grandly. We followed along the brink of the cliff and around the edges of great perpendicular chasms, the ground being bare of trees and covered with a scrubby plant, called the uba, with gnarled roots spreading like the branches of a grape-vine. At the point terminating the island, standing boldly upon the sea, was [a] lonely edifice. Below, rocking on the waves, was a small canoa, with our host then in the act of getting on board a turtle. It was the wildest and grandest scene we had looked upon in our whole journey.

The steps which led to the building are in good preservation, and at the foot is a platform, with the ruins of an altar. The front, on one side of the doorway, has fallen. On the top is a cross, probably erected by the fishermen. The interior is divided into two corridors, and in the wall of that in front are three small doorways leading to the inner corridor. The ceiling had the triangular arch, and throughout the hand of the builders on the mainland could not be mistaken.

We returned to the hut ready to embark, and at twelve o'clock we took leave of the fisherman, and were again on board our canoa. The wind was fair and strong, and very soon we reached the point of the island. Toward dark we doubled Catoche, and, for the first time coasting all night, day broke upon us in the harbor of Yalahao. After the desolate regions we had been visiting, the old pirates' haunt seemed a metropolis. At seven o'clock we were again under way, with the wind directly astern, and as much as we could carry, the canoa rolling so that we were compelled to take in the mainsail. The coast was low, barren, and monotonous. At three o'clock we passed an ancient mound, towering above the huts that constituted the port of El Cuyo, a landmark for sailors, visible at sea three leagues distant; but our patron told us that there were no buildings or vestiges of ruins.

CHAPTER SIXTEEN

Izamal and Aké

At daylight the next morning we crawled out from the bottom of the canoa, and found her anchored off the port of Silan, a few huts built around a sandy square on a low, barren coast. We gave portions of our tattered garments to the waves, and waded ashore. Silan is the port of Izamal, eleven leagues distant. We had a great enterprise in procuring breakfast, and after this in providing for dinner, which we determined should be the best the country afforded, to consist of fish and fowl, each of which had to be bought separately, and, with separate portions of lard, sent to different houses to be cooked.

During the interval of preparation I took a walk along the shore. Toward the end of a sandy beach was a projecting point, on a line with which I noticed on the water what seemed to be a red cloud of singular brilliancy, which, on drawing nearer, I found to be a flat covered with flamingoes. On my return I reported the discovery to Doctor Cabot. Our host gave us a glowing account of flamingoes, scarlet ibises, and roseate spoonbills at Punta Arenas. Doctor Cabot was anxious for closer acquaintance with the birds, and we determined to go that same afternoon. At dusk we reached a hut in a beautifully picturesque position, imbosomed in a small bay, with a frail bridge running out some distance from the shore. We swung our hammocks, kindled a fire, and when the occupant arrived had a cup of chocolate ready for him, and endeavoured to make him feel himself at home. He was a lad of about sixteen, the son of the proprietor. He had never seen a foreigner in his life, and was by no means reassured when we told him that we had come to shoot flamingoes and spoonbills.

In the gray of the morning we heard a loud quacking of ducks, which carried us out of doors. Below us the shore formed a large bay, with the Punta de Arenas, or Point of Sand, projecting toward us, bordered down to the water's edge with trees, and all over the bay were sand-banks covered with wild fowl. Doctor Cabot enumerated of ducks, the mallard, pin-tail, blooming teal, widgeon, and gadwall; of bitterns, the American bittern, least bittern, great and lesser egret, blue crane, great blue heron, Louisiana heron, night heron, two kinds of rail, one clapper rail, white ibis, willets, snipes, red-breasted snipe, least snipe, semi-palmated sandpiper, black-breasted plover, marble godwit, long-billed curlew, osprey or fish-hawk, black hawk, and other smaller birds, all together, forming, as we passed among them, an animated and exciting scene. It would have been slaughter to shoot among them. A single flock of flamingoes flew by us, but out of reach.

At the moment our canoe was stuck in the mud, and we continued to hit every flat till we entered a creek. Near the mouth a flock of roseate spoonbills flew over our heads, also out of reach, but we saw where they alighted. Setting toward them till we were stopped by a mud-bank, we took to the water, or rather to the mud, in which we found our lower members moving suddenly downward to parts unknown, and in some danger of descending till our sombreros only remained as monuments of our muddy grave. Moving in another direction, and again sinking and drawing back, for two hours we toiled, struggled, floundered, and fired, a laughing stock to the beautiful spoonbills in the free element above. At length Dr. Cabot brought one down, and we parted.

In following our separate fortunes along the shore I shot one, which fell at the other side of a stream. As I rushed in, the water rose above all my mud stains, and I fell back, and hastily disencumbered myself of clothing. A high wind was sweeping over the bay. My hat and light garments were blown into the water, and at the same moment the roseate bird stood up, opened its large wings, and fluttered along the beach. I gave chase to the bird. Holding it kicking under

93. *Page 268:* Catherwood drawing of stucco mask (now destroyed), Izamal

my arm, I pursued my habiliments into the water, and at length got back to dry land with my miscellaneous load, and stood on the beach a picture of an antiquary in distress, doubtless illustrating the proverb to the Indian, who now came to my relief, that no man can be a hero to his valet de chambre.

Before daylight the next morning we were again in the saddle. For some distance back from the port the ground had been over-flowed by the sea, and was a sandy, barren mangrove brake. Beyond commenced the same broken, stony surface, and at eight o'clock [we] reached the village of Silan. In the suburbs I discovered unexpectedly the towering memorial of another ruined city, and riding into the plaza, saw at one angle, near the wall of the church, [a] gigantic mound. At the base, and inside of the wall of the church, were five large orange trees, loaded with fruit. A group of Indians were en-gaged in getting stone out of the mound to repair the wall, and a young man was superintending them, whom I immediately recog-nised as the padre. He accompanied me to the top of the mound, one of the largest we had seen. There was no building or structure of any kind visible; whatever had been upon it had fallen or been pulled down. The church, the wall of the yard, and the few stone houses in the village, had been built of materials taken from it.

Walking along the top we reached a hole, at the bottom of which I discovered the broken arch of a ceiling, and looked through it into an apartment below. This explained the character of the struc-ture. A building had extended the whole length of the mound, the up-per part of which had fallen, and the ruins had made the whole a long, confused, and undistinguishable mass. The top commanded an extensive view of a great wooded plain, and near by, rising above the trees, was another mound, which, within a few years, had been crowned with an edifice, called El Castillo. The padre, a young man, but little over thirty, remembered when this Castillo stood with its doorways open, pillars in them, and corridors around. The sight of these ruins was entirely unexpected. If they had been all we had met with in the country, we should have gazed upon them with perplexity and wonder. They possessed unusual interest from the fact that they existed in a place, the name of which was known and familiar to us as that of an existing aboriginal town at the time of the conquest.

At ten o'clock we set out, and at half past twelve reached Temax, two and a half leagues distant. It had a fine plaza, with a great church and convent, and a stone casa real, with a broad corri-dor in front, under which the guarda were swinging in hammocks. Early in the evening, one of the guarda came to inform us that a caricoche had just arrived from Izamal, and wanted a return freight. At two o'clock, by a bright moonlight, we started. The caricoche was drawn by three mules, and had in it a bed, on which we reclined at full length.

At nine o'clock we entered the suburbs of Izamal, but fifteen leagues from Merida. Peeping through the curtain, we rode into the plaza, which was alive with people, dressed in clean clothes for the fiesta. There was an unusual proportion of gentlemen with black hats and canes, and some with military coats, bright and flashing to such a degree that we congratulated ourselves upon not having made our entry on horseback. We had on our shooting-clothes, with the mud stains from Punta Arenas, and by computation our beards were of twenty-eight days' growth.

It was the last day of the fiesta of Santa Cruz. The bull-fights were over, but the bull-ring, fancifully ornamented, still remained in the centre of the plaza, and two bulls stood under one of the corridors, pierced with wounds and streaming with blood, as memorials of the fight. Amid a crowd of Indians were parties of vecinos, gay and well dressed in the style and costume of the capital. Music was sounding to summon the people to a ball. But amid this gay scene the eye turned involuntarily to immense mounds rising grandly above the tops of the houses, from which the whole city had been built, without seeming to diminish their colossal proportions, proclaiming the power of those who reared them, and destined, apparently, to stand, when the feebler structures of their more civilized conquerors shall have crumbled into dust.

One of these great mounds blocked up the yard of the house we occupied, and extended into the adjoining yard. The part in our yard was entirely ruined, but in that of the señora it appeared that its vast sides had been covered from one end to the other with colossal ornaments in stucco, most of which had fallen, but among the fragments is [a] gigantic head [see Fig. 93]. The ground-work is of projecting stones, which are covered with stucco. A stone protrudes from the chin, intended, perhaps, for burning copal on, as a sort of altar. It was the first time we had seen an ornament of this kind upon the exterior of any of these structures. In sternness and harshness of expression it reminded us of the idols at Copan, and its colossal proportions, with the corresponding dimensions of the mound, gave an unusual impression of grandeur.

Two or three streets distant from the plaza, but visible in all its huge proportions, was the most stupendous mound we had seen in the country, being, perhaps, six or seven hundred feet long and sixty feet high, which, we ascertained beyond all doubt, had interior chambers.

On the north side of the plaza is the great church and convent of Franciscan monks, standing on an elevation, and giving a character to the plaza that no other in Yucatan possesses. Two flights of stone steps lead up to it; on three sides is a colonnade, forming a noble promenade, overlooking the city and the surrounding country to a great distance. This great elevation was evidently artificial, and not the work of the Spaniards.

At the earliest period of the conquest we have accounts of the large aboriginal town of Izamal, and, fortunately, we have authentic records which dispel all uncertainty respecting the origin of these ancient mounds. Testimony [from] the early monks proves that these great mounds had upon them temples and idols, and the habitations of priests, in the actual use of the Indians who were found occupying the country at the time of the conquest.

The next morning we started for Merida. Turning off from the main road, we entered the woods, and following a narrow path, a little before dark we reached the hacienda of Aké, and for the last time were among the towering and colossal memorials of an aboriginal city. A great mound towering in full sight from the door of the hacienda [is] called El Palacio. On the great platform on the top stand thirty-six shafts, or columns, in three parallel rows of twelve. But few have fallen, though some have lost their upper layer of stones. There are no remains of any structure or roof. If there ever was one, it must have been of wood, which would seem most incongruous and inappropriate for such a solid structure of stones. The whole mound was so overgrown that we could not ascertain the juxtaposition of the pillars till the growth was cleared away. It was a new and extraordinary feature, entirely different from any we had seen, and at the very end of our journey, when we supposed ourselves familiar with the character of American ruins, threw over them a new air of mystery.

In the same vicinity are other mounds of colossal dimensions, one of which is also called the Palace, but of a different construction and without pillars. On another, at the head of the ruined staircase, is an opening under the top of a doorway, nearly filled up, crawling through which, by means of the crotch of a tree I descended into a dark chamber called Akabna, or dark house. Near this is a senote, with the remains of steps leading down to water, which once supplied the ancient city. The ruins cover a great extent, but all were overgrown. They were more massive than all the others we had seen, bore the stamp of an older era, and more than any others, in fact, for the first time in the country, suggested the idea of Cyclopean remains. But even here we have a gleam of historic light, faint, it is true, but, in my mind, sufficient to dispel all unsettled and wavering notions.

In the account of the march of Don Francisco Montejo from the coast, it is mentioned that the Spaniards reached a town called Aké, at which they found themselves confronted by a great multitude of armed Indians. A desperate battle ensued, which lasted two days, and in which the Spaniards were victorious, but gained no easy triumph.

There is no other mention of Aké, and in this there is no allusion whatever to the buildings, but from its geographical position, and the direction of the line of march of the Spanish army from the coast, I have little doubt that their Aké was the place now known by the same name. It is, indeed, strange that no mention is made of the buildings, but regard must be had to the circumstances of danger and death which surrounded the Spaniards. At all events, it is not more strange than the want of any description of the great buildings of Chichen. We have the strongest possible proof that no correct infer-

94. Great Gallery, Aké
(Charnay, circa 1885)

ence is to be drawn from the silence of the Spaniards, for in the comparatively minute account of the conquest of Mexico, we find that the Spanish army marched under the very shadow of the great pyramids of Otumba, and yet not the slightest mention whatever is made of their existence.

I have now finished my journey among ruined cities. In our long, irregular, and devious route we have discovered the crumbling remains of forty-four ancient cities, most of them but a short distance apart, though, from the breaking up of the old roads, having no direct communication with each other. With few exceptions, all were lost, buried, and unknown, never before visited by a stranger, and some of them, perhaps, never looked upon by the eyes of a white man. Involuntarily we turn for a moment to the frightful scenes of which this now desolate region must have been the theatre; the scenes of blood, agony, and wo which preceded the desolation or abandonment of these cities. But, leaving the boundless space in which imagination might rove, I confine myself to the consideration of facts. If I may be permitted to say so, in the whole history of discoveries there is nothing to be compared with those here presented. They give an entirely new aspect to the great Continent on which we live, and bring up with more force than ever the question which I once undertook to consider: Who were the builders of these American cities?

My opinion has been fully and freely expressed, "that they are not the works of people who have passed away, and whose history is lost, but of the same races who inhabited the country at the time of the Spanish conquest, or of some not very distant progenitors." Some were probably in ruins, but in general I believe that they were occupied by the Indians at the time of the Spanish invasion. The grounds of this belief are interspersed throughout these pages, interwoven with so many facts and circumstances that I do not recapitulate them. In conclusion I shall only refer briefly to those arguments which I consider the strongest that are urged against this belief.

The first is the entire absence of all traditions. But I would ask, may not this be accounted for by the unparalleled circumstances which attended the conquest and subjugation of Spanish America? Every captain, on first planting the royal standard on the shores of a new country, made proclamation according to a form drawn up by the most eminent divines and lawyers in Spain, the most extraordinary that ever appeared in the history of mankind; entreating and requiring the inhabitants to acknowledge and obey the church as the superior and guide of the universe, the holy father called the pope, and his majesty as king and sovereign lord of these islands; and concluding, "But if you will not comply, or maliciously delay to obey my injunction, then, with the help of God, I will enter your country by force; I will carry on war against you with the utmost violence; I will subject you to the yoke of obedience, to the church and king; I will take your wives and children, and make them slaves, and sell or dispose of them according to his majesty's pleasure. I will seize your goods, and do you all the mischief in my power, as rebellious subjects, who will not acknowledge or submit to their lawful sovereign; and I protest that all the bloodshed and calamities which shall follow are to be imputed to you, and not to his majesty, or to me, or the gentlemen who serve under me."

The conquest and subjugation of the country were carried out in the unscrupulous spirit of this proclamation. The pages of the historians are dyed with blood; and sailing on the crimson stream appears the policy of the Spaniards, more fatal than the sword, to subvert all the institutions of the natives, and to break up and utterly destroy all the rites, customs, and associations that might keep alive the memory of their fathers and their ancient condition. One sad instance shows the effects of this policy. Before the destruction of Mayapan, the capital of the kingdom of Maya, all the nobles of the country had houses in that city, and were exempted from tribute. According to Cogolludo, in the year 1582, forty years after the conquest, all who held themselves for lords and nobles still claimed their solares (sites for mansions) as tokens of their rank. But now, he says, "from the change of government and the little estimation in which they are held, it does not appear that they care to preserve nobility for their posterity, for at this day, if they do not work with their own hands, [they] have nothing to eat."

If at that early date nobles no longer cared for their titles, it is not strange that the present inhabitants, nine generations removed, without any written language, borne down by three centuries of servitude, and toiling daily for a scanty subsistence, are alike ignorant and indifferent concerning the history of their ancestors, and the great cities lying in ruins under their eyes. It is my belief, that among the whole mass of what are called Christianized Indians, there is not at this day one solitary tradition which can shed a ray of light upon any event in their history that occurred one hundred and fifty years from the present time. In fact, I believe it would be almost impossible to procure any information of any kind whatever beyond the memory of the oldest living Indian.

Besides, the want of traditionary knowledge is not peculiar to these American ruins. Two thousand years ago the Pyramids towered on the borders of the African Desert without any certain tradition of the time when they were founded. So long back as the first century of the Christian era, Pliny cites various older authors who disagreed concerning the persons who built them, and even concerning the use and object for which they were erected. No traditions hang round the ruins of Greece and Rome. But for written records, Egyptian, Grecian, and Roman remains would be as mysterious as the ruins of America. To come down to later times and countries comparatively familiar, tradition sheds no light upon the round towers of Ireland, and the ruins of Stonehenge stand on Salisbury plain without a tradition to carry us back to the age or nation of their builders.

The second argument I shall notice is, that a people possessing the power, art, and skill to erect such cities, never could have fallen so low as the miserable Indians who now linger about their ruins. But the pages of written history are burdened with changes in national character quite equal to that here exhibited. And again, we have close at hand an illustration in point. The Indians who inhabit that country now are not more changed than their Spanish masters. Whether debased, and but little above the grade of brutes, as it was the Spanish policy to represent them, or not, we know that at the time of the conquest they were at least proud, fierce, and warlike, and poured out their blood like water to save their inheritance from the grasp of strangers. Crushed, humbled, and bowed down as they are now by generations of bitter servitude, even yet they are not more changed than the descendants of those terrible Spaniards who invaded and conquered their country. In both, all traces of the daring and warlike character of their ancestors are entirely gone. In contemplating this change in the Indian, the loss of mere mechanical skill and art seems comparatively nothing. In my opinion, teaching might again lift up the Indian, might impart to him the skill to sculpture stone and carve wood. If restored to freedom, and the unshackled exercise of his powers of mind, there might again appear a capacity to originate and construct, equal to that exhibited in the ruined monuments of his ancestors.

The last argument against the hypothesis that the cities were constructed by the ancestors of the present Indians is the alleged absence of knowledge of such cities by the conquerors. Even if this allegation were true, the argument would be unsound, for it goes to deny that such cities ever existed at all. Now there can be no doubt as to their existence. As it is never pretended that they were erected since the conquest, they must be allowed to have been standing at that time.

Whether erected by the Indians or by races perished and unknown, whether desolate or inhabited, beyond all question the great buildings were there. If not entire, they must at least have been far more so than they are now; if desolate, perhaps more calculated to excite wonder than if inhabited. In either case the alleged silence of the historian would be equally inexplicable.

But the allegation is untrue. The old historians are not silent. On the contrary, we have the glowing accounts of Cortez and his companions, of soldiers, priests, and civilians, all concurring in representations of existing cities, then in the actual use and occupation of the Indians, with buildings and temples like those presented in these pages. Indeed, these accounts are so glowing that modern historians, at the head of whom stands Robertson, have thrown discredit over them, and ascribed them to a heated imagination. To my mind, they bear on the face of them the stamp of truth, and it seems strange that they have been deemed worthy of so little reliance. But Robertson wrote upon the authority of correspondents in New Spain, one of whom, long resident in that country, and professing to have visited every part of it, says that "at this day there does not remain the smallest vestige of any Indian building, public or private, either in Mexico or any province of New Spain."

Robertson's informants were probably foreign merchants resident in the city of Mexico, whose travels had been confined to the beaten road, and to places occupied by the Spaniards. At that time the white inhabitants were in utter ignorance of the great cities, desolate and in ruins, that lay buried in the forests. But at this day better information exists. Vast remains have been brought to light, and the discoveries prove incontestably that those histories which make no mention of these great buildings are imperfect, those which deny their existence are untrue. The graves cry out for the old historians, and the mouldering skeletons of cities confirm Herrera's account of Yucatan, that "there were so many and such stately Stone Buildings that it was Amazing; and the greatest Wonder was that, having no Use of any Metal, they were able to raise such Structures, which seem to have been Temples, for their Houses were all of Timber, and thatched." And again, he says, that "for the Space of twenty Years there was such Plenty throughout the Country, and the People multiplied so much that Men said the whole Province looked like one Town."

These arguments then—the want of tradition, the degeneracy of the people, and the alleged absence of historical accounts—are not sufficient to disturb my belief that the great cities now lying in ruins were the works of the same races who inhabited the country at the time of the conquest. Who these people were, whence they came, and who were their progenitors, are questions that involve too many considerations to be entered upon at the conclusion of these pages. All the light that history sheds upon them is dim and faint, and may be summed up in a few words.

According to traditions, picture writings, and Mexican manuscripts written after the conquest, the Toltecs, or Toltecans, were the first inhabitants of the land of Anahuac, now known as New Spain or Mexico. They are the oldest nations on the continent of America of which we have any knowledge. Banished, according to their own history, from their native country, which was situated to the northwest of Mexico, in the year 596 of our era, they proceeded southward under the directions of their chiefs. After sojourning at various places on the way for the space of one hundred and twenty-four years, [they] arrived at the banks of a river in the vale of Mexico, where they built the city of Tula, the capital of the Toltecan kingdom, near the site of the present city of Mexico.

Their monarchy lasted nearly four centuries, during which they multiplied, extended their population, and built numerous and large cities. But direful calamities hung over them. For several years Heaven denied them rain; the earth refused them food; the air, infected with mortal contagion, filled the graves with dead. A great part of the nation perished of famine or sickness; the last king was among the number, and in the year 1052 the monarchy ended. The wretched remains of the nation took refuge, some in Yucatan and other in Guatimala, while some lingered around the graves of their kindred in the great vale where Mexico was afterward founded. For a century the land of Anahuac lay waste and depopulated. The Chechemecas, following in the track of their ruined cities, reoccupied it, and after them the Acolhuans, the Tlastaltecs, and the Aztecs, which last were the subjects of Montezuma at the time of the invasion by the Spaniards.

The history of all these tribes or nations is misty, confused, and indistinct. The Toltecans, represented to have been the most ancient, are said to have been also the most polished. Probably they were the originators of that peculiar style of architecture found in Guatimala and Yucatan, which was adopted by all the subsequent inhabitants. As, according to their own annals, they did not set out on their emigration to those countries from the vale of Mexico until the year 1052 of our era, the oldest cities erected by them in those countries could have been in existence but from four to five hundred years at the time of the Spanish conquest. This gives them a very modern date compared with the Pyramids and temples of Egypt, and the other ruined monuments of the Old World. It gives them a much less antiquity than that claimed by the Maya manuscript, and, in fact, much less than I should ascribe to them myself.

In identifying them as the works of the ancestors of the present Indians, the cloud which hung over their origin is not removed. The time when and the circumstances under which they were built, the rise, progress, and full development of the power, art, and skill required for their construction, are all mysteries which will not easily be unravelled. They rise like skeletons from the grave, wrapped in their burial shrouds; claiming no affinity with the works of any known people, but a distinct, independent, and separate existence. They stand alone, absolutely and entirely anomalous, perhaps the most interesting subject which at this day presents itself to the inquiring mind. I will now bid farewell to ruins. I leave them with all their mystery around them; and in the feeble hope that these imperfect pages may in some way throw a glimmer of light upon the great question, who were the peoplers of America?

ILLUSTRATION CREDITS

Photographs not otherwise credited were taken by the editor.

Cover: Photograph by Kenneth Garrett.

Maps: From *Incidents of Travel in Yucatán,* by John Lloyd Stephens with engravings by Frederick Catherwood. Edited by Victor Wolfgang von Hagen. New edition copyright © 1962 by the University of Oklahoma Press.

Figs. 1, 14, 22, 23, 27, 32, 36, 44, 80, 81, and 83: Photographs by Parney and Jacques VanKirk.

Figs. 2, 9, 15, 21, 28, 31, 34, 39, 41, 42, 47, 52, 56, 62, 65, 66, 69, 71, 72, 77, 84, 87, and 93: Drawings by Frederick Catherwood, reproduced from original 1843 edition of *Incidents of Travel in Yucatan,* by John Lloyd Stephens.

Fig. 4: From *Harper's Monthly Magazine,* January 1859.

Figs. 5, 8, 13, 18, 20, 24, 30, 35, 40, 48, 49, 50, 51, 54, and 55: Photographs by Edward H. Thompson, courtesy of Peabody Museum, Harvard University.

Figs. 7, 10, 17, 19, 26, 37, 38, 70, 78, and 94: Photographs by Désiré Charnay, courtesy of Peabody Museum, Harvard University.

Fig. 11: Photograph by Augustus Le Plongeon, courtesy of Peabody Museum, Harvard University.

Figs. 29, 43, 45, 63, 74, 75, 76, 79, and 85: Photographers unknown, courtesy of Peabody Museum, Harvard University.

Figs. 46, 58, 64, 67, 82, 86, 88, 89, 90, 91, and 92: Photographs by C.I.W., courtesy of Peabody Museum, Harvard University.

Figs. 60 and 61: Photographs by Teobert Maler, courtesy of Peabody Museum, Harvard University.

Figs. 68 and 73: Drawings by Tatiana Proskouriakoff, courtesy of Peabody Museum, Harvard University.

Main entries reflect current spellings of geographical and building names when these vary from Stephens' spellings, which can be found in brackets. Secondary English or Spanish variants of proper names are in parentheses. Generic subject entries relate to aspects of Stephens' journey and to the culture and customs of Yucatán. Page numbers set in italics refer to illustrations.